'The Hotties'

Excavation and building survey at Pilkingtons' No 9 Tank House
St Helens, Merseyside

'Like trying to obtain clear water by applying
heat to ice in a container made of sugar.'
(Maloney 1967, 75, on melting glass)

M Krupa
R Heawood

With contributions by

A J Bell
D Martlew
C Wild

2002

Published by
Oxford Archaeology North
Storey Institute
Meeting House Lane
Lancaster
LA1 1TF
(*Phone:* 01524 848666; *Fax:* 01524 848606)

Distributed by
Oxbow Books
Park End Place
Oxford
OX1 1HN
(*Phone:* 01865 241249; *Fax:* 01865 794449)

Printed by
Henry Ling Limited, at the Dorset Press, Dorchester, DT1 1HD

ISBN 0-904220-32-X
ISSN 1343-5205

Series editor
Rachel Newman
Copy editor
Martin Lister
Indexer
Sue Vaughan
Design, layout, and formatting
Andrea Scott

Front Cover: The cone of No 9 Tank House with the furnace foundations below
Rear Cover: 'The Hotties' in the 1970s, with steam from the glassworks being vented over The St Helens Canal

LANCASTER IMPRINTS   Lancaster Imprints is the publication series of Oxford Archaeology North. The series covers work on major excavations and surveys of all periods undertaken by the organisation and associated bodies.

Contents

List of figures iv
List of plates .... iv–v
Contributors vi
Abbreviations vi
Summaries .... vii-x
Acknowledgements xi
Glossary .... xii–xiii

1 INTRODUCTION 1
   'The Hotties' 1
   The re-development of the site 3
   The fieldwork programme 3
   The excavation and building survey report 4
   The archive 4

2 THE MAKING OF GLASS 5

3 HISTORICAL BACKGROUND 7
   The adoption of coal-fired glass furnaces in the seventeenth century 7
   The establishment of glassmaking in St Helens 7
   The development of Pilkington Brothers 9
   The development of the glass furnace, 1860-73 10
   The introduction of continuous tank furnaces by Pilkingtons 14

4 PHASE 1: PRE-TANK HOUSE ACTIVITY 17
   Documentary evidence 17
   Archaeological evidence — Phase 1.1 19
   Archaeological evidence — Phase 1.2 23

5 PHASE 2: CONSTRUCTION OF THE NO 9 TANK HOUSE COMPLEX 25
   Documentary evidence 25
   Archaeological evidence — Phase 2.1 32
   Archaeological evidence — Phase 2.2 71
   Functional analysis of the tank furnace 74

6 PHASE 3: POST-PRODUCTION TANK HOUSE MODIFICATIONS 83
   Documentary evidence 83
   Archaeological evidence 86
   Functional analysis of the Phase 3 structures 93

7 PHASE 4: MID- AND LATE-TWENTIETH CENTURY ALTERATIONS 97
   Phase 4.1 97
   Phase 4.2 100

8 WORKING CONDITIONS AND INDUSTRIAL RELATIONS 103
   Work in the tank house 103
   Wages and labour relations 104

9 DISCUSSION 107
   The use of continuous tank furnaces in the British glass industry 107
   Pilkingtons' development of the continuous tank furnace 108
   The archaeological evidence for contemporary bottle-making furnaces 110
   The expansion of production, and further development 111
   Conclusion 113

BIBLIOGRAPHY 115
INDEX 119

List of illustrations

Figures

1   Location of No 9 Tank House xiv
2   Map of principal places mentioned in the text 8
3   Schematic section through a regenerative furnace, showing flow of gas and air 12
4   Phase 1 remains, predating No 9 Tank House 20
5   Remains of the probable pit-head structure and winding house 21
6   No 9 Tank House and surrounding structures 24
7   Phase 2 buildings: No 9 Tank House and adjacent structures 32
8   Artist's reconstruction of No 9 Tank House, looking west 33
9   External elevation, cone house south–east gable wall 34
10   External elevation, cone house north–west gable wall 35
11   External elevation, cone house north–east wall 40
12   External elevation, cone house south–west wall 41
13   Transverse section across the width of the cone house 44
14   Longitudinal section along the length of the cone house 45
15   Phase 2 tunnels, flues, and swing pits 50
16   Detail of the Phase 2 working end switch room 53
17   Basal remains of the Phase 2 furnace 61
18   Longitudinal section through the cone house, with the position of the furnace reconstructed 63
19   Schematic reconstruction plan of the furnace base at the working end 65
20   Section through gas supply tunnels 512–7 69
21   Schematic plan of the regenerators, showing flow of gas and air 73
22   Schematic reconstruction of the working end switch room and regenerators 75
23   Transverse section through the cone house, with the position of the furnace reconstructed 78
24   Artist's reconstruction of the furnace 79
25   Reconstruction of the bridge wall 81
26   Phase 3 flues and shafts 88
27   Phase 3 adaptation of the north–west corner of the cone house 90
28   Phase 3 external ground-level features 92
29   Phase 4 remains 98
30   Plan of the Cannington Shaw Bottle Shop regenerators and associated sub-surface features 110

Plates

1   Aerial photograph showing Pilkingtons' Sheet Glass Works, December 1947 1
2   Extract from Ordnance Survey 1:2500 map, 1894 2
3   View south over the cone house 2
4   Excavation beneath the cone house floor 3
5   A worker wearing personal protective equipment 4
6   A teazer, wearing heat resistant clothing 5
7   Drawing of a regenerative pot furnace prepared by Siemens Brothers in 1873–4 11
8   Plan view of a continuous tank furnace from William Siemens' patent of 1872 13
9   Blower reheating a cylinder in the furnace, with the aid of a bicycle machine 15
10   Extract from Ordnance Survey 5 feet:1 mile map, 1849 17
11   Extract from Ordnance Survey 1:2500 map, 1882 18
12   Looking south–west across the foundations of the probable Phase 1 pit head (Structure 1) 19
13   View north–west to the probable Phase 1 winding house (Structure 2) 20
14   View south–west to concrete piers 854 and 855 22
15   Demonstration of a cylinder being blown without mechanical aids 27
16   Reproduction of an engraving showing the manufacture of hand-blown cylinder glass 28
17   A completed cylinder 29
18   Longitudinal section through a gas producer 30
19   An artist's impresssion of Pilkingtons' Sheet Glass Works in 1879 31

20	Extract from Ordnance Survey 1:500 map, 1891	33
21	Looking south–west towards the cone house north–east wall	36
22	External elevation of the cone house south–east gable wall	36
23	Internal elevation of the cone house north–east wall.	38
24	External elevation of the cone house north–east wall	38
25	External elevation of the cone house south–west wall	42
26	The cone house roof structure and the base of the cone, with the foundations of the furnace below	43
27	One of the cast iron sockets bolted to the top of each stanchion in the cone house north–east wall	46
28	One of the cast iron fixtures that secured the apex of each of the six complete roof trusses	47
29	A pair of cast iron plates securing the king bolt, ties, and braces of each truss	48
30	Aerial photograph of the Jubilee Side, 4 June 1939	48
31	Grove Street in the 1940s, with the old cone of No 15 Tank House in the background	49
32	The north–west extent of melt end regenerator 530	51
33	Looking south across the working end switch room	52
34	The south–west part of structure 535 in the working end switch room	54
35	Looking south–east along tunnel 524	55
36	View north–east into tunnel 504, with flue 532 in the foreground	57
37	View south–west to the brick arches above tunnel 504	58
38	Looking south–west along the foundations of the furnace working end	62
39	Looking north–west across the south-east swing pit to the working end furnace foundations	64
40	View south–east across the south-east swing pit	66
41	Looking north along gas supply flues 519 and 520	67
42	Shafts 808 and 810	68
43	View south–east along gas supply flue 514	70
44	Transverse section across a continuous tank furnace, from William Siemens' patent of 1879	72
45	Drawing showing a regenerative furnace butterfly reversing valve	76
46	Mechanised manufacture of cylinder glass using the Lubbers process	83
47	Early version of a Libbey-Owens machine	84
48	Looking north–west at the Phase 3 structures within chamber 503	87
49	The mushroom valve within shaft 807	94
50	View of the raking buttresses added to the cone house north–east wall during the conversion of the late 1940s	97
51	The exterior of the Cannington Shaw Bottle Shop, looking south–east	111
52	The base of the Cannington Shaw Bottle Shop cone	112

Contributors

Jo Bell
British Waterways, Brome Hall Lane, Lapworth, West Midlands, B94 5RB

Richard Heawood
Oxford Archaeology North, Storey Institute, Meeting House Lane, Lancaster, LA1 1TF

Mick Krupa
2 Kell Bank, Gosforth, Seascale, Cumbria, CA20 1JA

David Martlew
Models Laboratory, Pilkington Technology, Lathom

Chris Wild
Oxford Archaeology North, Storey Institute, Meeting House Lane, Lancaster, LA1 1TF

Abbreviations

LUAU	Lancaster University Archaeological Unit
OS	Ordnance Survey
PPG	Pittsburgh Plate Glass
RSJ	Reinforced Steel Joist

Summary

Between 1991 and 1997, Lancaster University Archaeological Unit (LUAU; now Oxford Archaeology North) conducted a phased programme of standing building survey, excavation, and oral and documentary research, targeted on the remains of Pilkingtons' No 9 Tank House, on the 'Hotties' site, in St Helens (NGR SJ 5135 9475). The cone house element of the complex still stands, and is an impressive Grade II* Listed building. The tank house was purpose-built by Pilkingtons in 1887 for the manufacture of window glass using the blown cylinder method, and housed a continuous tank furnace, which made use of the regenerative technology patented by the Siemens brothers. The site, which is bounded to the north by the 1757 Sankey Canal, had previously been used as the pit head of a coal mine and, until 1884–5, was occupied by the Bridgewater Chemical Works; thus, the history of this plot of land neatly illustrates the town's industrial progression from coal, through chemicals, to the glass industry, which still dominates the local economy.

By 1991, the area of the former glassworks had been earmarked for urban regeneration. The cone house and its immediate surroundings were acquired by the newly formed Hotties Science and Arts Centre Ltd, later the World of Glass Project, with the aim of recording and consolidating the remains of the glass furnace, and eventually opening the site as a visitor centre. In the same year, LUAU was commissioned to undertake the first of four stages of fieldwork, stage 1 involving a survey of the fabric of the cone house building, the planning of adjacent surface remains, and the archaeological recording of a number of geotechnical test pits. The investigations were commissioned and funded in the first instance by the Ravenhead Renaissance consortium, and latterly by English Heritage. A second phase of investigation, from November 1991 to March 1992, involved the removal of chemically contaminated overburden to a depth of 3.50 m from all areas around the tank house, with preliminary excavation of the sub-surface tunnel system located beneath the building. A third phase, conducted in 1993, saw the total excavation of the interior of the tank house, including clearance of the numerous underlying tunnels and flues. Between 1995 and 1997, building work to consolidate and repair the tank house remains proceeded; LUAU was commissioned to monitor these works, and also to carry out further excavation in two limited areas.

The investigations have revealed the surviving base-level remains of a continuous tank furnace, with its regenerator chambers and gas supply flues still largely intact. Though details of the original Siemens tank furnace design are well known owing to the survival of the original patent drawings, excavation of No 9 Tank House has demonstrated that very significant modifications of the standard design were made by Pilkingtons. Most notable was the division of the furnace into two distinct and independently-heated components, the 'melt end' and the 'working end', housed in two adjacent buildings, each with its own dedicated set of regenerators; this arrangement was developed in order to allow the different conditions needed for melting and refining glass, and gathering and working glass, to be achieved with maximum efficiency, cutting costs and increasing quality. As the commercial sensitivity of furnace design ensured that few detailed records were kept, elucidation of the modifications has been largely dependent on the detailed analysis of the surviving elements of the No 9 Tank House. Pilkington's development of standard furnace design was crucial to its commercial success, and the archaeological investigations have thus given a valuable insight into the reasons for the company's dominance of the British window glass trade from the late nineteenth century to the present day.

The No 9 Tank House remains represent a unique survival from an age of rapid technological development within the glass industry, a period characterised by innovative but short-lived design. No comparable continuous tank furnace site is known elsewhere in England; the Cannington Shaw Bottle Shop, also in St Helens, represents a second excellent survival of a late nineteenth century glass furnace, but was built for the manufacture of bottles rather than window glass, and exhibits a lesser degree of technological development. The World of Glass Project has succeeded in ensuring the preservation of a rare industrial monument, and the multi-million pound visitor centre and museum, constructed across the canal, now portrays the technical development and heritage of the glass industry to the public, using the surviving archaeological remains as the pivotal element.

Résumé

Entre 1991 et 1997, l'unité d'archéologie de l'université de Lancaster (ou LUAU) a dirigé un programme progressif comprenant l'inspection de bâtiments érigés, des fouiles et des recherches documentaires et orales, dont la cible était les vestiges de l'atelier à bassin No 9 de Pilkingtons, sur le site de 'Hottie', à St Helens (NGR SJ 5135 9475). L'élément conique du complexe est toujours debout, et c'est un édifice impressionnant classé Grade II. L'atelier à bassin était un bâtiment qui avait été spécialement construit par Pilkingtons en 1887 pour la fabrication du verre de fenêtre, utilisant la méthode du cylindre soufflé, et il abritait un four à bassin à passage continu, mettant à bon escient la technologie de chaleur récupérée brevetée par les frères Siemens. Le site, qui est bordé au Nord par le canal Sankey, lequel date de 1757, avait préalablement été utilisé comme bâtiment de puits d'une mine de charbon, et, jusqu'en 1884-5 était occupé par l'usine de produits chimiques Bridgewater. L'histoire de ce lopin de terre illustre ainsi de façon superbe la progression industrielle de la ville qui commence par le charbon, puis passe aux produits chimiques, et ensuite à l'industrie du verre, laquelle domine toujours l'économie locale.

Déjà, en 1991, la zone de l'ancienne verrerie avait été sélectionnée pour régénération urbaine. L'édifice conique et ses environs immédiats furent achetés par une compagnie nouvellement créée, Hotties Science and Arts Centre Limited, ensuite appelée World of Glass Project (Projet Monde du verre), dont l'objectif était de documenter et de consolider les vestiges du four à verre, et éventuellement d'ouvrir le site sous forme d'un centre de visiteurs. Dans la même année, la LUAU reçut mission d'entreprendre la première de quatre phases de recherches sur le terrain. Cette phase 1 comprenait l'inspection de la structure de l'édifice conique, la planification des vestiges adjacents en surface, ainsi que la documentation archéologique d'un certain nombre de puits d'exploration géotechniques. Les recherches furent tout d'abord commandées et financées par le consortium Ravenhead Renaissance, puis par l'organisme English Heritage (patrimoine anglais). La seconde phase de recherches, de novembre 1991 à mars 1992, comprenait l'enlèvement de la couche de morts-terrains contaminée par les produits chimiques de toutes les zones autour du bâtiment à bassin, ce, jusqu'à une profondeur de 3,5 mètres, avec des fouiles préliminaires du réseau de tunnels souterrains situés en dessous du bâtiment. La troisième phase, effectuée en 1993, vit l'exécution de fouiles complètes à l'intérieur de l'atelier à bassin, y compris le déblaiement de nombreux tunnels et conduits de cheminée sous-jacents. Entre 1995 et 1997, les travaux de consolidation et de réparation des vestiges de l'atelier à bassin furent exécutés. La LUAU avait pour mission de surveiller ces travaux et également d'effectuer d'autres fouiles dans deux zones limitées.

Les investigations out révélé des vestiges au niveau de base d'un four à bassin à passage continu, ses chambres avec récupérateurs de chaleur et conduites de gaz étant encore largement intactes. Bien que les détails de la conception du four à bassin Siemens d'origine soient bien connus, dû à la survie des plans de brevet d'origine, les fouiles de l'atelier à bassin No 9 ont prouvé que des modifications importantes par rapport à la conception de norme avaient été effectuées par Pilkingtons. La plus notable était la division du four en deux parties distinctes et chauffées indépendamment: 'L'extrémité fusion' et l'extrémité travail', situées dans deux ateliers adjacents, chacun ayant son propre jeu de récupérateurs de chaleur. Cet agencement avait été développé afin de permettre de satisfaire le plus efficacement possible les diverses conditions nécessaires pour fondre et affiner le verre, et pour cueillir et travailler le verre, réduisant les coûts et améliorant la qualité.

Comme la sensibilité commerciale de conception de four assurait que peu de documents détaillés soient conservés, l'élucidation des modiitications a largement dépendu de l'analyse détaillée des éléments de l'atelier à bassin No 9 qui ont survécu. Le développement d'un four de conception normalisée par Pilkingtons fut primordial pour le succès commercial de la compagnie, et les recherches archéologiques donnent ainsi une idée précieuse des raisons de la prédominance de cette compagnie dans le commerce du verre de fenêtre en Grande-Bretagne, de la fin du dix-neuvième siecle à nos jours.

Les vestiges de l'atelier à bassin No 9 offrent un témoignage unique sur une époque qui connut un développement technologique rapide au sein de l'industrie du verre, période se caractérisant par des conceptions innovatrices, mais de courte durée. Il n'existe aucun autre site comparable avec four à bassin à passage continu en Angletarre. Cannington Shaw Bottle Shop (l'atelier de bouteilles Cannington Shaw), également situé à St Helens, représente un deuxième bon exemple de survie d'un four à verre de la fin du dix-neuvième siècle, mais il avait été construit pour la fabrication des bouteilles, plutôt que pour celle du verre de fenêtre, et il est moins développé sur le plan technique. Le projet Monde du verre a réussi à assurer la conservation d'un monument industriel rare. Construits de l'autre côté du canal, le centre de visiteurs et le musée, d'un coût de plusieurs millions de livres sterling, offrent désormais au public une image représentative du développement technique et du patrimoine de l'industrie du verre, les vestiges archéologiques survivant en étant l'élément essentiel.

Zusammenfassung

Von 1991 bis 1997 führte die Lancaster University Archaeological Unit (LUAU) eine Untersuchung an stehenden Gebäuden, Ausgrabungen sowie mündliche und dokumentarisehe Untersuchungen in Form eines Phasenprogramms durch, die auf die Überreste von Pilkingtons Wannenhaus Nr. 9 auf dem „Hotties"-Gelände in St Helens (England) (NGR SJ 5135 9475) gerichtet war. Das konische Hauselement des Komplexes steht noch und ist ein eindrucksvolles denkmalgeschütztes Gebäude der Klasse II. Das Wannenhaus wurde 1887 von Pilkington als Zweckbau zur Herstellung von Fensterglas mit dem Zylinderglasverfahren errichtet. In diesem befand sich ein Durchlaufwannenofen, der auf regenerative Technik, einem Patent der Gebrüder Siemens, beruhte. Das Gelände, das im Norden vom Sankeykanal von 1757 begrenzt ist, wurde früher als das Schachtgebäude einer Kohlengrube und bis 1884-5 von der Firma Bridgewater Chemical Works benutzt. Die Geschichte dieses Grundstücks zeigt daher sauber den industriellen Fortschritt der Stadt von Kohle über Chemikalien bis zur Glasherstellung, die noch heute in der lokalen Wirtschaft dominiert

1991 wurde das Gelände des früheren Glaswerks für die Städtesanierung vorgesehen. Das konische Haus und seine direkte Umgebung wurden von der neu gegründeten Hotties Science and Arts Centre Ltd. erworben, die später den Namen World of Glass Project erhielt. Sie hatte das Ziel, Aufzeichnungen über den Glasofen zusammenzustellen, seine Überreste zu konsolidieren und schließlich das Gelände für Besucher zu öffnen. Im gleichen Jahr erhielt die LUAU den Auftrag, die ersten vier Phasen der Außenarbeiten auszuführen. Phase 1 bezog sich auf eine Untersuchung der Struktur des konischen Hausgebäudes, die Planung der benachbarten Oberflächenreste und die archäologische Registrierung mehrerer geotechnischer Schürfgruben. Die Untersuchungen wurden in erster Linie vom Ravenhead-Renaissance-Konsortium in Auftrag gegeben und finanziert und später von English Heritage. In einer zweiten Untersuchungsphase von November 1991 bis März 1992 wurde der chemisch kontaminierte Abraum bis auf eine Tiefe von 3,50 m von allen Flächen um das Wannenhaus abgetragen und eine vorläufige Ausgrabung des unterirdischen Tunnelsystems unter dem Gebäude vorgenommen. In der dritten Phase, die 1993 durchgeführt wurde, fand die gesamte Ausgrabung des Wannenhaus-Inneren statt, einschließlich der Räumung der zahlreichen darunter befindlichen Tunnel und Rauchzüge. Von 1995 bis 1997 wurden Bauarbeiten zum Konsolidieren und Ausbessern der Wannenhausüberreste ausgeführt. Die LUAU wurde mit der Kontrolle dieser Arbeiten beauftragt und ferner mit weiteren Ausgrabungen in zwei begrenzten Bereichen.

Bei den Untersuchungen wurden die noch bestehenden Überreste des Durchlaufwannenofens auf Basisniveau gefunden, wobei die Regenerativkammern und Rauchzüge der Gasversorgung noch weitgehend erhalten geblieben waren. Obgleich die ursprüngliche Konstruktion des Siemens-Wannenofens allgemein bekannt war, weil es noch die ursprünglichen Patentzeichnurigen gab, wurden nach den Ergebnissen der Ausgrabung des Wannenhauses Nr. 9 sehr bedeutende Änderungen an der Standardkonstruktion durch Pilkingtons vorgenommen. Am bemerkenswertesten war die Unterteilung des Ofens in zwei getrennte und unabhängig voneinander beheizte Teile, die Schmelzwanne und die Arbeitswanne, die in zwei benachbarten Gebäuden untergebracht waren. Jede hatte einen eigenen Generatorsatz. Diese Anordnung wurde entwickelt um die versehiedenen Bedingungen zu erzeugen, die zum Schmelzen und Läutern sowie zum Auffangen und Bearbeiten von Glas erforderlich waren um diese Arbeiten mit optimaler Effizienz auszuführen, die die Kosten senkte mid die Qualität verbesserte. Da die kommerzielle Empfindlichkeit der Ofenkonstruktion gewährleistete, dass nur wenige genaue Unterlagen geführt wurden, war die Klärung der Änderungen weitgehend von der genauen Analyse der noch vorhandenen Elemente des Wannenhauses Nr. 9 abhängig. Die Entwicklung der Standard-Ofenkonstruktion durch Pilkingtons war wesentlich für ihren kommerziellen Erfolg und die archäologischen Untersuchungen haben uns wertvolle Einsichten in die Gründe für die Dominanz des

Unternehmens in der britischen Fensterglasherstellung von Ende des neunzehnten Jahrhunderts bis auf den heutigen Tag vermittelt.

Die Überreste des Wannenhauses Nr. 9 stellen ein einzigartiges Beispiel für das Überleben aus einem Zeitalter rapider technischer Entwicklungen in der Glasindustrie bis zu einer Zeit dar, die durch innovative aber kurzlebige Konstruktionen gekennzeichnet ist. In England gibt es nirgendwo ein Gelände mit einem vergleichbaren Durchlaufwannenofen. Cannington Shaw Bottle Shop, ebenfalls in St Helens, ist ein zweites ausgezeichnetes Beispiel für Überreste eines Glasofens aus dem späten neunzehnten Jahrhundert, der jedoch zur Herstellung von Flaschen und nicht von Fenstergias gebaut wurde. Seine technische Entwicklung ist nicht so hochgradig. Das World of Glas Project war erfolgreich bei dem Versuch, die Erhaltung eines seltenen Industriebauwerks zu gewährleisten. Das Visitor Centre und Museum, die mit Kosten von mehreren Millionen Pfund Sterling über dem Kanal erbaut wurden, führen heute der Öffentlichkeit die technische Entwicklung und Tradition der Glasindustrie vor Augen, indem sie die archäologischen Überreste als wesentlichstes Element benutzen.

Acknowledgements

Many people have contributed to the archaeological recording programme at 'The Hotties' over the ten year life of the project. For the early phases particular mention must be made of Andrew Paterson (formerly of Ravenhead Renaissance) for his generous assistance and unbridled enthusiasm over the four years that he was associated with the scheme. Mike Davies (Carmichael Project Management) has seen the project through all its phases and has made a significant contribution towards ensuring cohesion between many people from diverse disciplines. During the later phases encouragement and assistance was provided by Frank Green (World of Glass Project Co-ordinator) and Dr David Martlew (Pilkington plc), who also provided valued technical advice and direction in the specialised field of furnace design. The contribution made by several English Heritage officers is also gratefully acknowledged, particularly Gerry Friell, Stephen Johnson, Frank Kelsall, Chris Scull, Tim Williams, and the project monitor, Tony Wilmott; their support was essential, both to the completion of the fieldwork programme, and to the production of this report.

Warm thanks must go to everyone who worked on the site, both local people and Lancaster University Archaeological Unit (LUAU) personnel; the bulk of the excavation and tunnel clearance was conducted by supervisors David Hodgkinson and Ian Scott, sometimes working with a team of former coal miners, often in extremely difficult conditions of chemical contamination. A significant contribution was also made by LUAU project assistants David Johnson, Malcolm Harrison, Richard Danks, and Chris Wild (latterly as a supervisor), and Chris Howard-Davis examined and commented on the finds. Jamie Quartermaine fulfilled the role of Field Officer during the early phases of work; subsequently, the project was directed in the field by Mick Krupa, who, through dedication and attention to detail, rapidly acquired an unrivalled understanding of this complex site. Jason Wood managed the 'Hotties' project for LUAU for the majority of its active life, and organised a very successful seminar funded by English Heritage on the theme of the glassmaking industry; the conclusion of the assessment, and the analysis phase, were managed by Alan Lupton. Analysis and report writing were conducted by Richard Heawood and Jo Bell, with the considerable assistance of Mick Krupa and David Martlew; the report drawings were designed by Chris Wild, and prepared by Chris Wild and Emma Carter, the volume being type-set with much patience by Andrea Scott. External reading of the text was performed by David Crossley and David Martlew, and the final draft was edited by Rachel Newman.

Documentary research was carried out in two stages by Nigel Neil and Jo Bell. Valuable assistance was provided by Joanne Howdle of St Helens Museum; by the staff of the Local Studies sections at St Helens Central Library and Manchester Central Library; by the staff of the libraries at Lancaster University and UMIST; and by Dinah Stobbs, custodian of the Pilkington archive at Information Management and Storage. Special acknowledgement must go to Ron Parkin (former Production Manager, Pilkington plc), whose unselfish sharing of personal research data, and contacts within the Pilkington organisation, enabled a greater understanding of the glassmaking trade to be rapidly assimilated.

The work at 'The Hotties' was initially financed by the 'Hotties' Science and Arts Centre Ltd. English Heritage became involved in 1993, when the extent and importance of the buried remains was recognised, and its subsequent large-scale funding has been crucial to the success of the project. English Heritage grants have made possible the Stage 3 excavation in 1993, the further excavation and monitoring carried out in 1995–7, the assessment of the project archive in 1998, and the programme of analysis and publication conducted between 1999 and 2001, of which this volume is the culmination.

Glossary

Alkali
Some form of alkali is required to reduce the melting temperature of the raw material mixture or batch. In the 1870s, glassmakers depended on alkali produced by the notorious Leblanc process. Sodium chloride (salt) was treated with sulphuric acid to produce sodium sulphate (known as 'saltcake') and hydrochloric acid gas (discharged to the atmosphere). A second treatment — calcining with coke and limestone — was needed to yield the desirable sodium carbonate (known as 'soda ash'). However, this was expensive, and the furnace on the Hotties site used sodium sulphate (saltcake) as the alkali source. This ingredient was sometimes termed 'soda', although modern usage of 'soda' usually refers to sodium carbonate, or sodium oxide. The glass industry was still a major user of Leblanc sodium sulphate in 1926 (Dick 1973).

Annealing
The process of reheating and gradually cooling finished glass, usually in a dedicated chamber or *lehr* close to the furnace. Without annealing, inequalities of tension between the surface and interior of the glass make it exceptionally brittle and prone to breaking.

Batch
The mixture of raw materials with which the glass-making process begins.

Broad glass
A term for *cylinder glass* used particularly in the eighteenth century and before. See *cylinder glass*, *German glass*, *muff glass*, *sheet glass*, and *spread glass*.

Cone
A distinctive cooling tower first built over early glass houses, but which remained in use until the end of the nineteenth century. Heat from the furnace was drawn upwards by the cone and dissipated, creating a more tolerable working environment for the glass blowers.

Continuous production
A method devised by Siemens which allowed a *tank furnace* to be simultaneously charged with raw materials at one end and have molten glass drawn off at the other. This meant that a single furnace could be worked without stoppage for several months.

Crown glass
Window glass produced by taking a gather of molten glass on the end of a blowing iron, blowing a sphere, and then spinning it out to form a thin circular sheet or table. The table is then cut into small panes and the central 'bullseye' used as *cullet* or upper window glass. The technique dominated the window glass market in the early nineteenth century, because glass manufacture was taxed on the weight of glass melted rather than the weight of saleable ware produced, and *crown glass* could be made with less waste than *cylinder glass*. It remained tax efficient until the 1840s.

Cullet
Broken or imperfect glass, which could be recycled as an important ingredient of the *batch*. When recycled, cullet requires less energy to fuse than is required to bring about the chemical reactions which convert raw materials into molten glass.

Cylinder glass
A general term for window glass produced by blowing or drawing a long tube of glass, splitting it open, and flattening it to produce sheets. The method was in general use until the late eighteenth century, when it was temporarily supplanted by *crown glass*; glass production was taxed on the total weight of glass melted until 1845, and in these circumstances, cylinder glass was not tax efficient. From the 1830s cylinder glass was revived to meet the growing need for larger panes of glass, and remained in general use until the early twentieth century. See also *broad glass*, *German glass*, *muff glass*, *sheet glass*, and *spread glass*.

Drawn glass
A term used for glass which was not blown by hand on the end of a tube, but drawn vertically from a pool of molten glass. The means to do this were the subject of experimentation in the late nineteenth and early twentieth centuries, in the hope of bypassing the expensive and time-consuming hand-blowing process. Initially, large cylinders of glass were drawn vertically, but by 1913, Pilkingtons' foreign competitors were able to draw flat sheet glass straight from the tank. The latter was sometimes termed 'direct drawn' glass; its quality was at first unreliable.

English bond
A brick bond consisting of alternate rows of headers and stretchers.

English garden wall bond
Brick bond employing one course of headers to three or five of stretchers.

Flint glass
A high quality glass manufactured to deliver uncoloured transparency, so called because it was originally made with crushed flints instead of sand. It has applications in the manufacture of certain types of containers, vessels, and optical glasses.

Frit	The part-fused or sintered mixture of materials which results from an initial heating of the *batch*, and in which chemical reactions essential to the melt begin.
German glass	A term for *cylinder glass* used around the 1830s. See *cylinder glass*, *broad glass*, *muff glass*, *sheet glass*, and *spread glass*.
Lehr	An annealing furnace, usually in the form of a long narrow structure close to the furnace.
Metal	Glass in its fully molten state.
Muff glass	A nineteenth century name for *cylinder glass*, on account of its similarity to the ladies' clothing accessory. See *cylinder glass*, *broad glass*, *German glass*, *sheet glass*, and *spread glass*.
Plate glass	Thick, high quality glass used for mirrors and stagecoach windows. From the early eighteenth century it was usually made by casting the molten glass on a table, and polishing it with sand and rouge (iron oxide).
Pot furnace	The type of furnace which, in various forms, was used to melt glass from the earliest times to the late nineteenth century. Clay pots or crucibles containing *frit* were arranged on a stone or fire-brick floor, above a furnace fuelled with wood or coal. Cooler or separate chambers allowed preliminary heating of the *batch* and post-production *annealing* of the product, whether for window- or vessel-glass.
Regenerative principle	A design developed by Siemens in the 1850s, which allowed waste heat from a furnace to be re-used, enormously increasing efficiency. The design was first applied to furnaces in the iron industry, but was transferred to the pot furnaces used for glassmaking following the introduction of remote gas producers in 1861, an innovation that allowed fuel gas to be generated away from the furnaces (Douglas and Frank 1972, 114–5). The technique was combined with the newly invented tank furnace in the 1870s and revolutionised glassmaking technology; as well as saving fuel, use of waste heat to preheat the combustion gases allowed higher furnace temperatures to be achieved. The regenerator itself is defined below.
Regenerator	One of a series of chambers sited below or adjacent to a furnace, containing a honeycomb arrangement of refractory bricks. Exhaust fumes were passed through the chamber, and heat absorbed by the bricks. The flow of gases was then switched, and instead of exhaust, either gas or air was now directed towards the furnace through the warmed regenerator, with the refractory bricks preheating the gas/air. When the bricks had cooled, exhaust was once again passed through, the fuel gases now being warmed by adjacent regenerators.
Sheet glass	Window glass made either as *cylinder glass*, or as *drawn glass*: the term was used from the 1830s until the *drawn glass* process became obsolete in 1959. See *cylinder glass*, *broad glass*, *German glass*, *muff glass*, and *spread glass*.
Spread glass	Window glass made by the cylinder method. A term thought to belong to the late eighteenth and early nineteenth centuries. See *cylinder glass*, *broad glass*, *German glass*, *muff glass*, and *sheet glass*.
Tank furnace	A furnace where glass is melted in, and drawn from, a single large container or tank, rather than a number of smaller pots. The use of a tank presented technical problems which were not overcome until the 1870s. The combination of the tank form with the principles of *regenerative* heating and *continuous* production allowed the window glass industry to expand hugely at a time of great demand.
Tank house	The building or buildings housing a tank furnace and its fixtures. In the case of No 9, the tank house was composed of two separate structures housing the melt and working ends, joined where the furnace passed from one to the other; the characteristic brick cone stood over the working end.

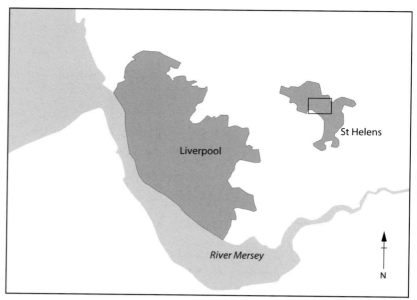

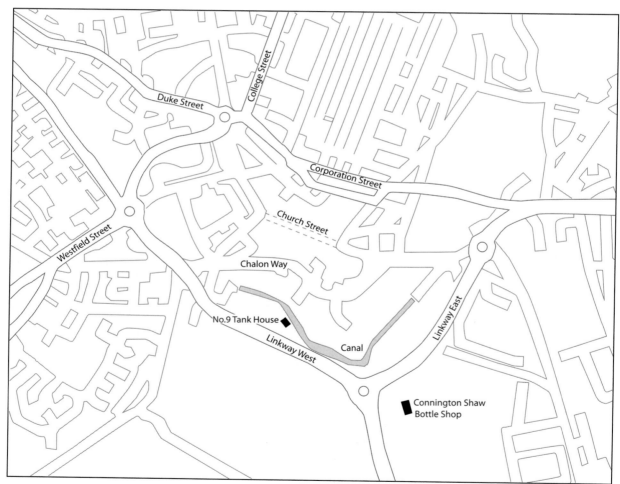

Fig 1 Location of No 9 Tank House within St Helens

1

INTRODUCTION

'The Hotties'

'The Hotties' lies 0.5 km south–east of the town centre of St Helens, the name referring specifically to the part of Pilkington plc's disused St Helens Sheet Glass Works that occupies the south bank of the Sankey Canal (SJ 5121 9501; Fig 1). The name is derived from a series of pipes, located on the south bank of the canal, which formerly discharged hot water/steam from the glass works, producing spectacular clouds of steam immediately over the canal's surface (see plate on rear cover of volume). 'The Hotties' lies within the area of the Jubilee Side, a part of the Pilkington works built in the late 1880s and 1890s; the Jubilee Side was an expansion of the much larger St Helens Sheet Glass Works to the south, which covered an area of c 9 ha (Pls 1 and 2). By the early 1990s, much of the former Jubilee Side was derelict land, Pilkington plc's modern glass making facilities having shifted to the south and east many years earlier. A single nineteenth century building survived from the former works, a Grade II Listed brick cone house which was formerly part of No 9 Tank House, a complex purpose-built by Pilkingtons for the manufacture of sheet glass, and completed in 1887 (Pl 3). As a result of the fieldwork programme described below, the listing of the brick cone house was upgraded to Grade II*.

*Plate 1 Aerial photograph showing Pilkingtons' Sheet Glass Works, December 1947
(Pilkington Archive PRM/AV/ZA)*

1

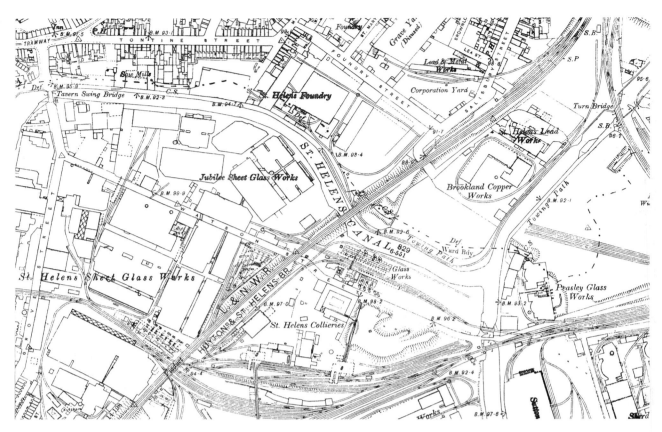

Plate 2 Extract from Ordnance Survey 1:2500 map, 1894, Sheet CVIII.1.10–4 (not to scale; reproduced by kind permission of St Helens Library). No 9 Tank House lies at the end of the caption 'Jubilee Sheet Glass Works'. The Cannington Shaw Bottle Shop lies within the Sherdley Glass Works, to the south–east of the Peasley Glass Works

Plate 3 View south over the cone house

The re-development of the site

By 1991, the area of the former Jubilee Side works was earmarked for urban regeneration, with two major developments being planned; the Chalon Court Hotel (now the Hilton) was to be built on the western portion, whilst to the east, a plot of land measuring *c* 80 m x 40 m, and including the remains of the Listed cone house, was acquired by the newly formed Hotties Science and Arts Centre Ltd. This organisation had been founded with the aim of excavating and consolidating the remains of the tank house complex, with a view to the eventual opening of the site as a visitor centre. However, in 1995, its backers redefined their plans, and a submission was made to the Heritage Lottery Fund with the name 'The World of Glass Project'. The cone house and adjacent archaeological remains were still to be consolidated for eventual display to the public, but additionally, it was planned to build a new museum with presentational facilities on the north bank of the canal.

The fieldwork programme

In 1991, the Hotties Science and Arts Centre Ltd commissioned Lancaster University Archaeological Unit (LUAU) to undertake the first of four stages of fieldwork on their site at the Hotties. Stage 1 involved a survey of the fabric of the cone house building, the planning of adjacent surface remains, and the archaeological recording of a number of geotechnical test pits. Stage 2 followed in November 1991 to March 1992; chemically contaminated overburden was removed from the area around the exterior of the cone house, and a variety of subsurface structures recorded. Stage 3 ran from January to September 1993, and was funded by English Heritage. The subsurface remains within the cone house were excavated and recorded (Pl 4), together with an external area between the cone house and the canal. This stage of the fieldwork was crucial, because it demonstrated that the basal remains of the working end of a continuous tank furnace survived largely intact below the floor of the

Plate 4 Excavation beneath the cone house floor. A total station was used to make a three-dimensional record of all structures revealed

Plate 5 A worker wearing personal protective equipment. Heavy metal contamination meant that staff had to wear clothing that was often hot and uncomfortable

cone building; heavy metal contamination was still present, and site staff had to excavate wearing personal protective equipment (Pl 5). Stage 4, in 1995–7, was a programme of archaeological recording to accompany the consolidation and repair of the fabric of the cone house, and of the underground brick flues and passages uncovered by earlier fieldwork. Additionally, two discrete areas were targeted for

further excavation, one within the cone house, the other immediately to the south–west.

The excavation and building survey report

The project results have been presented in terms of a chronological site narrative, divided into chapters by phase. For each phase, other than the final Phase 4 alterations, documentary evidence is presented first, followed by archaeological evidence. Additionally, for Phases 2 and 3, a functional analysis of the remains is provided at the end of the chapter. Interpretation is concentrated within the functional analysis sections and the final discussion, but a measure of interpretation has had to be included with the archaeological evidence in order to make it intelligible. Parallel systems of feature numbers and context numbers were used within the project archive, but in this report, context numbers only are cited.

The archive

The project archive is to be housed at Liverpool Museum. As well as *pro-forma* record sheets and indices, it consists of a context database, photographs, drawings on drafting film, and drawings in digital format which exist as CAD files. The majority of the finds from the project were derived from secondary and tertiary contexts, and proved to be of little use in the interpretation of the remains encountered. Most categories of artefact were discarded following a meeting between representatives of the Hotties Science and Arts Centre Ltd and Liverpool Museum, but three iron ladles and three work shoes have been retained for possible museum display. Full finds catalogues and assessment reports quantifying the discarded material are available in the archive.

2

THE MAKING OF GLASS

Jo Bell

All glassmaking, from its earliest days to the present time, has followed the same principles. The following section provides a brief description of the process, the terms in italic font being described in the *Glossary* at the start of this report.

The raw materials for glassmaking are silica (sand), *alkali* (potash, kelp ash, soda ash, or saltcake) and lime (from high-lime sand or limestone); colourants or decolorisers may also be added, the latter particularly to counteract a strong green tint caused by iron commonly present in sand. Glass can be formed from silica alone, but this requires a melting temperature of 1720°C, which was not achievable until the twentieth century (Crossley 1993, 6), and the addition of alkali reduces melting temperatures to 900–1200°C. The addition of lime gives durability to glass. This ingredient was not deliberately used until the seventeenth century, but earlier glassmakers achieved the best results by using sands and alkalis now known to have contained lime (*ibid*).

The mixture of raw materials is known as *batch*. Until the nineteenth century, it was common slowly to pre-heat the batch, to form *frit*, which was then transferred to the melting furnace (Pl 6). When fritting, the temperature is kept sufficiently below 800°C to prevent the formation of the liquid phases, with the aim being to obtain some sintering and pre-reaction without the mix becoming unhandlable. Fritting not only reduces the energy required by the main furnace by getting rid of some of the excess carbon dioxide gas, but sets in train chemical reactions essential for a homogeneous melt; in the furnace, the silicates formed during fritting melt early, and spread over the surface of the sand grains, aiding dissolution.

There is no such thing as waste glass, as broken or imperfect glass, *cullet*, makes a desirable addition to the batch, for three main reasons. Firstly, it requires less energy to fuse than is required to bring about the chemical reactions which convert raw materials into molten glass; secondly, it does not give off copious amounts of carbon dioxide, giving further savings in the energy required by the furnace; and thirdly, in large sizes, it can aid the entry of furnace radiation

Plate 6 A teazer, wearing heat-resistant clothing. The teazers kept the tank filling pocket full of frit and cullet (photograph kindly provided from the Pilkington Archive by David Martlew)

into the batch pile. For these reasons, some glasses use up to 50% of cullet in their make-up, and it is unusual to find much waste glass on a disused glass site; any fragments that remain are likely to date from the final period of operation of the furnace. This re-use of broken glass is an admirable economy for the manufacturer, but is less endearing to archaeologists. At most early furnace sites, so little glass remains that it is difficult even to identify the kind of vessels made.

In the body of the furnace, the raw materials melt fully and become *metal*, a highly corrosive liquid. Until the late nineteenth century, glass was melted in crucibles or pots made of refractory clay, with larger tanks being favoured thereafter; whatever the receptacle, it must be designed to withstand both extremely high temperatures, and the corrosive nature of molten glass — the melting process has been described as 'like trying to obtain clear water by applying heat to ice in a container made of sugar' (Maloney 1967, 75). The *metal* must not be contaminated with smoke or grit, and heat must be carefully conserved to melt the glass fully, and to minimise fuel consumption. Nonetheless, the furnace is usually greedy in its consumption of fuel, whether wood, coal or gas, and until the advent of natural gas, glassmaking has always had to be carried out near a plentiful source of fuel.

When it has been sufficiently refined, the metal is allowed to cool to a slightly lower temperature (usually about 1000°C), so that it can be worked by one of a number of methods. Metal may be taken from the furnace and cast onto a table to give a sheet of *plate glass*. Alternatively, a gather of molten glass may be taken from the furnace on the end of a metal rod; it may be blown to form a vessel, or to form a cylinder, which is subsequently opened up to obtain a sheet of *cylinder glass*, or to form a sphere, which is spun on the end of the rod to obtain a circular sheet of *crown glass*. At this stage, if plate glass is not being produced, a primary concern may be to avoid unnecessary contact between the molten glass and any other object, in order to give the article being manufactured a high quality 'fire-polished' surface, obviating the need for subsequent grinding and polishing.

The newly-formed article, either vessel or sheet of glass, must then be *annealed*, the process usually being carried out in a dedicated chamber or *lehr* close to the furnace (Douglas and Frank 1972, 119). Annealing involves the re-heating and gradual cooling of the product, and makes the glass less brittle and more durable. Some glasses, particularly plate glass, then need to be ground and polished to achieve a perfect surface. Finally, when the product is finished and ready for sale, a method of transport has to be found for this fragile commodity.

These, then, are the technical problems which have confronted all glassmakers, and their technology has been a constantly changing response to these difficulties. No 9 Tank House represents a rare survival of one of the major technological leaps in glassmaking, but in order that this may be appreciated, it is necessary briefly to review the history of glassmaking from the seventeenth century to the late nineteenth century, and then to consider the problems confronting the designers of furnaces in the years before No 9 was built.

3

HISTORICAL BACKGROUND

Jo Bell

The adoption of coal-fired glass furnaces in the seventeenth century

Although glass had been made in England since the Roman period, dramatic changes occurred in English glassmaking in the seventeenth century, and these had a profound effect upon the later development of the industry. The late sixteenth century had seen competition between the glass and iron industries for the products of coppice woodland, and increasing friction between both of these industries and the buyers of mature timber (Crossley 1993, 13). As a result of these tensions, attempts were made to develop coal-fired glass furnaces, and the granting of a patent to Sir Edward Zouch and others in 1611 has been interpreted as demonstrating that such a furnace had been successfully developed at Winchester House, Southwark (*ibid*). A further patent awarded to Zouch in 1614, and taken over by Sir Robert Mansell in 1615, gave the patentees control of the whole glass industry, allowing them to close down wood-fired furnaces, and to regulate glass imports. By 1620, the wood-fired industry had been virtually eradicated (Godfrey 1975, 59).

The change from wood to coal could only be made by altering the design of glass furnaces. Glassmakers initially struggled with the different and unfamiliar demands of coal; it was a potential contaminant of the glass metal, and burnt with a shorter flame than wood, so that fire had to be brought to the centre of the furnace. Over time, underground flues started to be constructed to provide draught for the central fire, the flues being vaulted over to give access to the fire for stoking (Crossley 1993, 8), but the importance of a chimney to create a draught and raise furnace temperatures was not at first appreciated (Godfrey 1975, 152). Only in the late seventeenth century did the characteristic glasshouse cone develop, and, in conjunction with draught flues at the foot of the furnace, it meant that 'the entire building acted as a giant chimney which created a strong draught' (*op cit*, 155). This removed much of the smoke from the process, and intensified the heat. With growing confidence, the industry was able to expand, and by the end of the seventeenth century there were 88 glasshouses in Britain (Vavra nd, 93).

The change of fuel had a dramatic effect on the location of the glass industry, and there was an almost complete shift from the woodlands, towards sources of coal. Since fuel was needed in much greater quantities than raw materials, the latter were often imported, and glassmakers particularly sought out the places in which their expanding new markets and coalfields coincided, exploring new markets and new technologies at the same time. Glass was made in the seventeenth century on coalfields in Gloucestershire, Lancashire, Nottinghamshire, Staffordshire, Tyneside, Worcestershire, and Yorkshire, as well as in London, which was supplied with coal by sea from the North East (Crossley 1993, 16–7). This distribution changed relatively little in the eighteenth and nineteenth centuries, although areas of specialisation slowly developed (*ibid*).

The establishment of glassmaking in St Helens

Glassmaking first came to Lancashire before 1605, with the establishment of a furnace at Haughton Green, to the south–east of Manchester (Hurst Vose 1994); later in the seventeenth century, the Leaf family set up a furnace at Warrington in 1650, and another at Sutton, in the Ravenhead area of St Helens, in 1688 (Harris 1968, 107; Fig 2). The early eighteenth century saw further modest development, the Huguenot Henzey brothers building a glass-house at Prescot in 1719, and another at Thatto Heath, St Helens, in 1725 (Harris 1968, 107; Barker 1960, 40; Fig 2). Glass manufacture continued on a small scale for several decades, but its expansion was limited by poor transport links. Glass was a commodity particularly unsuited to transport on the bad roads of eighteenth century Lancashire, and the glassmakers at Thatto Heath and Sutton found their markets limited.

The situation was to change with the expansion of the South Lancashire Coalfield. Coalmining had begun in Lancashire in the fourteenth century (Gould and Cranstone 1992, 12), and by the 1760s, the coalfield was becoming an increasingly important source of fuel for both industrial and domestic usage (Walton 1987, 119). The distribution of coal required an efficient means of transport, and the demand for cheap coal in Liverpool, which was then expanding rapidly, was sufficient to drive transport improvements around St Helens. The turnpike commissioners noted that 'the Inhabitants of this town [Liverpool] have suffer'd much for want of getting their Coales home During the Summer season' (Bailey 1936, 160), and turnpike roads were accordingly built and extended in the mid-1700s. However, roads remained a difficult, slow, and expensive means of transport for most commercial users, and a much more significant advance came with the opening in 1757 of the first British canal, the Sankey Navigation, built to supply Liverpool's demand for coal (Fig 2; Langton 1979, 165); within a few years, 75 % of the area's output was exported

down the canal, and production increased. St Helens grew rapidly in the last decades of the eighteenth century, with Lady Kenyon observing in 1797 that 'St Helens was a poor little place when I passed through it thirty years ago; and now is a very neat pretty country town' (Pilkington Brothers 1926, 16).

The new waterway benefited the coal mines, but also stimulated a range of other enterprises. By the 1770s the area was 'already well-stocked with furnaces and coal-using workshops' (Walton 1987, 119). The copper and chemical industries, attracted by good transport and cheap coal, became mainstays of the economy of St Helens, and their factories brought 'employment, prosperity and pungent fumes' (Pilkington Brothers 1926, 36). The canal provided a link between the coalfield and the coal-burning salt works of Cheshire, and a reciprocal trade in salt opened up; in the nineteenth century, the St Helens chemical industry used salt for some of its processes, in order to supply chemicals for the soap and textile factories of Merseyside.

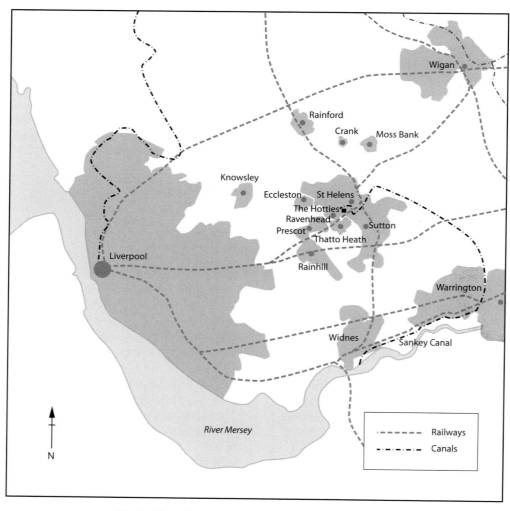

Fig 2 Map of principal places mentioned in the text

These economic developments made St Helens a very much more attractive place for the glassmaker. The first requirement was for a large supply of coal, and the town was literally built on it. Serviceable sand was also available locally, north-west of St Helens, and suitable fireclay could be extracted from within the coal-measure strata. However, there was now ready access to alkali as well, either from St Helens chemical factories, or via the canal. Initially, the glass industry used soda ash (sodium carbonate), produced in Liverpool by burning imported kelp. However, the Leblanc process, invented in the 1780s, offered a larger supply of cheaper alkali. Salt was treated with sulphuric acid to produce saltcake (sodium sulphate), and a second treatment, calcining with coke and limestone, could be used to generate soda ash if required (Barker and Harris 1959, 224). Saltcake was adequate for the manufacture of most types of glass, and from the 1830s was used even in the manufacture of high quality plate. The Leblanc process was commonly used by the Liverpool chemical industry after 1822, but Muspratt and Gamble eventually moved to St Helens itself, fearing that the Liverpool corporation would force them out because of the volume of hydrochloric acid gas which the Leblanc process released into the atmosphere (*op cit*, 229). With access to alkali, and with the canal at their backs providing an ideal means of transport for their fragile product, the glassmakers now had all their requirements to hand.

Growth in the regional market for glass also stimulated the Lancashire glass industry. In the 1820s, a building boom vastly increased the demand for glass (Barker 1977, 29), and the rapid growth of factory-based industry, particularly textiles, was especially significant; business premises were exempt from the window tax levied on private housing, and could afford to glaze extensively. The burgeoning textile industries of the North West led to the development of large mills and numerous weaving sheds, all of which needed to be well lit. Consequently, window glass was required in large quantities by an expanding local market.

These factors stimulated the establishment of a number of new companies around St Helens in the late eighteenth to mid-nineteenth centuries. These included the Eccleston Crown Glassworks (1792) and the very influential British Cast Plate Glass Company, established in 1773 at Ravenhead. The latter was relaunched at the end of the century as the British Plate Glass Company and became one of the country's most important manufacturers. It was world-famous for the quality of its glass and the size of its casting hall. Smaller firms in the Merseyside area included the Union Plate Glass Works, built in 1836, and the Manchester and Liverpool Plate Glass Company at Sutton Oak (Barker and Harris 1959, 216). More relevant to the present study, however, was the founding of the St Helens Crown Glass Company in 1826, by partners including Peter Greenall of the brewing family, and William Pilkington Jnr (Barker 1960, 55–8).

The development of Pilkington Brothers

The St Helens Crown Glass Company, the predecessor of present-day Pilkington plc, established itself in the later 1820s and early 1830s, when window glass was made in one of three ways. Casting plate glass gave the highest quality product. Glass was cast while molten into flat tables, leaving a thick but imperfect plate which had to be ground and polished on one side and then the other, in the process losing half its thickness and vastly increasing its price. It was used for mirrors and stagecoach windows where perfect smoothness or strength were requisite (Barker 1977, 28). Cylinder glass (*see above Glossary*) was relatively cheap to produce, but was of lesser quality because of its imperfect surface. It fell out of popularity in the late eighteenth and early nineteenth centuries, because the loss of glass at the thick moil where the cylinder was attached to the blowing iron, and at the other end where the cylinder was opened, meant that the method was not tax efficient, glass being taxed on the total weight of glass melted, not on the product. The third type, and at this time the most common, was crown glass, made by spinning a bubble of molten glass on a blowpipe until it 'flashed' into a flat circular plate (or 'table'). This was a long-established and simple technology, which gave a relatively smooth, fire-polished surface at the cost of severe optical distortion (Barker 1977, 25). Its revival in Britain was due to the fact that a table of crown glass could be split into window panes with little wastage, making it tax efficient. The fact that the table had to be cut into several small panes gave rise to the distinctive multi-paned windows of the time (Barker 1977, 25).

This, then, was the product that Pilkingtons' predecessors started to manufacture in 1826, and the firm was thus not a rival to the famous Ravenhead works, which dominated the St Helens area, specialising in expensive, high-quality plate glass. In its early years, the St Helens Crown Glass Works benefited from the decline and collapse of the Eccleston Works, whose customers switched to Pilkingtons, and from a brief crisis at their main Midlands rival Chances, in 1831. In 1837, the enterprise was so successful that the Pilkington family, who had formerly divided their energies between glassmaking and the wine and spirits business, were sure enough of the future of their glass business to dedicate themselves solely to the glassworks (Barker 1960, 78). From the 1830s, Chances of Birmingham had developed new polishing techniques to finish the imperfect surface of cylinder glass, and this product began to gain in popularity, now offering a good surface finish as well as the possibility of much larger window panes. Greenall and Pilkington began to polish 'German sheet glass' or cylinder glass in 1842 — without licence from Chances, who had tried to establish a monopoly on it (Barker 1960, 87). The lifting of excise duty on glass melting in 1845 further encouraged the manufacture of cylinder glass, and although crown glass remained in production at Pilkingtons until 1872, cylinder glass rapidly became the company's main product (*op cit*, 86).

The firm weathered a depression in the early 1840s, and went on to prosper whilst two local competitors collapsed (*op cit*, 216). The name Pilkington Brothers was adopted in 1849, when Peter Greenall was bought out, choosing to devote his efforts to brewing. A further tax repeal in 1851 lifted window tax from private houses, and at the same time, the Crystal Palace provided the best and most conspicuous possible advertisement for window glass, the panes being made by Chances, using the cylinder method (Hurst Vose 1980, 117). The tax repeals of 1845 and 1851 made glass cheaper at a time of enormously increased building (Crossley 1993, 15), and there was a huge surge in demand for domestic window glass, particularly for the larger panes made by the cylinder process. The continuing expansion of industry in the North West, particularly the manufacture of cotton, further stimulated demand for window glass, and Pilkingtons saw their output rise from 80 tons per week in 1851 to 150 tons per week in 1854 (Barker and Harris 1959, 358).

The development of the glass furnace, 1860-73

In the mid-nineteenth century, power in the window glass industry became concentrated in the hands of three families — Pilkingtons, Chances of Birmingham and Hartleys of Sunderland. The three giants occasionally formed alliances to close down emerging firms (Barker 1960, 124), but generally were in fierce competition and remained so for many years. It was invariably technological advance that gave a brief advantage over the others, and it was noted that 'Great jealousy is manifested by the proprietors in keeping secret the details of their processes — questions are answered with caution and any very minute enquiry is evaded' (Redding 1842). The secrecy provoked by a justified fear of industrial espionage remains a characteristic of the industry even today.

Pot furnaces of *c* 1860
In the 1860s, competition stimulated innovation in the technology of glassmaking, which had formerly been rather stagnant. Up to this point, despite the introduction of coal-firing, furnaces operated on the same principle as those of the earliest glassmakers. A number of fireclay pots were charged with batch, and the furnace temperature was increased beneath them, to melt the batch and aid the removal of bubbles. The temperature would then be lowered to allow small residual bubbles to shrink, and to condition the glass to the right consistency for gathering and working. When the glass was ready, the blowers worked a long day to empty the pots, and make as much product as possible, as quickly as possible. The pots were then recharged, and the temperature was increased again. The whole cycle took between two and three days.

This was a disruptive and inefficient method of working, with numerous problems of management and cost. Above all, the furnaces consumed enormous amounts of fuel, as they had to be kept alight throughout the cycle, but were only productive for the day when the blowers could work. Additional costs resulted from the inefficient use of the blowers themselves, and the need to replace the fireclay pots every few months, a dangerous and time-consuming process carried out while the furnace burnt, and again involving the loss of energy.

The regenerative furnace
With the market for window glass vastly expanded, the shortcomings of the pot furnace were increasingly apparent. Glassmakers who could increase their output or reduce their costs would achieve a significant advantage. In this climate, the relatively great expense of experimentation with new furnace types was worthwhile. At Pilkingtons, Windle Pilkington, an innovative and instinctive engineer, attempted to improve the pot furnace. At first conscious of the need to economise on fuel, he was drawn to the work of the Siemens brothers. A close working relationship began, which was the key to Pilkingtons' later dominance of the window-glass market.

The Siemens brothers were engineers who in the late 1850s had developed a regenerative coal-fired furnace for smelting metals. Alert to its potential for glassmaking, Friedrich Siemens adapted the invention, designing furnaces for glass manufacturers in Rotherham and Birmingham in 1860 and 1861, and with his brother William, obtaining a patent for the design (British Patent 167, 1861; Cable 2000, 213–4). The furnace was now to be fuelled with gas, a cleaner fuel than coal and less likely to contaminate the metal. More furnaces were soon built; Chance Brothers of Birmingham were quick to make use of the design, the Ravenhead Plate Glass Works soon followed, and in the autumn of 1863, Pilkingtons themselves installed a Siemens-type regenerative furnace at their St Helens Sheet Glass Works (Barker and Harris 1959, 362; Plate 7 reproduces a drawing of a regenerative pot furnace prepared for Chances by Siemens Brothers).

The essential idea behind Siemens' regenerative furnace is that hot exhaust gases are not immediately released to the atmosphere, but are used to pre-heat fresh incoming combustion gases, in structures termed regenerators. On each side of the furnace was a set of two regenerators, each regenerator being in essence a chamber nearly filled with a checkerwork of bricks, stacked in such a way as to allow freedom for gas or air to pass through (Fig 3). Hot exhaust gases leaving the furnace would flow downwards through one set of regenerator chambers and on to the chimney, drawn by the chimney draught. A substantial part of their heat would be taken up by the brick checkerwork, which would get progressively hotter as time went on. After 20 minutes or so, large valves were operated to reverse the direction of gas flow in the system. Now these hot piles of bricks would be used to heat up the air and the producer gas required to fire the furnace. By the time the fuel and combustion air reached the furnace, they had been pre-heated to over 1000° C. Using re-cycled heat in this way gave the flame a tremendous boost — instead of the prime heat of burning being wasted just to warm up lots of nitrogen, it could be liberated as useful heat in the furnace, resulting in hotter, more efficient flames. After this had been happening for a further period of 20 minutes, the bricks would be noticeably cooler, so the valves would be reversed, and the cycle begin over again (British Patent 167, 1861). Although each regenerator would carry hot exhaust gases while being warmed, after the flow was switched, one regenerator in each pair would carry combustion air drawn from the atmosphere, whilst the other would carry producer

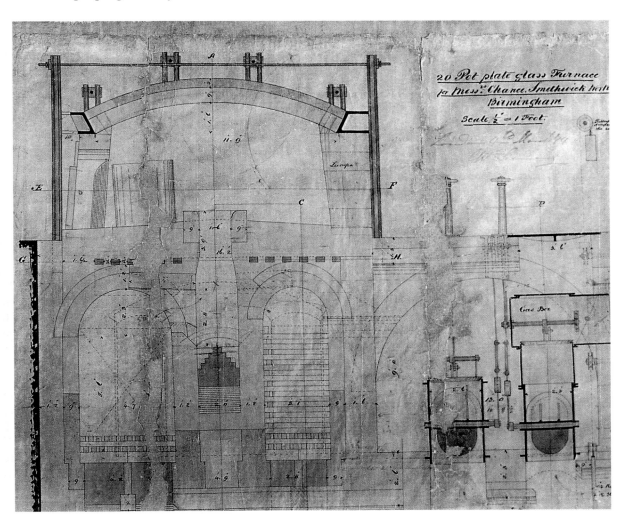

Plate 7 Drawing of a regenerative pot furnace prepared by Siemens Brothers in 1873–4 for Chances of Birmingham. The regenerator switch mechanism is in the bottom right hand corner (photograph kindly provided from the Pilkington Archive by David Martlew)

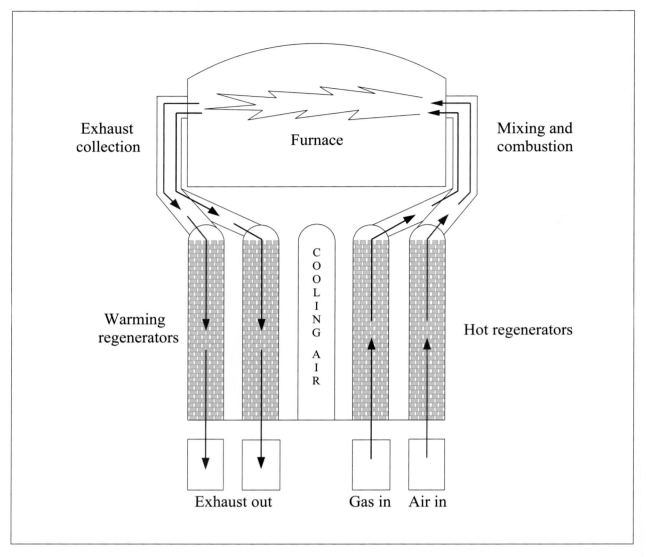

Fig 3 Schematic section through a regenerative furnace, showing flow of gas and air. The combustion gases were fed up from one pair of regenerators, ignited over the molten glass, and the exhaust gases then drawn down to the regenerators on the other side of the furnace

gas, drawn in from a nearby gas producer via a flue system.

This pre-heating of gases gave a considerable reduction in fuel. Siemens claimed that in one of his experimental furnaces the fuel savings had reached as much as 79% (Barker 1960, 139). Gas, chosen over coal as a clean fuel, had the additional advantage that it could be manufactured on the premises using the very cheapest type of coal or coal dust. Pilkingtons had its own collieries to hand, having sunk the first at Green Lane in 1845, and bought out the former St Helens colliery in 1857 (Barker and Harris 1959, 340), but they were now able to use the cheapest coal themselves, and sell a greater proportion of the better grades. However, perhaps more significant, especially to Pilkingtons, was the fact that the preheating of the combustion gases allowed the temperature of the flame in the

furnace to be lifted; this in turn allowed better and more efficient refining of the metal, and the production of glass of higher quality. It has recently been calculated that the glass produced by the first Rotherham regenerative furnace required a melting temperature of at least 1450° C, some 150° C higher than that required by glass produced by a previous furnace (Cable 2000, 213). In time, regenerative furnaces would be able to achieve temperatures of 2000–2200° C.

In use, the regenerative principle seemed a manufacturer's dream, almost too good to be true. It promised enormously improved yield and glass of much better quality than coal furnaces, using cheaper raw materials and positively requiring a fuel which at first was literally given away in coal yards. Friedrich Siemens summarised its benefits when describing its application in a pot furnace:

'Fewer pot breakages also occur, less repairs are required, and the amount of waste has decreased; moreover, the glass metal is obtained from a cheaper composition than that hitherto used, and proves to be of a far superior quality. The pots last fully double the time, and melt more than three times the quantity of material, whilst the furnace itself stands for three years; that is, *it lasts six times as long, and melts more than nine times the quantity of material it did previously to its reconstruction*' (Siemens 1873, 5: my italics).

The complete combustion of fuel which optimised radiating heat in the furnace also ensured that the furnaces were largely smoke-free. Siemens was aware of the opposition aroused by factories which belched out large quantities of smoke, and considered this feature one of the commercial advantages of regenerative firing. Dr Lloyd, one of those who first heard the furnace explained, said that 'The regenerative system appeared to him one of the most beautiful adaptations of science to practical art' (Siemens 1862, 38). JT Chance said that the furnace 'appeared not only perfect in theory, but also to present no insuperable difficulties in practice' (*ibid*).

The regenerative furnace installed at Pilkingtons in 1863 was instantly successful, and made vast economies in fuel costs. The principle quickly proved its worth and was always used henceforth at Pilkingtons: it remains in use today. Yet the inefficient system of using pots to contain the glass remained, with all its drawbacks. Pilkingtons now turned their attention to the possibility of melting glass in a single large container or tank. The idea of a tank was not new: it had first appeared in a British patent of 1769 (Douglas and Frank 1972, 119), but had never been applied successfully.

The development of the regenerative continuous tank furnace

From 1868 Windle Pilkington conducted experiments with tank or 'cistern' furnaces, in the hope of melting larger quantities of glass and economising on pots and fuel. If such a tank could further be simultaneously charged at one end and emptied at the other, then the furnace might be worked without stoppages to recharge or reheat. Pilkington's initial experiments, however, were unsuccessful (Barker 1960, 147).

The Siemens brothers had long been involved with experiments on tank furnaces, and saw that a furnace combining the regenerative principle with a single, large and long-lived container would be a great advance for the glass industry. They experimented independently on tanks from 1860, and after Hans' death in 1867 Friedrich continued the research at Dresden, just as Windle began his un-successful

attempts. The brothers obtained a British patent for a tank furnace in 1870, and continued to develop it. Windle Pilkington had visited Dresden to see their work in progress (Barker 1960, 147), and kept closely in touch with the developing research. It was evidently a close working relationship, for Pilkingtons decided to build a 'continuous tank' to Siemens' new design, a week before he patented it in 1872 (*ibid*). Plate 8 shows a plan view of a continuous tank furnace, reproduced from the 1872 patent.

The new tank combined the proven virtues of regenerative heating with the possibility of continuous working. It was based on Friedrich Siemens' observation that the bulk density of glass increases as glassmaking proceeds. Batch floats on molten glass, and if charged onto the surface of a large pot or tank, it will spread out and prevent the blowers gathering from the surface. However, a barrier wall with a low hole will keep back the light imperfectly melted batch, and allow the molten glass to pass to a second chamber. There the bubbly new glass can be refined, the bubbles rising to the surface and bursting. The bubble-free

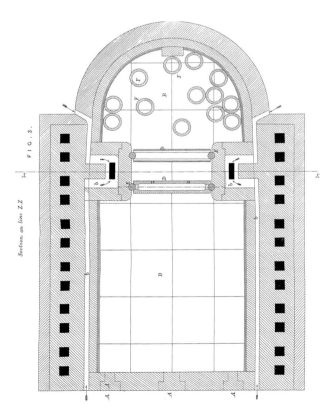

Plate 8 Plan view of a continuous tank furnace from William Siemens' patent of 1872 (British Patent 3478, 1872, fig 3). The drawing shows a relatively short furnace with a semi-circular working end divided from an almost square melt end by two floating bridges

glass accumulates at the bottom, and again, a barrier with an opening at the base will allow it to pass through to a third chamber when ready for working. The principle operating there is exactly the same as that used in the kitchen, for separating meat juices from floating fat (Lakeland Limited 2001, 6). Siemens' new design gave rise to the division, still observed, between the 'melt end' and 'working end' of a tank furnace, the melt end being that where the raw materials are fed in, and the working end that where the molten glass is drawn off.

The introduction of continuous tank furnaces by Pilkingtons

The first continuous tank started production at Pilkingtons in April 1873. For three days it ran successfully and made a great impression on those who saw it. The board of directors heard that it was 'beating any pot furnace on the ground' (Minutes of Board, 17/4/1873), and it seemed that the exciting potential of the tank furnace had indeed been realised. The day after the board meeting, however, the tank leaked badly. The resultant fire destroyed the furnace building (Barker 1977, 134). Many decades later, Cecil Pilkington was of the opinion that this first furnace had failed because the side walls and crown of the furnace were built directly on top of the refractory blocks which contained the highly corrosive metal; as the blocks started to wear, the upper part of the furnace was left unsupported (*ibid*). The failure appears to have occurred too quickly to be the product of block wear, but the supporting of the crown on the side refractory blocks may indeed have been at the root of the problem. If the expansion of the crown during warm-up were to push the sides outwards, there could easily have been a leak via a joint which had sprung open, most likely at low level, where the pressure of the molten glass would be greatest.

Pilkingtons' directors were appalled by the destruction and the concomitant expense. They considered the experiment conclusively unsuccessful and decided to abandon the tank furnace principle. Windle Pilkington was vehemently opposed to this. Having seen the Siemens' experiments for himself, he was convinced of the merits of the continuous tank and insisted that a replacement should be built. If the company would not undertake the project, he made it clear that he would build one at his own expense (Barker 1977, 134). Faced with this commercially dangerous threat from their most dynamic board member, the firm recanted. A new tank furnace was built. Starting production in August 1873, it ran for over three months (Barker 1960, 148). It was not a particularly long run, but the quantity, quality and cost of the product were convincing. Indications from the abortive first furnace suggest that the quality of the glass was particularly impressive (Minutes of Board, 17/4/1873).

Once converted, the company acted with alacrity to commit their whole operation to the tank furnace. Within four years, Pilkingtons had 12 tank furnaces in use to make cylinder or 'sheet' glass, and Siemens was charging them a preferential royalty rate for bulk use (Barker 1977, 135). In the mid-1880s Pilkingtons were expanding sufficiently to buy the land north of their existing premises on which they laid out the Jubilee Side works, including No 9 Tank House. Pilkingtons' willingness to invest heavily in the new technology set them apart from Chances, their main rival. JT Chance had been enthusiastic for the regenerative principle, but did not commit his company to its application in tank furnaces. Chances' failure to grasp the commercial implications of the tank furnace cost them their predominant position in the sheet glass trade, and they eventually abandoned sheet glass manufacture altogether in 1933 (Barker 1960, 154, 213); in contrast, Pilkingtons went on to establish a monopoly in flat glass manufacture in the UK.

Having reaped the dividends of technical innovation, Pilkingtons continued to explore and embrace technological change wherever possible. Willingness to experiment was a keystone of their success in the late nineteenth and early twentieth centuries. In a pattern common to many industries, Pilkingtons' innovation tended always towards mechanisation and the integration of various processes into a streamlined system. Because glass is made from raw material through to finished product in one location, it 'lends itself ideally to continuous processes and automation' (Maloney 1967, 73). Coal, sand and salt are taken in as raw materials and can be prepared on site. The raw materials are fritted and melted, the glass is drawn off and blown, annealed and stored, and finally distributed. By the late nineteenth century all these stages could be carried out on the company's own premises. From the 1870s Pilkingtons converted coal into gas on site, via inclined-grate gas producers (Barker 1977, 190–1; *see Ch 5, Pl 18*). The salt too was processed at the works: Pilkingtons used it from 1853 to produce much of their own alkali in the form of saltcake, by using the first part of the two-stage Leblanc process (Barker and Harris 1959, 224). The spirit of innovation at Pilkingtons is further illustrated by Windle Pilkington's patents for the 'bicycle' machine, to aid the manipulation of the larger cylinders being produced (British Patent No 207, 1871; Pl 9).

Plate 9 Blower reheating a cylinder in the furnace, with the aid of a bicycle machine (photograph kindly provided from the Pilkington Archive by David Martlew)

4

PHASE 1: PRE-TANK HOUSE ACTIVITY

Documentary evidence

Jo Bell

Coal mining

The earliest Ordnance Survey map covering the site of No 9 Tank House suggests that, in the 1840s, it bordered the St Helens Colliery (Ordnance Survey 1849; Pl 10), later purchased by Pilkingtons in 1857 (Barker 1960, 129). No buildings or shafts are shown within the footprint of the tank house itself, but a row of structures, possibly cottages, stood immediately to the south, in the position occupied by flattening kilns in 1914 (*see Ch 5, p 25*). An engine house and a mine shaft are shown a short distance away, some 60 m to the south–east of the gable ends of No 9 Tank House, in a position occupied by the L&NWR railway by 1882 (compare Plates 10 and 11).

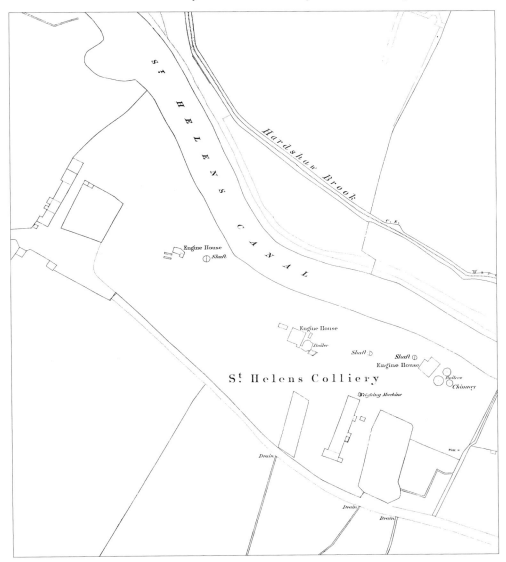

Plate 10 Extract from Ordnance Survey 5 feet:1 mile map, St Helens Sheet 7, 1849 (not to scale; reproduced from the Pilkington Archive)

Although the 1849 map shows no structures within the Hotties redevelopment area, mining records place two mine shafts within the site, one below the south–east end of the extant cone building component of the tank house, a second 35 m to the south–east, where a possible pit head structure was found (Fig 4; *see below Structures related to coal mining*; British Coal Corporation refs SJ59NW/428 and SJ59SW/231 respectively; Wardell Armstrong 1991, 4 and fig 2/5092/L). The positions of the shafts must be regarded as approximate, with the Abandonment Plan which shows SJ59NW/428 having few surface features to aid the fixing of the shaft's location on modern maps (AH Leach Son and Dean 1990, 17); equally, it would not be unusual if additional, unrecorded mineshafts had been present in the area. There is no written information about the two recorded mineshafts, so it is not known whether they were air or access shafts, or to which seams they were sunk (*ibid*). Thus, although it is clear that the area between Watson Street and the Sankey Canal was used extensively for coal mining in the early and mid-nineteenth century, the paucity of documentary evidence means that details such as the

period of use of each of the recorded shafts remain unknown.

The importance of coal to the local economy has been touched upon above, and was summarised frankly in a publication celebrating Pilkingtons' own centenary: 'St Helens owes everything to its coal. The coal brought the canal. The canal and coal together brought the original glass works to Ravenhead and other industries to the town. These in turn brought the railway' (Pilkington Brothers 1926, 11). Although coal was crucial to the development of St Helens, it was nevertheless obtained through great hardship on the part of the coal miners themselves. The colliery north of Watson Street is likely to have been one of those inspected in 1833 by the Commissioner for Factories. He found that the collieries in St Helens were particularly exploitative, and commented that 'the hardest labour in the worst room in the worst conducted factory is less hard, less cruel and less demoralising than the labour in the best of coal mines' (Aspin 1969, 89). Conditions remained difficult after the St Helens Colliery had passed into Pilkingtons'

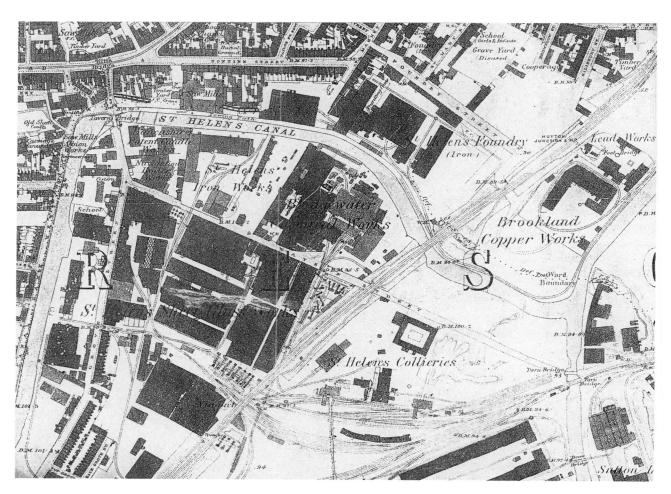

Plate 11 Extract from Ordnance Survey 1:2500 map, 1882, Sheet CVIII.1 (not to scale; reproduced by kind permission of St Helens Library). The Bridgewater Chemical Works lies to the south–east of the annotation 'St Helens Canal'

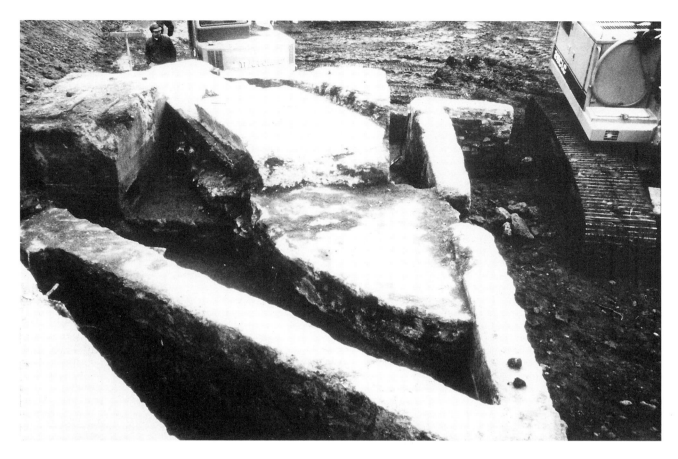

Plate 12 Looking south-west across the foundations of the probable Phase 1 pit head (Structure 1)

ownership; William Hopton was engaged by Pilkingtons to improve the ventilation, and he recalled that on his arrival in the late 1860s, 'the ventilation…was very bad. Only 19,000 ft of air per minute passed through the workings and the mine gave off much explosive gas. The lamps in several parts were unsafe to work with, and the inspector found it necessary to stop some parts of the mine' (Barker 1960, 183).

Chemical works

More intensive occupation of the site came in the mid-nineteenth century, when the Bridgewater Alkali Works was built in 1853–4 by John Knowles Leathers, 'brother of a Liverpool Merchant' (Barker and Harris 1959, 346) in partnership with T Watson and J Wilson (Nigel Neil pers comm). The factory was part of the Bridgewater Smelting Company, which made copper and sulphuric acid from iron pyrites; the firm did well in this trade until 1878, when a financial depression forced its closure. After attempts to sell the works as a going concern, its plant was auctioned in 1884. The works buildings are shown on the Ordnance Survey map of 1882 (Pl 11).

The Leather family who owned the works were fully aware that Pilkingtons wished to acquire their land in

order to expand the existing glass works, and dragged their feet over details of the sale. However, on 31 January 1885 the sale was finalised. On 21 May an instruction to 'prepare three tracings' (PB 138, 9) suggests that plans for the site were being drawn up. It is believed that the site was cleared, with Pilkingtons keen to seize the opportunity to lay out a group of new furnaces on a site largely unconstrained by existing buildings.

Archaeological evidence — Phase 1.1

Structures related to coal mining

The earliest remains uncovered were two isolated structures revealed during the excavation of the contaminated overburden in the extreme eastern sector of the site. Both structures contained elements of original brick construction, with later components added in mass concrete. Although the structures were physically detached from each other, being about 13 m apart, they shared a common orientation.

Structure 1 *(Figs 4 and 5; Pl 12)*
The earliest element of the most northerly of the two structures was a short section of eroded brick wall,

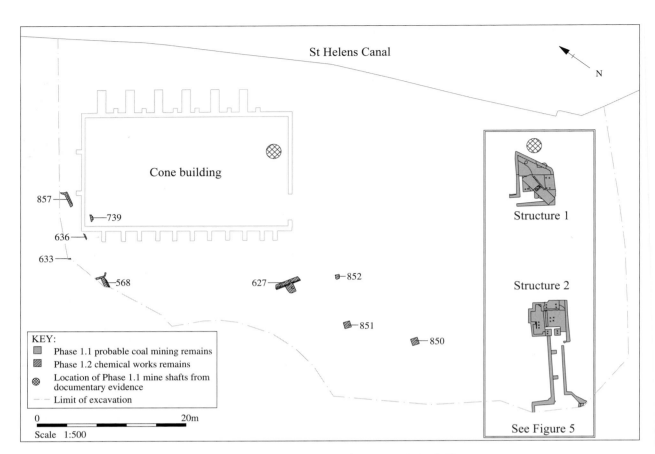

Fig 4 *Phase 1 remains, predating No 9 Tank House*

Plate 13 *View north-west to the probable Phase 1 winding house (Structure 2), with Phase 2 gas supply flues 519 and 520 beyond, and the cone house in the background*

641, aligned north/south. This was abutted on either side by later walls, 642, 643, and 644, which had been constructed in mass concrete to form an irregular polygonal enclosure on a north–east/south–west alignment, measuring 7.7 m by 6.2 m (Pl 12). A corridor-like entrance appeared to give access from the north–west. Several large RSJs had been inserted into the concrete walls, but had subsequently been cut to allow the emplacement of additional mass concrete features. These were located centrally within the structure (Pl 12), and comprised a complex multi-phase construction with two elevated piers, 858 and 859, that had the remains of substantial hold-down bolts on their upper surfaces. The concrete emplacements had later been cut by the concrete footings of the Phase 4 brick perimeter wall, 609. Structure 1 lay at exactly the estimated position of a

nineteenth century mineshaft, SJ59SW/231 (Fig 4; *see above Documentary evidence, p 17*), between 30 m and 35 m south–east of the gable of the extant cone house.

Structure 2 (*Figs 4 and 5; Pls 13 and 14*)
The remains of a largely brick-built building were uncovered 13 m to the south–west of Structure 1. The extant portion had overall dimensions of 15.6 m by 7.4 m, and consisted of a roughly square cell at the north–east end, a narrow central corridor aligned north–east/south–west, and a second wider cell which lay mostly beyond the site boundary to the south–west.

The north–eastern cell of the structure was enclosed by brick walls. The south–east wall, 628, had been built with a well-pointed interior face, whereas the

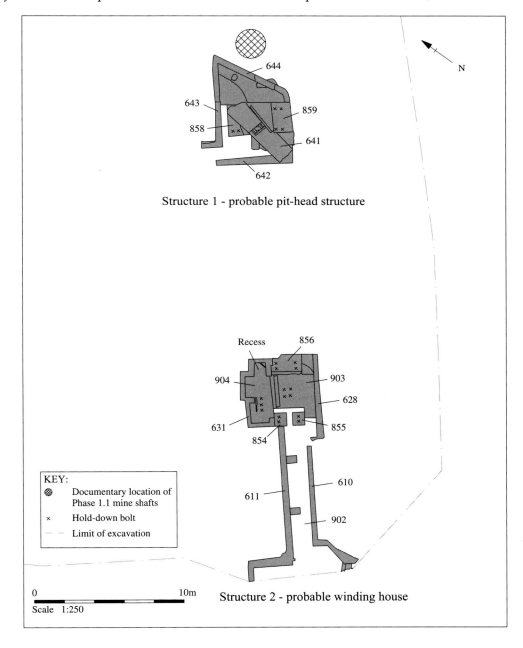

Fig 5 Remains of the probable pit-head structure and winding house

Structure 1 - probable pit-head structure

KEY:
⊗ Documentary location of Phase 1.1 mine shafts
× Hold-down bolt
– – – Limit of excavation

0   10m
Scale 1:250

Structure 2 - probable winding house

external face had been left rough and unfinished. To the north–west, wall 631 had been constructed in two phases; the earlier brickwork to the south–west again had a pointed interior face and unpointed external face, whereas later work added at the north–east end of the wall was pointed on both faces. Internal floor surfaces were formed in concrete, on two levels. In the eastern part of the structure, a low-level floor, 903, still contained the remains of hold-down bolts and wooden baulks. In the west of the structure, floor 904 stood 0.80 m higher than 903, but also retained the stumps of some hold-down bolts, arranged in a linear orientation alongside the broken remains of a vertical cast iron plate. Several pieces of flat woven machine belting were recovered during excavation above 904, and a distinctive groove had been worn in the floor surface, oriented towards a narrow recess in the north–east wall. Two concrete piers had been let into the north–east and south–west walls. The northern pier, 856, was formed from a single block, with the remains of hold-down bolts located in the upper surface. The southern pier was formed as a single block at low level, but two square piers, 854 and 855, separated by a small gap, sat on its upper surface (Pl 14). Again evidence for hold-down bolts was located on the upper surfaces.

To the south of piers 854 and 855, a narrow corridor, 1.4 m wide internally, had been constructed, bounded by brick walls 610 and 611, and floored with brick. It led away to the south–east into a large room at least 7.4 m wide, which had been truncated by the construction of gas supply flues for the tank house. Two large iron castings, which had the remains of plummer blocks with phosphor-bronze bearings attached to the upper surface, were set into the western wall of the corridor.

Function of Structures 1 and 2

As part of the Hotties site consolidation works, boreholes were cut in order to locate and then grout any possible voids associated with mining activity. The remains of a shaft close to Structure 1 were discovered, confirming the documentary evidence for a mineshaft here (Fig 4). This proximity seems to confirm that the structures were indeed related to nineteenth-century coal mining. Structure 2, the southern building, shows evidence of having contained an engine of some type, that appears to have driven both flat belting and line shafting, possibly in tandem or at differing times, whilst Structure 1, the northern building, was sited immediately adjacent to the shaft. The two buildings appear to be linked by their common orientation, and it can be suggested that Structure 1 represents the surviving remains of a

Plate 14 View south-west to concrete piers 854 and 855, within the probable Phase 1 winding house (Structure 2)

pit head, and Structure 2 a winding house. As such, these buildings, and the associated coal shaft remains, represent the earliest features identified on the site.

The winding hole

Towards the end of the planned programme of Stage 3 works, it was agreed with English Heritage that excavations should be carried out on the land lying between the north–east wall of the cone house and the bank of the St Helens Canal. One reason for this was to establish the location with respect to the cone house of the 'winding hole' for the canal traffic shown on the Ordnance Survey map of 1849 (Pl 10). No evidence for the 'winding hole' could be found within the excavated trenches.

Archaeological evidence — Phase 1.2

Structures relating to the Bridgewater Chemical Works

Several isolated fragments of masonry were recorded which appeared not to relate to the coal mining remains, to the tank house, or to known twentieth century structures. Some of these fragments had been truncated by the foundations of the tank house complex, indicating an earlier origin.

Wall fragment 739 *(Fig 4)*

During the excavation of Test Pit 4, sited in the western corner of the cone house, the foundation courses of a wall were uncovered at a depth of 2.60 m below the concrete floor slab. The wall ran at a slightly oblique angle to the north–west gable of the tank house building and was interpreted as an earlier feature, cut through during the construction of the tank house.

Piers 850, 851, 852 *(Fig 4)*

The remains of three brick-built piers, 850, 851, 852 (Fig 4), were found to the south–east of the tank house. The alignment of all three appeared to be consistent with the presence of buildings oriented north–north–east/south–south–west and east–south–east/west–north–west. Piers 850 and 851 measured *c* 1 m square, whilst 852, which appeared to have been subject to disturbance, measured *c* 0.66 m square.

Wall 627 *(Fig 4)*

Part of a wall containing a level platform and two small openings was located close to the external face of tunnel 508 (*see Ch 5, p 56*). The wall had been cut at its west end to allow the tunnel to be built, indicating that construction of the tank house complex had not been preceded by wholesale site clearance. The wall was aligned roughly east-south–east/west-north–west, the remaining fragment extending for 3.5 m in length. The surviving portion of the platform measured 1.1 m x 1.2 m.

Wall 568 *(Fig 4)*

Another fragment of walling, situated close to, and cut by, the western side of tunnel 502 (*see Ch 5, p 71*), was located in an area of very high levels of contamination and was removed without full detailed recording on the grounds of health and safety. Overall, the masonry measured 2.5 m x 1.75 m. It appeared to represent part of a wall aligned north-north–east/south-south–west.

Pier 857, and walls 633 and 636 *(Fig 4)*

Further fragments of masonry were recorded close to the north–west gable wall of the cone house. Although numbered as a pier, fragment 857 may in fact have been part of the same length of wall as 568. It was 2.3 m long and for the most part 0.43 m wide, and was aligned north-north–east/south-south–west.

Wall 636 shared the same alignment, and may have been part of the same wall, lying between 857 and 568. It measured 0.9 m long x 0.15 m wide. Wall 633 measured only 0.37 m x 0.19 m, but appeared to be aligned at right angles to 857 and 636, being potentially part of the same structure.

Date and function

These fragments of masonry appear to be the disturbed remnants of a group of structures laid out on a different orientation to that of both the coal mining remains and the later cone house, and documentary and cartographic evidence would suggest that they may represent part of the Bridgewater Chemical Works known to have existed on the site prior to its purchase by Pilkington Brothers in 1885 (*see above Documentary evidence*). The fragmentary remains show the same alignment as the depiction of the Bridgewater Chemical Works on the Ordnance Survey map of 1882 (Pl 11). It should be noted, however, that none of the remains can be associated with a particular function or structure within the works, in which copper and sulphuric acid were manufactured from iron pyrites (*see above Documentary evidence*).

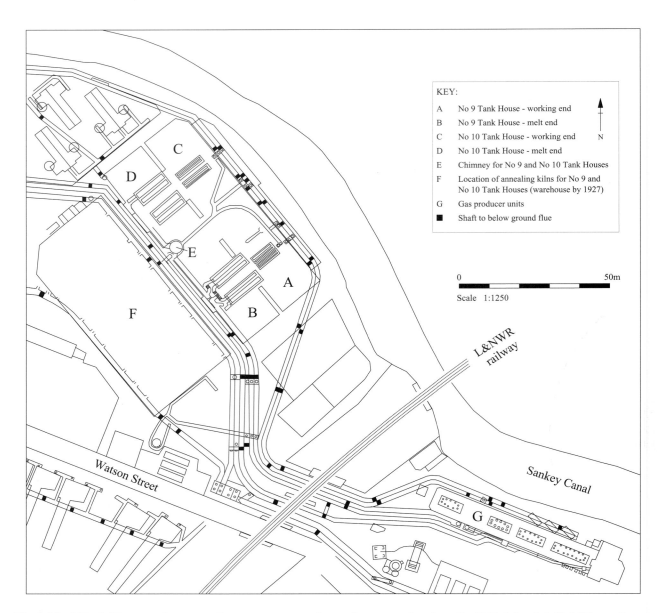

Fig 6 No 9 Tank House and surrounding structures, redrawn from a works plan of c 1912 (plan labelled 'Flues. Crown Glass Works'; reproduced by kind permission of David Martlew)

5

PHASE 2: CONSTRUCTION OF THE NO 9 TANK HOUSE COMPLEX

Documentary evidence

Jo Bell

Pilkingtons' tank furnaces

Three continuous tank furnaces were built by Pilkingtons in the late 1880s, following the acquisition of the former site of the Bridgewater Chemical Works to the north of Watson Street in 1885. Two of the new furnaces, Nos 9 and 10, were built on the new site, which came to be known as the Jubilee Side; the third was built under the old First House cone to the south of Watson Street (Fig 6; Pl 2). All three of the new tank furnaces were larger than the firm's existing thirteen sheet glass tanks (RE 1, 14; Barker 1960, 151; Barker 1977, 136). Another two furnaces, Nos 11 and 12, were built on the Jubilee Side in the 1890s, as demand for sheet glass increased, and the construction of No 13 in *c* 1900 exhausted all the available space in this part of the works (RE 1, 17, 20). Pilkingtons went on to build a further two furnaces for the production of hand-blown sheet glass, before the process was superseded by direct-drawn glass; these were the No 14 and No 15 tanks, laid out a short distance to the south–west of the Jubilee Side, between Grove Street and Watson Street, in 1904–5 (*ibid*).

The acquisition of the Jubilee Side gave Pilkingtons space to lay out new structures as they wished, on a site not hemmed-in by existing structures; in consequence, Windle Pilkington may have had a freedom to experiment that he had not previously enjoyed. Works' plans show that most of the new furnaces were built in pairs within adjoining tank houses, Nos 9 and 10 being built within contiguous buildings (Fig 6). The plans also illustrate the fact that the furnaces themselves were only one part of the development of the works; producer units had to be built to supply them with gas, flattening kilns were needed to flatten and cool the cylinders of glass after splitting, and warehousing facilities were also required. The furnaces on the Jubilee Side drew their gas supply from a series of inclined-grate producer units sited across the L&NWR railway to the south–

east (Fig 6), which would have been capable of providing a cheap supply of producer gas, a mixture of carbon monoxide, nitrogen, and hydrogen (*see below Raw materials and transportation, p 29*; LUAU 1998, 7–12; Cable 2000, 210). A plan dated 1914 shows that two very large buildings, one immediately to the south–west of No 9 and No 10 Tank Houses, one to the south of Nos 11 and 12, each housed 12 flattening kilns, with further kilns in buildings between No 10 and No 11 Tank Houses, and south and west of No 13 (Unlabelled works plan dated 1914; Fig 6). The remaining space on the Jubilee Side was taken up by two warehouses, built in 1896 and 1898, fronting onto Watson Street. Together, the new furnaces and ancillary buildings represented a massive investment in the regenerative continuous tank furnace technology first patented by Siemens in 1870.

The No 9 Tank House furnace was lit on 22 February 1887, and it remained in use for the production of hand-blown cylinder glass until 1920 or 1921 (Parkin 2000, 80). However, it should not be thought that the design of the furnace remained unchanged throughout this period; the base and walls of the tank needed much maintenance and rebuilding because of the corrosive power of the molten glass, and the furnace was typically put out every two to three years to allow the more major repairs to be carried out (PB 129). It is clear that there was scope for considerable alteration of the original furnace design during the 34 years of its working life, although subsequent improvements must have been constrained to some extent by the tank house building, and by the layout of the regenerators below.

There seems to be relatively little documentary evidence available to help elucidate the constructional details of the first furnace within No 9 Tank House. The lack of evidence is clearly partly the result of the loss of documents and drawings, including all material from the Pilkingtons drawing office prior to 1960 (Parkin nd), but it also derives from the fact that many developments in furnace design were never documented, either because of concerns over industrial espionage, or because furnaces were designed in traditional face-to-face meetings on-site between bricklayers and glassmakers. The reminiscences of SE Baddeley (RE 1) have often been quoted to illustrate the absence of preparatory plans for furnaces. In *c* 1890, Mr Baddeley started work in the Sheet Works drawing office, and was asked to measure up several tanks. He found it strange that tanks were drawn only after they had been built, but was told that Windle Pilkington was accustomed to tracing the outlines of new tanks out on the ground with his foot (RE 1, 15). Mr Baddeley's drawings were not found during this documentary study; he emphasised in his reminiscences that for reasons of security, he was the only draughtsman allowed to work on the tank furnaces, and 'kept a careful guard on all drawings and records associated with them' (RE 1, 21).

Despite the paucity of records relating explicitly to the first build of the furnace within No 9 Tank House, documentary evidence for Pilkingtons' furnaces in the 1870s can be used to make some suggestions as to the form of the 1887 furnace. Ron Parkin, a former manager at Pilkington plc, has recently studied a range of documentary sources not accessible within the scope of this present project, including the General and Executive Board minutes, and statements given by informants to Pilkingtons' main rivals, Chances of Birmingham (Parkin 2000). These represent a further significant source of information for Pilkingtons' furnaces of the 1870s. This documentary evidence can be supplemented from the reminiscences of former glass workers who began their employment with Pilkingtons just before No 9 Tank House ceased production in 1920/21 (Parkin 2000, 80).

Construction
Pilkingtons' first attempt at building a tank furnace in 1873 may have failed because the side walls and crown had been built on top of the lower part of the tank wall that was in contact with the molten glass (Barker 1977, 134). In later furnaces, they were independently supported, with the crown being carried on springers and pillars; this meant that corroded sections of the sides could be cut out and replaced where necessary, prolonging the life of the furnace (RE 2, 404). J Semple, writing to Chances in 1876, noted that the crowns of Pilkingtons' tank furnaces were very flat, and so furnaces were very firmly bound, presumably with a metal frame (Keenan 1995, 13). Parkin believes that there is evidence to suggest that Pilkingtons started to apply heat to the working ends of their tank furnaces in 1881 (Parkin 2000, 71), with the heating of the two ends independently controlled (*op cit*, 76). He also refers to there being seven stacks at either side of the melt end of the furnace, these structures funnelling the pre-heated gas and air up into the furnace from the regenerators below; accompanying illustrations show

three stacks at either side of the working end (Parkin 2000, 71, and figs 48–9). It is believed that this information about the disposition of stacks is derived from oral evidence.

Use of a 'bridge' within the tank furnace
J Semple's letter of 1876 stated that Pilkingtons' tanks were constructed with a broad bridge about five yards from the gathering end (Keenan 1995, 13). It has been suggested that a letter written in the same year, by an informant who signed himself EJF, indicates that Pilkingtons' bridges *c* 1876 were floating structures, albeit placed in tanks with constricted, air-cooled waists (*op cit*, 12). Parkin has found evidence to suggest that Pilkingtons introduced the use of a fixed bridge wall to divide tank furnaces into separate melting and gathering ends in 1881 (Parkin 2000, 71), making exclusive use of divided tanks for the manufacture of blown cylinder flat glass until 1912 (Parkin nd). SE Baddeley remembered that No 11 tank, built on the Jubilee Side shortly after 1889, 'was divided into two, roughly, equal parts by a stone weir, one end running at a very high temperature for melting purposes and the other forming a bath of cleaner and cooler metal' (RE 1, 19).

It is difficult to make a judgement on the nature of the bridges used by Pilkingtons without further documentary research, but it does seem probable that a fixed bridge, constructed from two separate walls with a space in between, was used for the No 9 furnace in 1887, or at the latest by 1889, when the furnace was put out for renovation work. The tank repair book notes that when the furnace was lit in 1887, it had an 'all Stourbridge clay circular bridge', but an entry for 29 September 1887 notes 'metal in the bridge' (PB 129, 34). The latter entry appears to suggest a two-walled structure with a void in the centre. When the furnace was lit for the second time in May 1889 after a five week cold repair, the tank repair book notes 'all Strourbridge clay double bridge' and an entry dated 20 September 1892 notes 'bridge down all but one wall'. These references suggest a fixed structure, and certainly one which was capable of being cooled; Ron Parkin has tried to reconstruct its likely form (*see p 80*; Parkin 2000, 65–6). By the end of the century, it is clear that Pilkingtons' bridges were subject to sophisticated cooling; when the tank was started on 6 December 1897, the repair book noted 'three air passage bridge' (PB 129, 49).

Dimensions
Information given to Chances by a furnace builder named Thomas May demonstrates that, by 1877, Pilkingtons were already using tanks that could hold 2 ft 6 in of molten glass when new (Barker 1960, 149), anticipating by at least two years the Siemens' patent which first envisaged the use of deep tanks (British

Patent 4763, 1879). T Semple noted that the crowns of Pilkingtons' tank furnaces stood no more than 5 ft 6 in above the bottom of the tank in 1876 (Keenan 1995, 13). The new furnaces on the Jubilee Side appear to have held c 200 tons of metal, compared with the 100–20 ton capacity of earlier Pilkingtons' furnaces (RE 2, 404); if of a similar height and width to the earlier furnaces, it might be thought that they were up to twice the length of the earlier tanks, said to be 45 ft long (Keenan 1995, 13).

Materials

The materials used for the construction of early tank furnaces appear to have been the subject of experimentation. A letter to Chances by the informant who signed himself EJF indicates that, in 1876, the body of a Pilkingtons' tank furnace was made of firestone from North Wales (Keenan 1995, 12), this material being a naturally-occurring sandstone typically containing 80–90% silica and 6–11% alumina (Hartley 1995). The tank base and walls may later have been made of fireclay bricks and blocks; these were manufactured from siliceous clays containing 70–90% silica, alumina, and smaller quantities of other compounds (Hartley 1995, 2–3). Brick samples taken from rubble deposits found on the No 9 Tank House site were marked with the names of manufacturers based south and east of Glasgow and in North Wales, and proved to be fireclay bricks; such bricks were certainly used in the construction of the regenerators (see p 49). The hard, downward flame used in the Pilkingtons' tank furnaces from the 1870s meant that the furnace crown was subject to very high temperatures, and evidence has been found to suggest that, at this time, Pilkingtons began to use silica for furnace crowns rather than the fireclay bricks employed earlier (Parkin nd). Silica appears to have been used in the form of silica bricks, made from crushed rock to give a silica content of at least 98% (Hartley 1995, 1). The tank repair book (PB 129) makes frequent reference to the need to tile the 'sides' at frequent intervals during the operation of the furnace. Tiles are used in the construction of modern glass furnaces, but it had not hitherto been recognised that tiles were employed in the 1880s and 1890s.

Cooling

It has been observed that information supplied to Chances in 1876 by EJF suggests the direction of cooling air to the waist of the furnace (Keenan 1995, 13). Later references to 'metal in the bridge' and to a 'double bridge' likewise suggest that the bridge of the No 9 furnace may also have been designed to allow cooling (PB 129, 34). Ron Parkin has also referred to the use of waterboxes to cool furnaces, with water brought in from the canal and piped along the furnace flux line, but it is not clear when this practice was carried out (Transcript of interview with Ron Parkin);

Gas supply

Gas was fed into the furnace regenerators from nearby inclined-grate producers under a slight pressure to keep it moving, and combustion air was drawn directly from the atmosphere. The melt end and working end of the tank were supplied independently, from separate gas producers, and a tall chimney provided the draught, drawing out exhaust gases so that combustion air was in turn pulled into the furnace via the regenerators. All inlets and outlets for gas and air were controlled by valves and dampers, to maintain the equilibrium between draught and supply, and control the temperature of the two ends of the furnace (Parkin 2000, 76–7).

Glassblowing

Knowledge of the glassblowing process itself comes largely from the oral evidence of former Pilkingtons' employees. It is believed that the No 9 furnace had five gathering holes sited at the canal-side end of the working end, and ten blowing holes, five on each side

Plate 15 Demonstration of a cylinder being blown without mechanical aids. The gather of glass is shaped in a mould block at the start of the blowing process (photograph kindly provided from the Pilkington Archive by David Martlew)

Plate 16 Reproduction of an engraving showing the manufacture of hand-blown cylinder glass in the mid-nineteenth century. Cylinders were elongated by being manually swung down into the swing pits. The furnace is in the background (photograph kindly provided from the Pilkington Archive by David Martlew)

of the furnace. A gatherer, time gatherer, and block minder worked at each gathering hole, and were responsible for gathering sufficient molten glass for blowing a cylinder. The gather was then handed to one of ten blowers, who would blow a cylinder of glass using compressed air, reheating the glass up to six times in his blowing hole, and swinging the emerging cylinder down into the swing pit below to obtain the desired elongation. Plate 15 shows a demonstration of a cylinder being blown my mouth, whilst Plate 16 is an engraving of cylinders being swung in *c* 1850. Towards the end of the process, the two ends of the cylinder were blown, or cracked off (Pl 17), and the cylinder was then removed for splitting and flattening to form a flat sheet of glass (Parkin 2000, 49–53). In this period, most cylinders were exclusively hand-produced by workers who were effectively craftsmen, although limited mechanisation was attempted. In 1871, Windle Pilkington had patented a device, nick-named 'the bicycle', designed to help blowers to manipulate the larger cylinders, and to allow them to use compressed air in the blowing process (Pl 9). The device was used with some success, but there was only one per tank in 1887, and two per tank in 1900 (Barker 1960, 192).

Modifications made during the life of the furnace, 1887–1921

The corrosive power of molten glass, allied to the high furnace temperatures, meant that glass furnaces had to be continually repaired and rebuilt. This gave ample opportunity for refining furnace design, and making improvements in the light of experience. There appears to be considerable documentary evidence for this process of development, but for the purposes of this volume, only the tank repair book entries for No 9 Tank in years 1887–1900 have been used (PB 129, 34–51).

The modifications documented during the early years of the operation of No 9 Tank House mainly involved the repair and rebuilding of the above ground superstructure of the tank, although there are references to lengths of the regenerators being 'taken out' (*op cit*, 34). Certain repairs were clearly routinely performed, and the tank repair book seems to imply that they were undertaken whilst the furnace was still lit, but dampered down. The most common repair noted was 'tiled sides', and this might vary from 'part of each side' to 'both sides'. Re-tiling typically seems to have been needed every two months or so. Another common repair was 'repaired filling end', 'new filling end', or 'new front', typically being noted every four to six months, whilst repairs to the stacks and ports were often needed every six months. An entry for 7/8 January 1895 noted 'three new stacks & ports a side (Ports B). Patched the other stacks'. The repairs appear to have been carried out at weekends. The entry for 6 February 1900 notes 'Four ports. Tiled and front. Dampers in at 4 am Fri, finished at 1 am Sat'. Problems with the bridge were also recorded, and have been briefly discussed above (*see p 26*).

These appear to have been 'hot repairs', but further repairs were made when the furnace was put out every two to three years. Thus, when the furnace was lit in July 1893, it had 'Stourbridge clay 10 in bottom through. Thin sides. Double bridge. New crown to bridge. Extra ports to bridge blowing stacks, stackless melting end next to bridge.' The statements concerning the bottom, sides, and bridge had been made before in previous years, and appear to represent routine repair rather than innovation, but the references to the stacks imply development of the furnace design. There is evidence of further innovation when the furnace was lit in December 1897, in an entry reading 'Stourbridge clay three air passage bridge. Tank four inches shallower'. The reference to the bridge has already been mentioned (*see p 26*), but it seems clear that the disposition of the ports and stacks, and the depth of the tank, were also subject to modification over time.

This demonstrates that the above-ground elements of the furnace were subject to constant change; had they survived to be recorded archaeologically, they would represent evidence for the last use of the tank house, rather than its design in 1887. However, the regenerators, access tunnels, and furnace foundations which did survive represent parts of the tank house that were more difficult and costly to amend, and the documentary evidence does not suggest that these elements were repeatedly or radically altered.

Raw materials and transportation

The availability of local coal was perhaps the main factor that had first drawn the glass industry to the St Helens area (*see Ch 3*), and in the mid-nineteenth century, glassmakers still needed coal in greater quantities than any other material. In 1851, Pilkingtons were using at least eight tons of coal for every one ton of glass produced, and their works was consuming 650 tons of coal per week (Barker 1960, 128). In view of this dependency, Pilkingtons had been perturbed by strikes in 1843, and had decided to secure their fuel supply by entering the coal mining business (*ibid*). Their first venture was at Green Lane on the Ormskirk

Plate 17 A completed cylinder. The cap end is about to be removed, and the cylinder will then be sent for splitting and flattening, creating a sheet of window glass (photograph kindly provided from the Pilkington Archive by David Martlew)

Road, but in 1857 they purchased the St Helens Colliery, which lay immediately to the east of their glassworks, turning it into one of the largest and most profitable mines in the area (*op cit*, 129). With the coming of the regenerative gas-fired furnace, and then the tank furnace, coal was used with much greater efficiency (*see Ch 3*), but remained the vital source of producer gas. When new tank furnaces, including No 9, were laid out on the Jubilee Side in the 1880s, it is notable that the new gas producers were built to the east of the L&NWR railway, immediately north of the St Helens Collieries (compare Figure 6 and Plate 2). It thus seems probable that when No 9 tank furnace began operating, Pilkingtons were able to bring their own coal to the surface right next to their producer units, incurring no transport costs at all.

In the late 1880s, gas would have been obtained from inclined-grate producers, based on a design first developed by William Siemens (Parkin 2000, 85); the operation of this apparatus was described in the specification to the patent obtained by William and Frederick Siemens in 1861 (Pl 18; British Patent 167, 1861). Coal was fed downwards through openings fitted with lids or covers, into a hopper (O) placed at a moderate inclination. From there, it passed on down a ramp of brickwork (P), inclined at about 45°, and over a grate (Q), inclined at about 30°. A fire on the grate produced heat, and a brick arch (R), above the grate, helped to radiate heat onto the fresh coal passing down the ramp above, causing its partial decomposition and volatization. This process was augmented by the passage of air, which entered through the grate, was decomposed on contact with the heated fuel there into carbon dioxide and nitrogen, and passed on through the cooler coal, forming carbon monoxide. On reaching the fresh fuel on the ramp, it mixed with the gases being evolved there, then passed up through a passage (S), and on to a pipe (U) which carried it to the regenerators. Steam, rather than air, could periodically be applied to the coal on the grate, leading to the formation of hydrogen as well as carbon monoxide. Thus, producer gas was usually a mixture of carbon monoxide, nitrogen, and hydrogen, with smaller quantities of carbon dioxide and hydrocarbons also present (LUAU 1998, 7–12; Cable 2000, 210).

Cartographic evidence indicates that the producers which fuelled the Jubilee Side furnaces were sited on the canal bank some 80 m south–east of No 9 Tank House (Fig 6; Pl 2); however, the number and arrangement of inclined-grate producers built in the late 1880s is not known, as the available works' plans depict the later 'brick producers' known to have been used by Pilkingtons in the first decade of the twentieth century (Parkin 2000, 85). It is suggested below that the melt end of the furnace may have had a dedicated producer, whilst the working end shared one or more

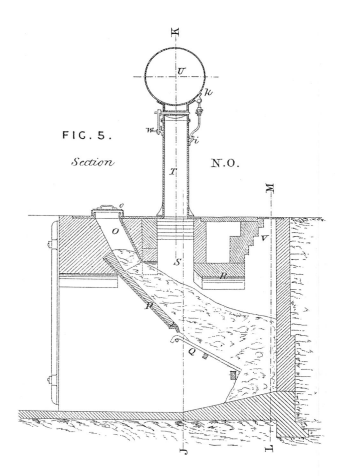

Plate 18 *Longitudinal section through a gas producer from William and Friedrich Siemens' patent of 1861 (British Patent 167, 1861, fig 5). Fuel passes down to the inclined fire-grate Q, arch R is heated by the fire and radiates heat onto fresh fuel passing down inclined plane P, causing its partial volatilization, a process completed by the introduction of air through grate Q*

producers with other furnaces (*see below p 75*). The replacement of the early inclined-grate producers suggests that their remains may not survive to the present day. The archaeological potential of the Jubilee Side producer site is in any case uncertain, because it lies almost exactly within the footprint of a modern pump house; it seems likely that deep remains may be intact, but that shallower features will have been destroyed.

The producer gas was combusted to heat sand, alkali, and limestone in the melt end of the furnace (*see Ch 2*). Sand for No 9 furnace was obtained locally from sandfields at Knowsley, Rainford, and Crank, villages to the north–west of St Helens which lay no more than three miles from Pilkingtons' sheet glass works (Fig 2; Parkin 2000, 75). After the opening of the railway to Rainford in 1851, sand was brought to the works by rail from railheads at Rainford, Crank, and Mossbank; horse-drawn tramways and continuous wire ropes appear to have been used to transport sand to the railway (*op cit*, 110). In 1881, a new sandwash plant and siding was installed at Mill Lane, south–east of Rainford, and in the following years, sand extraction was concentrated to the south of the railway (*ibid*). By the early twentieth century, silver sand was being imported by sea from Belgium, being landed at Liverpool and brought to the glassworks by rail (*op cit*, 75); it may have been used in the manufacture of specialist glasses. Shares in a Belgian sand company were purchased in 1901, and by 1907 the enterprise was wholly owned by Pilkingtons (Barker 1960, 167).

In the early nineteenth century, alkali was readily available from the thriving St Helens chemical industry, but by 1848, it had become cheaper to transport St Helens coal to the Mersey end of the St Helens canal than to move salt, limestone, and pyrites up to St Helens. Once more, Pilkingtons decided to secure a supply of an essential glassmaking material by producing it themselves; in 1864, William Pilkington opened the Mersey Chemical Works at Widnes, in partnership with his two younger sons (*op cit*, 130). Limestone was also included in the batch, and initially came from local quarries such as that at Hard Lane, but was later mainly derived from North Wales (Parkin 2000, 75; it has not been established exactly when this change occurred). Refractory materials for the construction of furnaces and associated flues and regenerators were another important material which the glass maker had to procure. Documentary sources suggest that Pilkingtons made use of firestone from North Wales

when building early tanks in the 1870s, but the bases and walls of tanks seem later to have been constructed of fireclay blocks. Ron Parkin has argued that for the period 1873-1902, most furnace blocks were bought from specialist manufacturers in Stourbridge, in the West Midlands (Parkin 2000, 43).

In the third quarter of the nineteenth century, both the canal and the railway appear to have played an important role in supplying the works. It has been shown above that sand was brought in by rail from the 1850s, and a plan of the works in 1856 confirms the importance of rail transport at this time (Barker 1960, plan 2); the plan shows the central part of the works encircled by railway sidings, one being sited immediately outside the doors of the mixing room, whilst another passed into the main warehouse. A later plan of 1878 indicates that the works had expanded westwards to the bank of the canal (Parkin 2000, fig 12), and shows three rectangular inlets in the canal bank which appear to be small docks or quays. An artist's impression of the works in 1879 (Pl 19) confirms that the inlets were used for mooring boats, and shows several other barges being loaded or unloaded at quays laid out along the canal bank. It is not certain exactly what was being transported, but it is possible that alkali, limestone, and timber for packing, were being brought in from the Mersey, and that finished glass was being sent to Liverpool. In the period 1877–87, Pilkingtons' production of sheet glass for the domestic market remained static, whilst exports of sheet glass increased seven-fold (Barker 1960, 170).

Plate 19 An artist's impresssion of Pilkingtons' Sheet Glass Works in 1879, viewed from the west (Pilkington Archive)

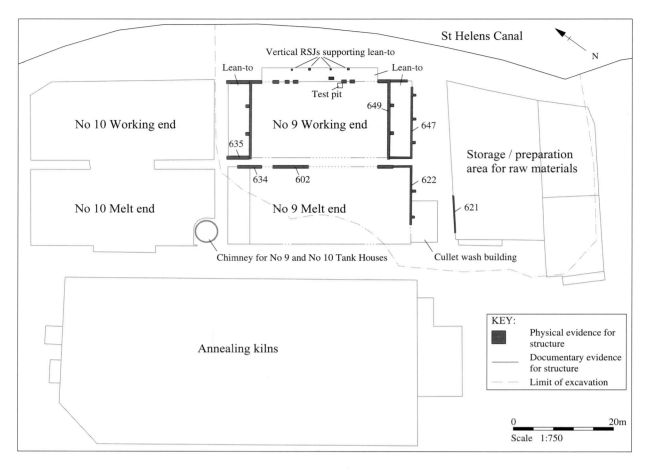

St Helens Canal

N

Vertical RSJs supporting lean-to

Lean-to

Lean-to

Test pit

No 10 Working end

No 9 Working end

649

647

635

Storage / preparation area for raw materials

634   602

622

621

No 10 Melt end

No 9 Melt end

Chimney for No 9 and No 10 Tank Houses

Cullet wash building

Annealing kilns

KEY:

■ Physical evidence for structure

— Documentary evidence for structure

– – Limit of excavation

0   20m

Scale   1:750

Fig 7 Phase 2 buildings: No 9 Tank House and adjacent structures

The company's shipping office at Drury Buildings in Liverpool is known to have handled a growing volume of glass at this time (*op cit*, 169), and by 1887, a significant proportion of the total sheet glass output is likely to have been going overseas via Liverpool docks. The extent to which glass was moved to Liverpool by canal rather than rail in the 1880s has not been established.

By the early twentieth century, the situation had changed, in that Pilkingtons appear to have relied almost exclusively on the railway for the supply of the works and the distribution of their product. An Act of Parliament in 1898 allowed the Ravenhead spur of the canal to be closed, and the canal was filled in to the west of Pilkingtons' Sheet Glass Works, where the busy quays depicted in 1878 had formerly stood (Barker 1960, 192).

Archaeological evidence — Phase 2.1

The raised platform around No 9 Tank House

Documentary and cartographic evidence clearly demonstrates that the structures ascribed to Phase 2

are the remains of the No 9 Tank House erected by Pilkingtons in 1886 (Fig 6,7; Pl 2; *see above Documentary evidence*). The existence of fragmentary remains of masonry which can be attributed to the Bridgewater Chemical Works (*see p 23*) suggests that the site was not completely cleared after the closure of the works, but that the former buildings were largely dismantled. Subsequently, stratigraphic relationships recorded during excavation appear to indicate that the Pilkingtons' building programme began with the laying out of a thick platform above the earlier remains. The earliest Phase 2 contexts identified were thick deposits, predominantly of mixed rubble and glass waste, which had been dumped to build up the ground level to a height roughly 2.5 m above the remains of the earlier wall foundations.

Given the problems of excavating through contaminated ground, it was difficult to determine exactly which deposits constituted part of the platform, and which were already *in situ* before the demolition of the chemical works. However, in Test Pit 4, sited in the western corner of the cone house, masonry considered to be associated with the chemical works was identified *c* 2.45 m below the cone house floor (Fig 4). Above the masonry, but below the south–west wall foundation trench, a banded deposit of

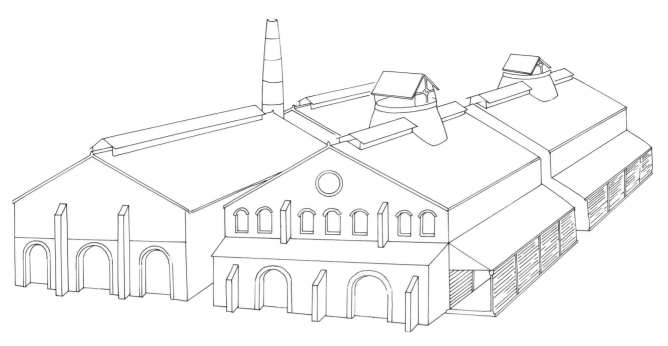

Fig 8 Artist's reconstruction of No 9 Tank House, looking west. No 10 Tank House is depicted in the background

mortar and brick rubble, 45 (not illustrated), was interpreted as being a demolition deposit associated with the dismantling of the former works and construction of the platform. Elsewhere within the tank house footprint, deposits of gritty sandy clay, and clay sand with brick and glass fragments, 249 and 253 (not illustrated), were found underlying the south–east swing pit, and may also derive from the deposition of make-up over the old chemical works. Similarly, the foundation trench for the south–east wall of the cone house had cut through several deposits, including layers of gravelly sandy clay and cinders. Several of these deposits were brightly coloured, and were thought to have been produced by chemical processes, but it could not be determined whether the deposits had been redeposited during the raising and levelling of the ground which accompanied the redevelopment of the site, or whether they were earlier in date.

The tank house buildings: introduction

The tank house complex consisted of a pair of parallel and interlinked buildings, together with a complex system of brick flues, access / ventilation tunnels, and regenerators laid out beneath the floor level (Figs 6, 7, 8; p 50 Fig 15; Pl 20). It appears that the buildings and underground components were built together as part of the same phase of construction, although some elements were clearly completed before others. Stratigraphic relationships recorded at foundation level suggest that the tank house buildings were constructed first, and that some if not all of the regenerators and flues were subsequently installed by cutting through the newly-built foundation walls.

The two tank house buildings were oriented south–east / north–west (Fig 7; Pl 20). The north–eastern of the two buildings was a 'cone house', distinguished by a brick cone structure passing up through the centre of the roof. The building contained a large, open, central cell, measuring 27.4 m x 15.5 m, defined to either end by gable walls extending up to the full

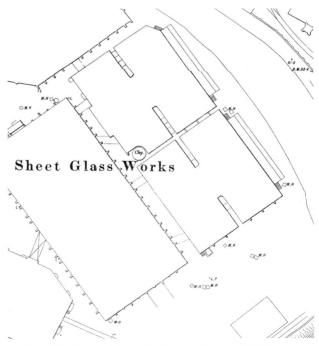

Plate 20 Extract from Ordnance Survey 1:500 map, 1891, Sheet CVIII.1.10-14 (not to scale; reproduced by kind permission of St Helens Library). No 9 Tank House lies to the east of the anotation 'Sheet Glass Works'

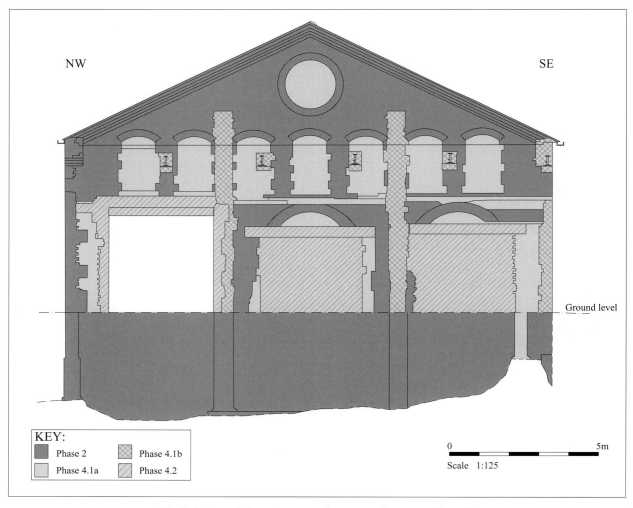

Fig 9 External elevation, cone house south–east gable wall

KEY:

- Phase 2
- Phase 4.1a
- Phase 4.1b
- Phase 4.2

0   5m

Scale   1:125

NW

SE

Ground level

10 m height of the roof; this part of the cone house had survived largely intact as a standing structure. Beyond each of these gables was a 'lean-to' structure, housing a subsidiary cell measuring 4.1 m x 15.5 m, but with a maximum roof height of only 4 m. Although built with roofs probably supported against the gables of the central cell, these end structures appear nevertheless to have been integral to the original layout of the building. The lean-to structures at each end of the cone house, and the second, parallel tank house building to the south–west, had been demolished in the late twentieth century, and their form had to be reconstructed from excavation evidence, and with reference to maps, documentary sources, and photographs. The cone house component housed the working end of a continuous tank furnace, and the building immediately to the south–west the melt end.

The cone house component
The cone house wall foundations *(Fig 7)*
The evidence for this structure was in part contained within the fabric of the present building, in part derived from excavation. Excavation to the south–

east of the extant central cell of the structure revealed the foundation walls of the south–east gable and of the south–east lean-to beyond. These foundations had survived almost completely intact, with the exception of a small area of truncation in the north–east corner. The gable foundation wall, 649 (Fig 7), was of orange-red brick constructed in English bond using a black ash mortar. The brickwork was 0.37 m thick, the thickness of a header and stretcher. Two rectangular section external buttresses survived, aligned with scars on the upper elevation demonstrating that that they had formerly continued to a high level on the gable. Towards the bottom, the foundation had wider stepped brick footings, set on a concrete base. Its full depth was not revealed externally, but the excavation of test pits within the surviving building showed the foundation to be 4.5–4.6 m deep, revealing that the wall had been constructed in spits, with the foundation trench being backfilled periodically during the building of the wall.

The foundation wall of the structure adjoining the gable, 647 (Fig 7), was again built of orange to red

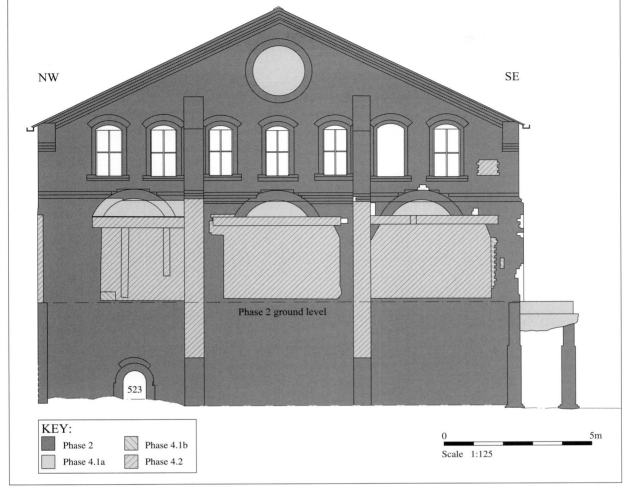

NW

SE

Phase 2 ground level

523

KEY:

▉	Phase 2	◨	Phase 4.1b
▨	Phase 4.1a	◪	Phase 4.2

0   5m

Scale   1:125

Fig 10 External elevation, cone house north–west gable wall

industrial brick in English bond with black ash mortar, and the return at its south–western end was clearly keyed into the brickwork of the gable. The stepped brick footings at the bottom of the wall had been laid onto a concrete base. No foundation trench was observed, but excavation of this area had to be conducted largely by machine, so it cannot be assumed that no such trench was present. Gas supply flues 519 and 520 (*see below* p 50, Fig 15) passed below the north–east corner of the structure; the foundation wall appeared to have been cut to allow them to be constructed, and was subsequently supported above the flues by brick piers and iron rails. The foundation appeared to be of a similar thickness and depth to that supporting the south–east gable.

Similar remains were revealed by excavation to the north–west of the standing structure of the cone house. The gable foundation wall mirrored that of the south–east gable, with internal test pits here showing the foundation to be *c* 4.4 m deep; a foundation trench was again recorded. The wall foundation had subsequently been cut at a low level to allow the passage of chimney flue 523, which passed through it

and then curved round to the west towards the known position of the tank house chimney (Fig 7). This demonstrates that some parts of the underground flue system were constructed after the building foundations. Beyond the gable, the foundations of the lean-to structure were less completely revealed than to the south–east, but the position of all three walls was established.

Excavation to a limited depth along the external face of the north–east long wall of the cone house revealed further fragmented portions of the original foundations, surviving between and below some of the later buttresses. An internal test pit (Fig 7) demonstrated that the north–east wall foundation was here 4.2 m deep but no foundation trench was observed, nor was one noted elsewhere which may have been related. Across the cone house, the probable position of the south–west wall foundation was located within an internal test pit. However, this foundation must have been present only at either end of the wall because of the passage of five parallel tunnels across the wall line. Cartographic evidence indicates that the wall above was correspondingly only present at either

Plate 21 Looking south–west towards the cone house north-east wall. Shaft 807 to the left is partially sealed by later masonry. To the right, a concrete pier and girder probably supported a lean-to verandah which extended along the north–east wall. The pier stands between the tops of gas supply flues 521 and 522

Plate 22 External elevation of the cone house south–east gable wall

end, with the two buildings forming the tank house being linked together centrally (Pl 20; Ordnance Survey 1891); this arrangement suggests that the tank furnace itself passed through the gap in the walls of the adjoining tank house buildings.

The Ordnance Survey 1:500 map of 1891 indicates that, in addition to these elements of the cone house described above, there was also a narrow structure adjoining the north–east wall of the building (Pl 20). During excavation to the north–east of the extant cone house, several small rectangular concrete piers, some still containing the cut stumps of vertical RSJs, were found lying between gas supply flues 521 and 522 (Fig 7; Pl 21). As the excavations between the gas flues and the canal revealed no other evidence for structural remains, it is thought that these concrete stumps may have been the surviving remnants of the structure suggested by the cartographic and documentary evidence.

Original fabric within the present gable walls of the cone house (Figs 9 and 10; Pl 22)

The extant south–east and north–west gable walls of the cone house appear to date largely to the first phase of construction of the building, although some modifications are evident. The original form of the two gables was virtually identical, and the two walls can be described together.

A large circular window was centrally placed near the top of each gable, each window having an internal diameter of c 1.75 m. No framing or glazing survived in either window, that to the south–east having been boarded-up, and that to the north–west bricked-in. Below, each gable contained a line of seven windows. The windows in the south–east gable had been bricked-up, obscuring the original form of the apertures, but those in the north–west gable had merely been blocked with sheets of plywood. Here wooden frames and glazing had survived. The frames divided the windows into four rectangular lights, which had last been glazed with wired glass. It could also be seen in this gable that the apertures were recessed into the wall by the width of one brick. At the opening of the recesses, the windows measured approximately 2.0 m high by 1.1 m wide. The tops of the apertures were gently arched, formed from bricks set on end, whilst the sills appeared to be of moulded tiles. The windows in the south–eastern gable appeared to have been of the same size and form, though only the outer edges of the recesses were exposed.

Each gable façade would have been subdivided by two buttresses, dividing the windows into groups of two, three, and two. On the south–east gable, these buttresses had been removed above foundation level, their positions higher up the elevation being indicated by the refacing in stretcher bond of the scars left by their removal. On the north–western elevation, the buttresses had survived in their original form above a height of c 3.4 m, and were rectangular in plan, measuring c 0.7 m x 0.6 m, with gently-angled tops capped with tile. Below 3.4 m, they appear to have been replaced or repaired; here, the external buttress corners were built of bull-nose bricks.

Below the windows on the north–west elevation was a form of string course, formed of either two or three courses of bricks protruding slightly from the external face of the wall (Fig 10). A band of mortar infill present at the same height on the south–east gable suggested that a similar feature had existed here. These features appear to correlate with the roof lines of the two lean-to structures formerly present at either end of the cone house (Fig 7). The bonding of the brickwork on the external elevations suggested that original cone house fabric existed both above and below the string courses, but the upper part of the string course and the brickwork above had been subject to considerable external blackening, whilst the brick below had not. The implication is that the upper parts of the external faces of the gables has been exposed to air pollution, whilst below, the brickwork had been protected. This represents further evidence for structures at either end of the cone house, with the walling below string course level having originally been internal to each of the two end cells. The two end structures appear to have been removed during Phase 4 (see Ch 7).

Towards the bottom of the north–west gable evidence for three arched openings, now blocked, survived. Only two such openings were discernible in the south–east gable, but it is probable that a third had existed here as well, as the insertion of the present large rectangular entrance through the gable would have completely removed any trace of an earlier arched aperture here. The gentle arches above the apertures were formed of three courses of bricks set on edge. Below arch level, all evidence of the openings had been removed by the insertion of later, rectangular doorways. The arched openings were at least 2.0 m wide internally, with an internal crown height some 3.4 m above modern ground level. The apertures appear to have been doorways, communicating between the central cell of the cone house, and the smaller rooms at either end. Their large size was probably intended to allow the easy passage of finished glass cylinders from the furnace area to the adjacent rooms. It is possible that one of these smaller rooms may have been the 'palace' referred to in oral accounts of the tank house, a temporary storage area for the cylinders, before they were taken to the flattening kilns (Transcript of interview with Harry Langtree, 1).

Plate 23 Internal elevation of the cone house north-east wall. The upper parts of three stanchions are visible above the Phase 4 brickwork

Plate 24 External elevation of the cone house north–east wall

As has been noted above, all the doors and many of the windows within the gables of the cone house had been subject to later blocking with brick. Much of the rest of the brickwork of the two gables appears to date to the first construction of the building, with the exception of disturbance caused by the later insertion and blocking of rectangular doorways beneath the earlier arched openings. All the brickwork considered to be original had been laid using English bond. Two context numbers were used for all phases of the south–eastern and north–western gables: 550 for the former, and 551 for the latter.

Original fabric within the long walls of the cone house *(Figs 11 and 12; Pls 23, 24, and 25)*

The interior of the north–east wall had been re-skinned in brick to a height of *c* 4 m, but above, the upper portions of seven tapering cast iron stanchions were visible, *c* 0.25 m wide (Pl 23 shows the upper portions of three of the stanchions; additionally, parts of six of the stanchions are visible on the external elevation of the cone house, Fig 11; Pl 24). At the top, each stanchion incorporated a cast iron bracket that held a principal rafter supporting the roof. The stanchions appear to have formed the main structural component of the original north–east wall. Their presence suggests that the wall was not at first of solid brick; oral evidence suggests that the spaces between stanchions were filled by louvred doors (Transcript of interview with Harry Langtree, 17). Excavation of a test pit alongside the internal face of the wall (Fig 7) indicated that the third stanchion from the south–east continued down for a depth of 3.7 m below the floor surface of the cone house, there resting on a sandstone block measuring at least 0.5 m high x 0.8 m long.

Externally, original brick walling was visible extending along from each end of the wall as far as the first stanchion, for the full height of the elevation (Fig 11). The gaps between the stanchions had, at the top of the wall, been filled with timber boarding 1.45 m high. Below, an extant brick wall in English garden wall bond, together with adjacent buttressing, clearly post-dated the construction of the cone house. The stanchions were visible at the top of this wall, but lower down were obscured by the later raking buttresses. The timber infill at the top of the elevation may have been contemporary with the secondary walling below, there again being no surviving evidence for the nature of the primary infill between stanchions.

The south–west long wall of the cone house had been largely re-built. Small areas of original brickwork laid in English bond had survived at either end of the external face of the wall, but the brickwork elsewhere was in stretcher bond, and represented a complete re-build (Fig 12; Pl 25). However, a composite, riveted, cast iron girder ran along the top of the central part of the wall, at eaves level, and represented further evidence for the original construction of the wall; it was visible on the internal elevation (not illustrated), whereas on the outer face of the wall, its position was represented as a disruption in the pattern of the brick bond (Fig 12). It was 13.2 m in length, and supported the middle three principal rafters of the south–west pitch of the roof. The presence of the girder strongly suggests that the south–western wall had originally contained a large, centrally-located opening. To either side of the girder, the two principal rafters were supported by stone blocks. The foundations of the long wall were not accessible for recording because of the presence of surviving structures to either side.

The brick cone *(Figs 13 and 14; Pls 26 and 3)*

A large brick cone passed up through the centre of the pitched roof . It was built on a rectangular frame of four cast iron beams, supported by a round section cast iron column at each corner, which carried the base of the cone *c* 4 m above the probable original cone house floor level (Pl 26). At its base the cone measured 7.00 m south–east/north–west x 9.90 m south–west/north–east, its long axis being aligned with the furnace base below. The bottom six courses of brickwork were built up to form a rectangle, but above, the brickwork was carefully staggered inwards to form an elliptical shape. The cone steadily narrowed in diameter to a point close to its top, although the final 0.55 m again rose vertically. The top of the cone was *c* 1.7 m higher than the apex of the cone house roof, and *c* 12.3 m above floor level. It measured 7.26 m across externally, from south–west to north–east.

The cone house roof *(Fig 13 and Pl 26)*

During the repairs to the roof, an opportunity arose to examine some of its components in detail. Evidence for at least two episodes of replacement of the roof covering was apparent, but the main elements of the roof structure appeared to date to the original building of the cone house.

Roof trusses

The roof was carried at either end by the brick gable walls of the cone house, and in between, by seven wooden trusses, and by the brick cone. The principal rafters were *c* 8.2 m long, and typically measured 155 mm wide by 335 mm deep. On the north–eastern side of the building, the north–east principal rafter of each truss was supported by one of the seven cast iron stanchions of the north–east wall. The upper ends of the stanchions were jowled, and were topped by flat plates. The ends of the principal rafters were housed within cast iron sockets bolted to these plates (Pl 27). Two sets of wall plates ran along the top of the north–east wall, one on top of the other. Neither was in direct contact with the principal rafters, the lower, more

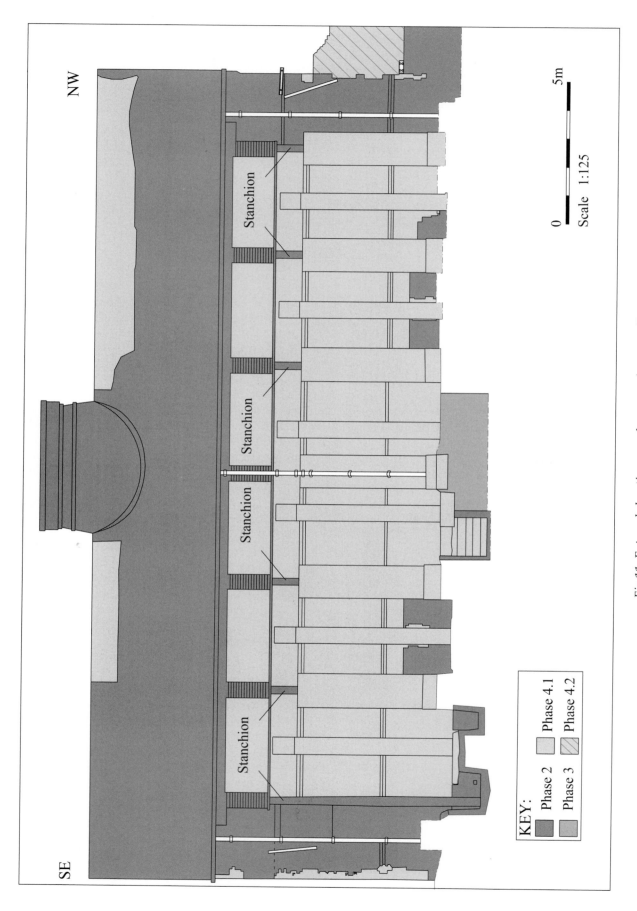

Fig 11 External elevation, cone house north–east wall

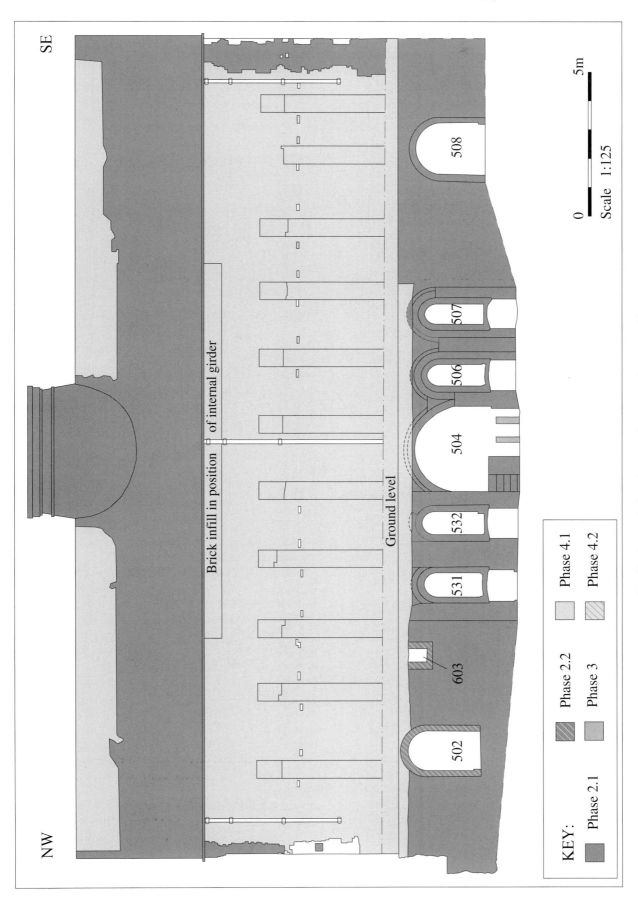

SE

NW

Brick infill in position of internal girder

Ground level

508

507

506

504

532

531

603

502

KEY:

Phase 2.1

Phase 2.2

Phase 3

Phase 4.1

Phase 4.2

0   5m

Scale   1:125

Fig 12 External elevation, cone house south–west wall

41

Plate 25 External elevation of the cone house south–west wall

substantial, wall plates being bolted to the back of the cast iron socket assembly on top of each stanchion.

On the south–western side of the building, the trusses were supported differently, as the south–west wall structure did not contain cast iron stanchions. The four principal rafters closest to the ends of the roof were supported by large rectangular stone pads built into the brickwork of the later wall, and which were probably also present in the original build of the wall. It was not possible to view the bottoms of these timbers, but they may have been bolted into the stone pads below. The three central principal rafters were housed within cast iron sockets bolted to the cast iron beam which ran along the centre of this wall, spanning the former wide opening through the wall to the south–western building of the tank house.

The central truss of the seven did not extend up to the apex of the roof because of the presence of the brick cone (Fig 13). Instead the upper end of the principal rafter on each side of the roof was housed in a cast iron socket resting against the external brick face of the cone. The socket was at the upper end of a cast iron strap bolted flush with the face of the cone in a near vertical position. At the lower end of the strap, a cast iron tie ran back out to the top of each wall.

The trusses contained no wooden components apart from the principal rafters, but the six complete trusses at either side of the central cone were strengthened by steel bolts, braces, and ties. The two principal rafters of each truss were joined at the roof apex by a cast iron fixture with sockets at either side (Pl 28). A king bolt, *c* 25 mm in diameter, ran vertically downwards from the sockets at the roof apex to a square plate located slightly above the level of the tops of the walls (Pls 26 and 29). From here, two wider braces ran diagonally upwards, being bolted to the undersides of the principal rafters at the level of the second purlin down from the apex. Two ties, again of *c* 25 mm diameter, also extended from the central plate outwards to the tops of the walls. Additional bracing was provided by thin rods extending vertically from the tops of the diagonal braces to the mid points of the ties. Thicker longitudinal ties also linked the square plates central to the ties and braces of each truss.

Purlins
A ridge purlin extended from each gable wall as far as the cone, which emerged through the centre of the roof. Each appeared to be a single timber, *c* 11.5 m long and measuring 220 mm wide by 195 mm high. The ridge purlins were carried on rectangular stone pads set within the internal face of each gable wall, the

Plate 26 The cone house roof structure and the base of the cone, with the foundations of the furnace below

other ends being supported by brick corbels built out from the cone. Additionally, the ridge purlins were bolted to the tops of the cast iron fixtures at the apex of each of the six complete roof trusses (Pl 28).

Below the ridge purlins, three runs of side purlins were present on each pitch of the roof. These were shorter and of lesser scantling than the principal rafters. The side purlins were trenched slightly into the upper faces of the principal rafters, were bolted in position, and were further secured by wooden wedge-shaped cleats attached to the upper faces of the principal rafters above and below the purlins. At the gable ends, the purlins were carried on stone pads set into the inner faces of the gable walls, and additionally,

the ends of the top runs of purlins were supported by projecting brick corbels where they abutted the cone. Each set of purlins appeared to consist of either four or five individual timbers, each a maximum of 7.6 m long. The individual purlins were joined by longitudinally-bevelled halved joints, the joints being placed over every second principal rafter. These joints were also staggered up the pitch of the roof, so that the joints of the top and bottom runs were aligned, whereas the joints of the second runs occurred over adjacent trusses.

Windbraces
Eight sets of windbraces extended diagonally across each pitch of the roof, from the wall plates to the ridge

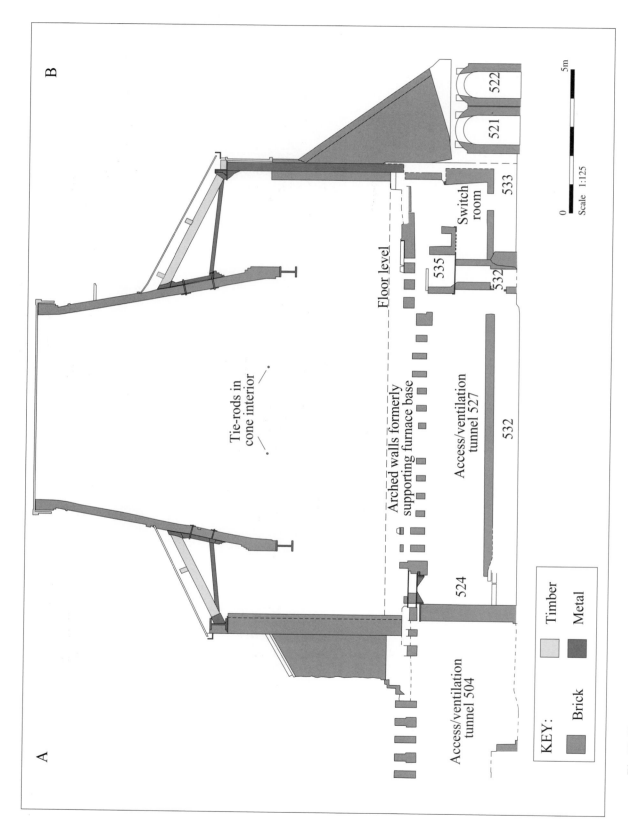

A

B

Tie-rods in
cone interior

Floor level

Arched walls formerly
supporting furnace base

Access/ventilation
tunnel 527

Access/ventilation
tunnel 504

524

532

532

533

Switch
room

535

521

522

KEY:

Brick		Timber
		Metal

0   5m

Scale 1:125

Fig 13 Transverse section across the width of the cone house. Compare with Figure 23, which reconstructs the probable position of the furnace

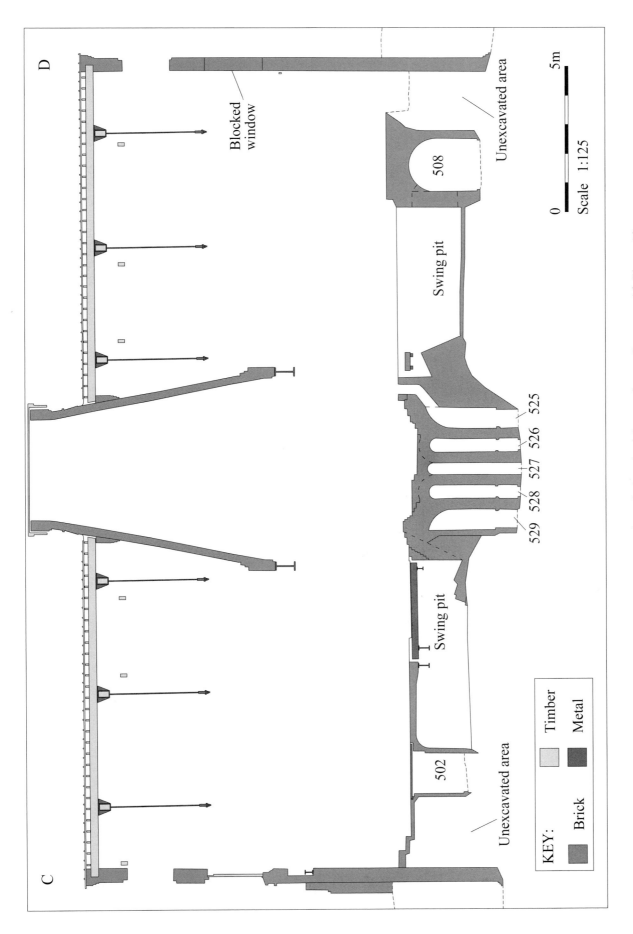

Fig 14 *Longitudinal section along the length of the cone house. Compare with Figure 18*

purlin. They were trenched into the principal rafters. Those located between the gable walls and the end trusses were set at a more acute angle to the principal rafters than the other windbraces.

Rafters

Rafters from three different periods were distinguished on the roof. The earliest may have been contemporary with the construction of the cone house. They were dark in colour, and measured *c* 115 mm x 60 mm. Where individual rafters passed right across a side purlin, they were double cogged and nailed into the purlin. Where the ends of two rafters abutted one another at a side purlin, each formed half of a double-cogged joint, each side being nailed. Nailed 'birdsmouth' joints had been used where the rafters met the ridge purlin, whilst at the base of the roof, they had been let into shallow notches in the upper wall plates, and nailed in position. A high proportion of the rafters appeared to be of this phase, but there were very few at the top of the roof, between the upper runs of side purlins and the apex (*see below Collars*).

Wall plates

The wall plates at the foot of the north–eastern pitch of the roof were exposed and examined during the repair programme, but it was not possible to view those of the south–west pitch. Two sets of wall plates, one on top of the other, were present at the top of the north–eastern wall. The lower set were the more substantial, measuring typically 230 mm wide by 220 mm high, and these rested on top of the cast iron stanchions, and were bolted into the back of the cast iron sockets which housed the principal rafters (Pl 27). Smaller wall plates measuring typically 100 mm wide by 145 mm high were bolted to the top of these, and it was to the upper wall plates that the common rafters were attached. Like the purlins, the individual upper wall plates were joined together using longitudinally-bevelled halved joints.

Roof covering

Lateral timber rails had been fixed above the rafters, and slates laid directly above. The slates below, roughly, the upper run of side purlins were darker in colour to those above (Pl 3), and may represent largely the original roof covering.

Collars

In addition to the roof structure described above, six wooden collars survived out of a probable original total of eight. They were 4 m long, and typically 120 mm wide by 220 mm high. These timbers spanned

Plate 27 One of the cast iron sockets bolted to the top of each of the stanchions in the north-east wall of the cone house. Each socket held the end of a principal rafter, and was bolted at the rear onto the lower of two wall plates

Plate 28 One of the cast iron fixtures that secured the apex of each of the six complete roof trusses. In the foreground, the stubs of two braces can be seen protruding from a collar; it is suggested that these had supported a structure which originally projected above the apex of the cone house roof

the gap between the upper run of side purlins on either side of the roof, but they were sited away from the roof trusses (Pl 28). Three were located to the north–west of the cone, whilst bolts remaining in the purlins indicated the position of a fourth. Three collars remained *in situ* on the other side of the cone, and it can be suggested that a fourth had existed here as well.

These collars appear superfluous to the extant roof of the cone house, and it can be suggested that their function was to support an additional structure. Two timber braces remained jointed into the collar nearest to the north–west gable of the cone house, rising steeply but not vertically, and being cut-off flush with the pitch of the present roof. The stubs of two further such braces were found protruding from the collar immediately to the north–west of the cone (Pl 28). An aerial photograph taken in 1939 indicates that two longitudinal structures originally projected above the roof of the cone house, one on either side of the cone, aligned parallel with the roof, and covering the roof apex (Pl 30). Similar structures are shown by a photograph of No 15 Tank House in the 1940s (Pl 31). They appear to have resembled louvres, with vertical sides and a pitched roof, but they must have been

c 8m in length, covering much of the roof apex. The upper structures may have been partially supported by the braces described above, for it seems probable that the latter originally projected above the present roof-line. The former presence of these structures capping the roof may also explain why most of the rafters at the top of the roof appeared to be secondary insertions (*see above Rafters*), and why the colour of the slate along the top of the roof differed from that lower down (Pl 3). Initially, the portion of the roof between the upper sets of side purlins and the apex may have had few if any rafters, and may not have been covered.

The south–western tank house building
Wall foundations (*Fig 7*)
Historic maps and old photographs demonstrated that a building of similar appearance to the cone house had originally formed the south–western element of No 9 Tank House (Pls 20 and 30; Figs 6 and 8). This structure had been demolished in 1984 (Plan of usage, Pilkingtons' Watson Street drawing office).

Some physical evidence for the south–western tank house building was recorded at foundation level. The foundations of the south–east gable and north–east long wall had both survived in part (wall 622, Fig 7),

Plate 29 A pair of cast iron plates securing the king bolt, ties, and braces of each truss

Plate 30 Aerial photograph of the Jubilee Side, 4 June 1939 (Pilkington Archive PRM/AV/2A). No 9 Tank House is just left of centre, towards the top of the photograph

48

and were built of orange-red brick laid in English bond using black ash mortar. The shape and form of the gable foundation closely matched the south–east wall of the cone house extension to the north–east, and two rectangular section buttresses keyed to the external face were very similar to those supporting the latter wall. They measured c 0.50 m wide by 0.80 m deep. The bottom of the gable foundation had stepped brick footings set on a concrete base. No evidence for an internal gable wall matching that of the extant cone house building could be found within the space defined by the foundation wall. This may suggest that the south–western building was not internally subdivided in the same way as the cone house.

Part of the north–east wall foundation was revealed further to the north–west (wall 602; Fig 7), between tunnel 502 and the north–west external wall of regenerator 530 (Fig 15). The upper part of the foundation had been truncated by the concrete footings for a later Phase 4 rebuild of the north–east wall, 632 (see Ch 7, p 97; Fig 29). The underlying brickwork was again constructed in orange-red bricks laid in English bond using black ash mortar, with the wider base stepped outwards. The wall had been truncated at its north–west end to allow the insertion

of tunnel 502; it had also been truncated to the south–east by north–east wall of regenerator 530, demonstrating that, although tank house and regenerators are thought to have been constructed during the same phase, the tank house foundations were built before some, at least, of the regenerators were installed.

A further length of wall foundation, 634, appears to represent the north–west end of the same wall (Fig 7). It was again sealed below a later wall on the same alignment, and was likewise cut by tunnel 502. However, the wall was constructed in English garden wall bond, thus differing from the other primary elements of the tank house.

Working end regenerators and central tunnel

A system of five contiguous brick tunnels was discovered below the floor level of the cone house, aligned across the width of the structure, and centrally-placed relative to its long axis (Figs 14 and 15). They lay between an underground chamber close to the north–east wall of the building, and a transverse tunnel parallel with, and immediately within, the south–west wall (tunnel 524, Fig 15). The central tunnel

Plate 31 Grove Street in the 1940s, with the old cone of No 15 Tank House in the background

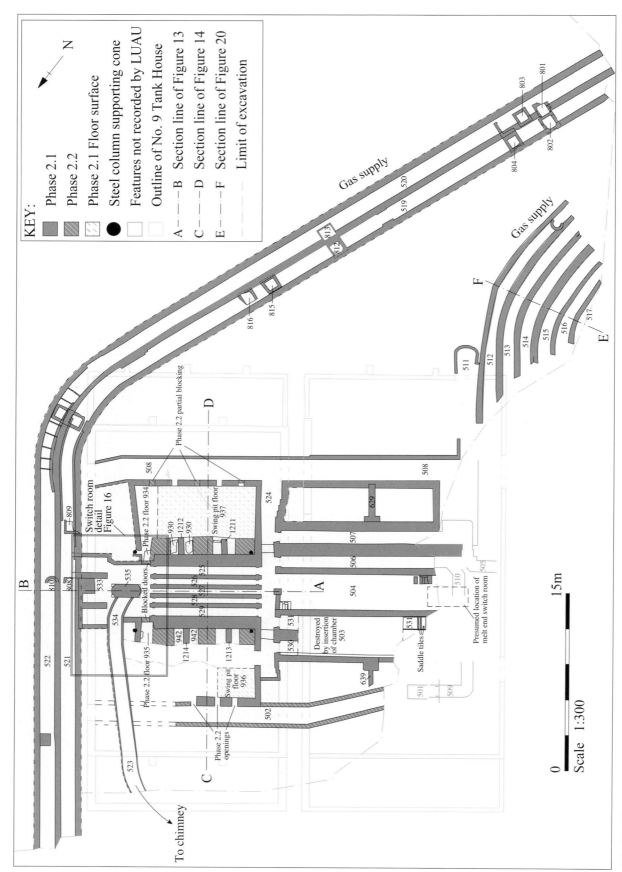

Fig 15 *Phase 2 tunnels, flues and swing pits. The relatively narrow working end regenerators, 525, 526, 528 and 529, are visible towards the top of the plan, with the wider melt end regenerators, 506, 507, 530 and 501, lying to the south–west*

of the five (527) had not been completely roofed over, but was spanned by a number of narrow brick arches, with spaces in between; the pair of tunnels to either side were completely enclosed. In each case, the outer tunnel was wider than both the inner tunnel of the pair, and the central tunnel. The form and location of these two pairs of tunnels suggested that they were regenerators (*see above Ch 3 The development of the glass furnace, 1860–73, p 10*). Each regenerator had a brick ledge located at approximately one-quarter of its total height (Plate 32 shows the ledges within one of the melt end regenerators), and documentary sources suggest that saddle tiles would have been laid on this ledge, to support regenerator bricks arranged in an open lattice above (for example, see British Patent 167, 1861). Thus, the lower part of the structure was in fact a flue, with the regenerator proper above the saddle tiles. Many probable examples of regenerator bricks were removed when the material infilling the tunnels was cleared. The central, intermittently-arched tunnel appeared to be intended to provide access and ventilation to the furnace located immediately above. The relatively small widths of this set of regenerators, compared to the larger ones immediately to the south–west, was consistent with their location below what is regarded as having been the cooler, working end, of the furnace.

Regenerators 525, 526, 528, and 529, and central tunnel 527 *(Figs 14 and 15)*

The regenerators and central tunnel were all 9.15 m long. Of the two outer regenerators, 525 was 0.62 m wide below the ledge, and 0.72 m wide above, 529 0.60 m wide below, and 0.71 m above. Inner regenerator 526 was 0.37 m wide below the ledge and 0.49 m wide above, and regenerator 528 was 0.35 m wide below, and 0.45 m wide above. The central tunnel, 527, was 0.41 m wide. All the regenerators had a stepped reveal above ledge height, 0.24 m from either end, standing 0.07 m proud of the tunnel walls. It is thought that this may have been to facilitate the blocking of the upper portions of the tunnels once the regenerator bricks were in place.

The central tunnel showed no obvious signs of the effects of severe heat, but the pairs of tunnels to either side bore the marks of intense thermal activity. For example, 525, the outer regenerator on the south–east side, had wall surfaces which appeared to be heavily vitrified with a dark reddish brown coating. This deposit was much more uniform than in the corresponding regenerator at the melt end, 507, but it was again largely confined to the wall surfaces above the level of the ledge. The two outer regenerator tunnels, 525 and 529, had three sets of matched pairs of flues distributed along the length of the roof, each pair communicating with the outer two flues of upcast stacks above. The two inner regenerator tunnels, 526

and 528, had three sets of single flues, each leading to the central flue of an upcast stack. This configuration allowed greater volumes of gas to be drawn from the outer regenerator tunnels than from the corresponding inner tunnels. At the extreme north–east end of 527, below the ledge level, an arched opening was revealed. This appeared to give access to flues below the floor of the chamber to the north–east, and again appeared to be repeated in regenerators 526, 528, and 529. No such openings were recorded at the opposing ends of the regenerators, suggesting that once they had been blocked at their stepped reveals, there was no corresponding access or egress for gases at the south–west end. The flue component at the base of each regenerator had been floored with brick.

The working end switch room

An underground chamber was discovered to the north–east of the working end regenerators and central ventilation tunnel (Fig 15). This room was roughly rectangular, with some irregularities, and had maximum dimensions of *c* 5.75 m south–east/north–west by 5.55 m south–west/north–east. The floor of

Plate 32 North–west extent of melt end regenerator 530. Saddle tiles would have bridged the gap between the ledges towards the base of the side walls, giving a platform on which the regenerator stuffing could be built up

Plate 33 Looking south across the working end switch room, to the portal of gas regenerator 528 (left of scale). The next opening to the left is that of central access/ventilation tunnel 527

the room was at an equivalent height to the ledges on the sides of the regenerator tunnels; the upper part of each tunnel opened into the room, whilst the lower part communicated with flues below the floor of the room.

Walls *(Fig 16)*

The portals of the regenerator tunnels and central ventilation tunnel formed the south–west wall of the room (Pl 33). The top of each tunnel opening was formed of an arch built of two courses of headers set on their sides. Below the level of the arches, the openings to the regenerator tunnels, but not the central tunnel, were constructed of bull-nose bricks. An iron beam had been laid along the length of the wall immediately over the tunnel arches, with three courses of brickwork above, stretchers, headers, and then stretchers. The ends of two iron roof beams oriented south–west/north–east were built into the wall above the level of the tunnel apertures. The tunnel openings appeared to be contemporary with the primary construction of the regenerators and switch room, but it was difficult to be certain whether the lateral iron

beam and three courses of bricks above were of the same date or later.

The north–west and south–east walls of the switch room, 666 and 667, also appeared to consist largely of original fabric. With the exception of two areas of blocking at the south–west end of each wall, the brickwork was of the English bond characteristic of the primary elements of the tank house. The two areas of blocking indicated the former presence of doorways giving access from the switch room to each of the two swing pits. Both walls were stepped outwards *c* 3.5 m along their length, so that the room became wider at its north–east end. A flight of stone steps immediately adjacent to the south–east wall allowed the switch room to be accessed from the north–east.

The north–east end of the switch room was divided into three bays by two walls, 664 and 715, which projected 1.74 m into the room from the north–east. These were again built in English bond, and were thought to be primary features. They supported the brick vault of the roof within the three end bays, as well as carrying the north–east ends of two iron roof beams, the other ends of which were bedded into the south–west wall above the level of the regenerator tunnel arches.

In the northern corner of the switch room, the original north–east wall appears to have been formed by the external face of gas supply flue 521, suggesting that the gas supply flue was constructed at the same time as the tank house complex was laid out. To the south–east, a brick wall in English bond, 734, was built butting the tunnel, and projecting at right angles into the room for 1.0 m, then turning south–east as far as the stone steps (Fig 16). This also appears to be an original wall, which served to enclose a vertical flue descending immediately to the south–west of 521. The wall contained a bricked-up arched aperture *c* 0.9 m high. Given its position adjacent to the vertical gas flue (*see below Under-floor flues*), it seems likely that the aperture gave access to this flue, to allow for the removal of tarry deposits, or any other blockage. The recess to the north–west of this wall was subsequently partially blocked by the construction of an elevated wall in English Garden Wall bond, 665.

Roof *(Not illustrated)*

Projecting walls 664 and 715 (Fig 16) supported three arched brick vaults and also carried iron beams, oriented north–east / south–west, which supported the remainder of the working end switch room roof. Evidence was recovered for at least three phases of vaulting, and it seems likely that the brickwork of the main part of the roof, beyond the north–eastern bays, had been partially replaced at least once.

Floor *(Fig 16)*

A brick floor, 909, was recorded within the switch room. It was constructed of red bricks which had been laid as stretchers, and bonded with black ash mortar. The floor contained several rectangular openings giving access to a system of under-floor flues *(see below Under-floor flues)*. The openings varied in dimensions from *c* 0.48 m x 0.64 m to *c* 0.62 m x 0.71 m. The floor butted the openings of the four regenerator tunnels and central ventilation tunnel to the south–west, and also the south–east and north–west walls of the switch room, extending north–east to the more southerly of the two roof support walls. However, an area of disturbance recorded around brick structure (535) standing in the centre of the room may reflect the position of the original switching mechanism *(see below Under-floor flues)*, suggesting that the brick floor may have been a primary feature within the switch room.

Under-floor flues *(Fig 16)*

Excavation below the switch room floor revealed a system of small flues. They appeared to provide a gas and air supply to the working end regenerators, via a switch mechanism *(see below Functional analysis of the tank furnace, p 74)*.

During excavations beyond the external face of the north–east wall of the cone house, the basal remains of two shafts, 808 and 810, were found adjacent to the switch room, sited above external gas supply flues 521 and 522 (Fig 16; *see below External gas supply flues, p 67*). It seems probable that the shafts allowed gas to be drawn from either of the two external flues. From the shafts, a vertical flue led downwards alongside the foundations of the north–east wall of the cone house, which also represented the north–east wall of the switch room. The wall here dog-legged inwards to accommodate the flue. Below the floor level of the

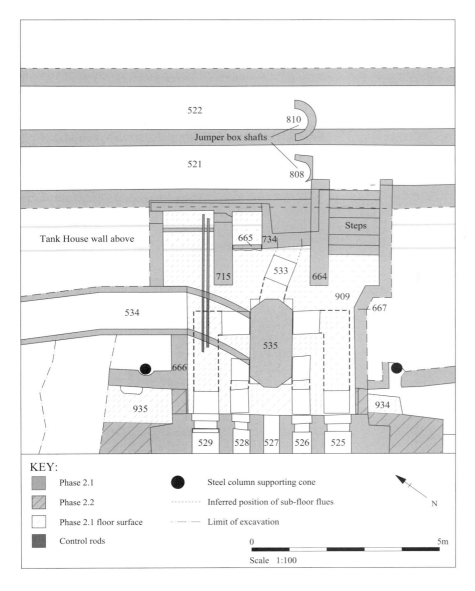

Fig 16 Detail of the Phase 2 working end switch room. Gas was drawn from flues 521 and 522 via flue 533 to a switch mechanism underneath structure 535; the switch directed the gas to regenerators 526 and 528 in turn. Air was drawn through a grill at the north-east of 535, and directed via the switch mechanism to regenerators 525 and 529 in turn. The exhaust gases were gathered alternately from regenerators 525 and 526, and then 528 and 529, and funelled via the switch and structure 535 to the chimney pull flue, 534

Plate 34 The south–west part of structure 535 in the working end switch room. Below the metal rails lies structure 738, inserted during Phase 3, which has removed evidence of the original switch mechanisms

The central brick structure and the working end chimney flue *(Figs 15 and 16; Pl 34)*

A large upstanding brick structure, 535, was found 0.8 m above floor level within the switch room. It was positioned above the junctions of the under-floor flues described above, but its base, H-shaped masonry 738, was clearly a secondary insertion (Pl 34; *Ch 6, Fig 26*), the bond and brick colour differing from those of the original parts of the chamber. The rebuilding of the base appeared to have disturbed evidence for the original means by which air was introduced into the regenerators, and exhaust gases removed (*see below Functional analysis of the tank furnace, p 74*).

Above the inserted base, fabric survived which appeared to date to the original construction of the switch room. Up to six courses of orange-red bricks in English bond formed the outer face of an elevated, multi-sided brick box or chamber, 535, carried on an iron frame of matching shape, with a pulley wheel attached to one side (Pl 34). The box measured *c* 2.25 m long by 1.15 m wide, and may originally have been *c* 0.9 m high. The metal frame at the bottom of the box was in turn supported by re-used rails, resting on top of inserted base 738. The rails appeared to have been provided in Phase 3, to carry the brick chamber whilst the base was being inserted, but had never been removed. A heavy steel door allowed access into the box, although it was unclear whether this was a primary or secondary feature. An elevated brick flue, 534, had been built as part of the same rise as the original courses of the box structure (Fig 16). The flue was attached to the north–west face of the box, and curved round in a northerly direction, cutting through the north–west wall of the switch room. It measured *c* 1.2 m high by 1 m wide. It was carried on curved iron beams integral with the frame supporting the original elements of the box, and its walls were also topped by an iron frame. A set of vertical iron bands provided additional support for the sides. The flue was again built in English bond of orange-red bricks. An area of later brick blocking in the south–east face of the flue may indicate the position of an original access door.

The curved, elevated flue is known to have continued to the north–west, before emerging from the gable of the cone house at foundation level (here numbered 523), and turning towards the chimney at the north–west corner of the tank house (Figs 6 and 7). It seems to have functioned as a chimney flue, but bore no external signs of having been heat-affected. Investigation of the interior of the flue demonstrated that, between the gable and the switch room, it was blocked by a brick infill panel, beyond the point at which a later structure (*Ch 7, Fig 27; 730*) accessed this

switch room, an aperture in the north–east wall is thought to have allowed gas to enter the cone house from the vertical flue. An horizontal sub-floor flue led south–west from the aperture towards the regenerators. At a point *c* 1.4 m inside the north–east wall of the switch room, two flues branched off to either side, and then turned through 90° to connect with the passages at the bases of the two air regenerators. Beyond this intersection, two more side flues branched off, leading to the passages below the two gas regenerators. It is suggested below that later activity has here removed evidence for switching mechanisms that would have directed the gas to the two gas regenerators, via the second set of branching flues, and air to the air regenerators via the first set, the air being drawn vertically down into the system from an inlet above (*see below Functional analysis of the tank furnace, p 74*). Thus, the surviving below-floor flues represent only a part of the original system for introducing gas and air to the regenerators, and for switching the supply from one set of regenerators to the other.

system of flues. Here the arched profile gave way to a box-like chamber with recesses for a vertical sliding damper.

It is suggested below that exhaust gases from the four regenerators passed along flues below the switch room floor, before being drawn up through holes in the floor and funnelled via the brick box, 535, into the chimney flue, 534, (*see below Functional analysis of the tank furnace, p 74*).

Control rods (*Fig 16*)

Two horizontal steel rods 75 mm apart were found on the floor of the switch room, oriented south–west/north–east, and extending for *c* 3.8 m, parallel with the north–west wall of the room. Both were *c* 50 mm thick, and passed below the later elevated north–east wall of the switch room, before turning upwards, beyond the line of the cone house wall, and adjacent to the external face of gas supply flue 521. Their disconnected upper ends were revealed by excavation between the cone house and the canal. It is uncertain whether the rods allowed valves in shafts 808 and 810,

atop the external gas supply flues, to be controlled from within the switch room, or if their purpose was to allowed the regenerator switching mechanism to be operated from ground level.

Access / ventilation tunnels

Tunnel 524 (*Figs 13 and 15; Pl 35*)

Tunnel 524 was discovered running parallel with the south–west long wall of the cone house, immediately within the line of the wall. The crowns of the arched tunnel roof were revealed by excavation, and the interior was also cleared of infill and recorded.

Tunnel 524 extended from roughly the mid-point of tunnel 528 to a square terminal 16.5 m to the north–west (Fig 15). Five arched openings to the north of 524 led to the four working end regenerators and central tunnel, and five openings to the south to the corresponding structures of the melt end. The tunnel appears to mark a division between these two functional components of the tank furnace above. As described above (*see above Working end regenerators and central tunnel, p 49*), raised reveals protruded from

Plate 35 Looking south-east along tunnel 524. The portals on the left lead to the working end regenerators, those on the right to the melt end regenerators

the faces of the regenerators close to their intersections with 524, suggesting that the openings to the tunnels would have been periodically blocked and unblocked, to service the regenerator 'stuffing'. The edges of the regenerator apertures were built using bull-nose bricks, contrasting with the regular bricks used for the openings of the central tunnels. A further opening was also present on the north–east side of 524, beyond the working end regenerator entrances. This led to the north–west swing pit (*see below The swing pits, p 65*). It differed from the other openings in the tunnel walls, the top being in the form of a shallow arch rather than a semi-circular arch, and the bottom edge of the arch being formed of bull-nose bricks in addition to the sides of the aperture. It is also in marked contrast with the lack of a similar opening to the south–east swing pit.

Tunnel 524 was built in English bond using red brick bonded with black ash mortar. It was a maximum of 1.72 m wide close to its south–eastern entrance, but narrowed to 1.00 m in width a short distance to the north–west, by virtue of bull-nosed vertical corbelling. In contrast to all the other tunnels and flues thought to be part of the original tank house layout, the roof of the central portion of 524 was formed of shallow arches aligned perpendicular to the orientation of the tunnel. These transverse arches were carried on cast iron beams with webs and flanges, which crossed the tunnel and were embedded in the tops of the vertical side walls (Pl 35). The arches were also strengthened by round steel bars serving as tie-rods. The presence of the beams appear to be related to the need to support the tank furnace passing above 524. The wall had stepped brick footings, and was constructed on a concrete base. The tunnel's north–western end was closed by a brick wall, 663, built in English bond of dark red brick and black ash mortar. The south–western internal face of 524 was seen to extend beyond the end wall of the tunnel at foundation level. This may suggest that it had originally been intended to extend the tunnel further to the north–west. Above foundation level, the nature of the junction of the brickwork between the end wall and internal faces of 524 was not discernible.

Tunnel 508 (*Fig 15*)
Tunnel 508 extended across almost the full width of both tank house structures, from close to the external wall of the south–western building, to the north–east wall of the cone house. The tunnel lay parallel with the south–east gable walls of both buildings, being 2 m within the inner gable wall of the cone house, 650, and 6.5 m within the gable of its associated partner structure. It was 28.5 m long, and was straight apart from a slight deviation to the north 2.6 m from its north–eastern end, and had clearly been constructed within a narrow foundation trench. The form of the

tunnel was gradually revealed by excavation of the deposits with which it had been infilled. Excavation began at the south–western entrance, and gradually progressed along the full length of the tunnel.

The tunnel had a south–western entrance, accessed via an underground chamber reached from entrance tunnel 511 (*see below Entrance tunnel 511 and the melt end switch room, p 59*). Roughly half-way along its length, it communicated with transverse tunnel 524, positioned just inside the line of the south–west wall of the cone house, and dividing the two sets of regenerators. Further north–east, five narrow rectangular openings through the north–west wall of 508 gave access to the south–east swing pit adjoining the working end of the furnace (*see below The swing pits, p 65*). Most of these had been partially bricked-up at a later date. The far end of 508 had been truncated and subsequently blocked by a rebuild of the cone house north–east foundation wall, but the survival of a number of bull-nose bricks in this location at foundation level demonstrated that it had originally communicated with the canal bank. The tunnel appeared to be rising slightly as it approached the blocking in order to pass over the crowns of the external gas supply tunnels.

Tunnel 508 was built with red non-refractory bricks, laid in English bond using black ash mortar. It was 1.80 m wide and 2.31 m high, with a semi-circular arched roof, with internal crown height of 29.14 m OD. The floor was composed of layers of compacted ash. Excavation of a sondage through these deposits showed that the walls were built on extended brick footings, which in turn had been laid on strip concrete foundations. Several iron plates were let into the floor surface just before the junction of 508 with tunnel 524. It seems clear that the function of the tunnel was to give access to the south–east swing pit, as well as to the north–west swing pit and the central entrances of the melt and working end regenerators via tunnel 524. However, the fact that the openings to the south–east swing pit were modified (*see below Alteration of the swing pits and furnace, p 71*) suggests that this tunnel was also a significant source of ventilation.

Melt end regenerators and central tunnel
The remains of four parallel, closely-spaced regenerators, and a central tunnel, were recorded to the south–west of the surviving cone house, their north–east terminals being almost immediately below the later south–west wall of the building (Fig 15). The regenerators lay largely within the footprint of the south–western of the two structures believed originally to have formed the tank house (*see above The south–western tank house building, p 47*), below the putative position of the melt end of the furnace. They were much larger than the comparable structures

recorded below the cone house, and their physical appearance following clearance demonstrated that they had been associated with much higher temperatures. They were in a correspondingly poorer state of preservation; regenerators 506 and 507 were in a very degraded state with bulging walls and delaminating brickwork. All their associated vertical rising flues had been partially blocked, either during the productive life of the furnace, or later; the purpose of the modification was not established. Regenerators 530 and 531, which were the gas and air regenerators to the north–west of the central tunnel, had been truncated a short distance from their portals to tunnel 524. In addition, two large concrete plinths had been inserted along the north–west wall of central tunnel 504, leading to the removal of one of the narrow arches that formed its roof.

Regenerators 530 and 531 *(Figs 13 and 15)*

The two north–western regenerators had been substantially truncated by the creation of the later Phase 3 rectangular chamber, 503 (Fig 26; *see below Ch 6, Changes to the melt end regenerators, p 86*), but their extreme north–east and south–west ends had survived. The surviving portions showed a close similarity with the south–eastern pair of melt end regenerators, 506 and 507, suggesting that the two pairs of tunnels had originally had the same function.

The south–west end of 531 still contained the *in situ* remains of three saddle tiles, supported by the ledges at either side of the tunnel, differentiating the narrower lower passage of the tunnel from the wider upper component (Plate 32 shows identical ledges within regenerator 530). Oral accounts of the use of glass furnaces demonstrate that lattice-work piles of refractory bricks would have been placed on these tiles (Transcript of interview with Ron Parkin). The tiles at this end of 531 were the only saddle tiles to be recovered *in situ* from the 'Hotties' site.

Tunnel 504 *(Figs 12 and 15)*

Tunnel 504 was exactly centrally-placed along the long axis of both the cone house and structure to the south–west, being perpendicular to both. It was built of non-refractory brick, with a semi-circular arched roof. Its internal width was 3.2 m, markedly greater than the width of the pairs of tunnels to either side, and its internal crown level was 29.05 m OD. Its north–east terminal lay 0.4 m inside the line of the later internal wall of the cone house. From this point, its surviving fabric was recorded extending south for *c* 6 m. An earlier survey, conducted in 1991 by MN Oliver and Co, before the archaeological recording of the site began, suggested that the tunnel might have extended a further 6 m to the south–west, and the south–west end was later found to be intact, having

Plate 36 View north-east into tunnel 504, with flue 532 in the foreground

Plate 37 View south–west to the brick arches above tunnel 504, which formerly supported the melt end of the furnace. The two surviving pairs of melt end upcast flues can be seen to the left of the photograph

escaped destruction during building works relating to the construction of the adjacent Hilton Hotel.

At its north–east end, the tunnel was partitioned centrally by a brick-built pier carrying a cast iron roof support for the multiple arched roof of tunnel 524, running perpendicular to 504. Tunnel 504 itself was braced throughout its length by vertical and horizontal steel tie-rods (Plate 36 shows a horizontal tie). The top of the tunnel was formed by a series of arches and apertures, running transversely across its longitudinal axis (Pl 37). The arches were brick-built, again using refractory bricks, and were 0.22 m wide. On the south–east side, they were recorded springing from the junction of 504 and regenerator 506; to the north–west, they had been truncated by the insertion of walls 658 and 659, part of a later brick-built channel. The apertures between the arches were 0.40 m wide (Pl 37). It is suggested that these spaces had been left in order to allow the passage of air to ventilate and cool the base of the tank furnace, which is thought to have stood immediately above, supported by the arches. However, despite the proximity of the furnace, the brickwork of 504 appeared to have been largely unaffected by heat. Additionally, a number of arched apertures, which had been blocked at ground level,

appeared formerly to have communicated with the adjacent regenerator 506, and a further arched aperture, later blocked, was recorded in the south–west wall of 504. A heavy steel door remained *in situ* below the arch.

Regenerator 506 *(Figs 12 and 15)*
Regenerator 506 lay parallel and immediately to the south–east of 504. Its north–eastern terminal lay 0.4 m inside the later inner wall of the cone house, the tunnel extending to the south–west for *c* 11.5 m, at which point it was found to have been truncated by recent building work associated with the erection of the Hilton Hotel. Earlier survey work carried out before the start of the archaeological fieldwork, and before the partial destruction of the tunnel, suggested that it had originally been *c* 13 m long.

The structure was found to be subdivided into upper and lower passages (Plate 32 shows the corresponding division in regenerator 530). The upper portion was 1.15 m wide and 2.18 m high, with a semi-circular arched roof and internal crown height of 29.15 m OD. At its north–east end, the upper portion of the tunnel had a junction with transverse tunnel 524. At this north–east portal, a stepped reveal was recorded, standing 20–50 mm proud of the tunnel profile and set back from the external face. This may have facilitated closure of the regenerator from the north–east. A moderate degree of surface corrosion, possibly representing the early stages of vitrification, was observed at the regenerator portals. Above, two flue orifices 0.35 m square were seen to emerge through the regenerator roof. They were heavily vitrified with a milky white glaze with greenish blue streaks, and were connected to the south–east side of the regenerator crown. They appeared to have been subject to intense temperatures, suggesting that this was where the products of combustion had entered the regenerators.

The lower component of the structure was a flue 0.99 m wide, offset by 0.16 m to the south–east of the upper portion. It was square-roofed, with an internal ceiling level of 26.72 m OD, 0.25 m below the floor of the upper passage.

Regenerator 507 *(Figs 12 and 15)*
Regenerator 507 lay immediately adjacent to 506, and was of very similar form. It was 1.12 m wide, with an internal crown height of 29.16 m OD, and a semi-circular arched roof. Again, a raised reveal at the north–east portal produced a narrowed entrance. The structure was waisted, being narrower towards its base. Although no intervening floor was found between the two portions, the tunnel was again clearly divided into upper and lower components.

Regenerator 507 again showed varying degrees of vitrification. At the lower levels and at the tunnel extremities, the brickwork showed only moderate signs of the effects of heat. Discolouration intensified towards the top of the tunnel, and was especially pronounced around six flues, emerging from the north–west face of the regenerator. Here, a milky white glaze with greenish-blue streaks was observed, closely comparable to the discolouration present within 506. A teapot-brown glazing had formed at the south–west end of the regenerator, and represents evidence for the substoichiometric operation of the first two ports; here, the furnace must have been fired with far more fuel than could be burnt, producing a reducing environment which helped the alkali to react with the sand grains, particularly important when saltcake was the alkali source.

Entrance tunnel 511 and the melt end switch room
A large part of the footprint of the south–western tank house structure lay beyond the limits of the World of Glass site. Substantial disturbance to this area had already occurred by the start of the programme of archaeological recording, leading to the destruction of hitherto surviving below-ground structures just within the south–west wall line of the tank house. However, although the details of the form and precise layout of flues here have been lost, the surviving remains, and the evidence of a survey carried out by commercial surveyors before the truncation, mean that the functions of the structures at this end of the building are largely understood.

Entrance tunnel 511 *(Fig 15)*
Entrance tunnel 511 appears to have provided an entrance to a below-ground chamber sited just within the south–west wall of the melt end tank house building. The tunnel's south–east portal was flush with the south–east gable of this building, as represented by the surviving foundation wall, 622 (Figs 7 and 15), uncovered by excavation. The tunnel entrance was surrounded externally by a sunken apsidal wall, through which access was gained by a flight of brick steps in the south–west corner. The apsidal wall appears to have been built from the interior, and was not keyed into the tunnel walls. It nevertheless appears to be an original feature, and is clearly depicted on the Ordnance Survey 1:500 map of 1891 (Pl 20).

From its entrance at the base of the south–east gable, the tunnel led north–westwards down a ramp, the tunnel floor being inclined downwards for a length of 4 m, as far as its intersection with tunnel 508. The south–western external face lay immediately adjacent to gas supply flue 512, the most northerly of seven flues, to which it here ran parallel.

The tunnel was built of red brick bonded with a black ash mortar, the roof forming a semi-circular arch. The south–west wall had been partially disturbed, but the north–east wall was largely intact as far as the junction with tunnel 508, the feature having been truncated at that point. The exterior face suggests that the tunnel was built up to arch spring level from the interior, as the external finish was rough and unpointed. Tunnel 511 showed no signs of being heat-affected and as such was interpreted as an access tunnel.

The stratigraphic relationships of the tunnel's fabric gave some indication of the order in which the tank house complex was laid out. The north–east face butted against tunnel 508, suggesting that 511 was built after 508. It was also recorded as cutting the south–east gable wall, 622, at the tunnel entrance, further indicating that the access tunnel was inserted after the south–west tank house building has been constructed (*see above The south–western tank house building, p 47*). It appears that the wall had been partially demolished down to the height of the tunnel arch spring and as far back to the north–east as the first buttress. The wall below this was cut to accommodate the passage of the tunnel, and subsequently rebuilt up to ground level after the tunnel arch was completed. However, these relationships are considered to indicate the sequence of primary construction, rather than implying that access tunnel 511 was the product of a later phase of activity. The tunnel had certainly been built by 1891 at the latest (Pl 20; Ordnance Survey 1891).

The melt end switch room *(Fig 15)*

The existence of a below-ground chamber to the south–west of the melt end regenerators is known from oral testimony, and its position would have mirrored that of the switch room to the north–east of the working end regenerators (*see above The working end switch room, p 51*). Former glass workers referred to a sunken room beyond the melt end regenerators, known as 'the cave'. This structure was found to have been largely destroyed, with the exception of a 4.3 m length of its north–eastern wall, surviving between regenerator 507 and tunnel 508 (Fig 15). However, an earlier survey of the southern part of the site by a non-archaeological survey company revealed the former existence of several brick tunnels at a low level, which may have been gas and air flues sited below the floor of 'the cave' (Fig 15). Ron Parkin's account of the use of the tank furnace suggests that the melt end regenerator switching mechanism would have been sited here (Parkin 2000, 76 and fig 51), and it now seems certain that this south–western chamber was a switch room closely comparable with the more intact switch room north–east of the working end of the furnace. However, the melt end regenerator tunnels were much larger than those at the working end, and the gas and air flues supplying the melt end appear to have been correspondingly larger than their counterparts at the working end, probably necessitating a different layout for the switching mechanism.

A four-way junction of brick flues appears to have occurred at a low level 2 m south–west of melt end regenerators 506 and 507. Flue 505 was located opposite the south–west entrance of 506, and was truncated 2.55 m south–west of the junction (Fig 15); it was 1.01 m wide internally and had an arched roof. Flue 510 showed the same form and dimensions as 505, and survived for a length of 2.42 m (Fig 15). Both flues had internal crown heights of 26.74 m OD, which corresponds to the height of the division between the flues at the base of the melt end regenerators, and the regenerator chambers above (see the ledges shown by Plate 32). The fact that flue 510 appears to approach regenerator 506, whilst flue 505 turns towards regenerator 507, suggests the possibility that these were gas and air flues respectively, which probably also have carried exhaust gases when the direction of gas flow was reversed. Similar structures probably existed in a corresponding position to the south–west

of the north–western set of melt end regenerators, but there the destruction of archaeological remains had been complete. In between would have been the melt end switching mechanism.

Fragments of two further tunnels or flues were recorded and destroyed prior to the commencement of archaeological fieldwork: 509 extended north–west from the putative melt end switch room, turning a right-angled corner to the north–east (Fig 15). The structure was 1.02 m wide internally, but no other information was recorded. Its north–eastern end appeared to join 501. Plan evidence suggests that flue or tunnel 501 came to a square butt end 2.6 m north of its intersection with 509 (Fig 15), but written records appear to indicate an intersection with 502, 1.95 m further north–east. The structure is believed to have been two-tiered. The lower portion was 1.03 m wide, with a flattened arched roof, but no established floor level. Above, the upper passage was 0.8 m wide, with a level floor at 26.94 m OD; this height corresponds roughly to the base of 502. The roof of 501 had been removed by later disturbance. The phasing of the possible relationship with tunnel 502 is unclear from the available evidence. The functions of these structures have not been established, and it is uncertain why 501 should have been of two-tier construction.

Walls 629 and 639

Two foundation walls were found within the footprint of the south–west tank house building, but not underlying any of its external walls; they were almost in line, and oriented south–east/north–west.

Although not identical, these two walls were of broadly similar form, and were built in equivalent positions on either side of the melt end regenerators. The north–western wall, 639, was built in English bond and cut by tunnel 502 (Fig 15); it seems clearly to have been part of the original layout of tunnels and foundations below the south–western tank house building. The date of construction of the south–eastern wall is more ambiguous, it being constructed in English Garden Wall bond, and butting against regenerator 507. It is uncertain from the keying of this wall into tunnel 508 whether it was contemporary with, or later than, tunnel 508. It may thus have been an original support for regenerator 507, or a later addition. As well as supporting the external faces of the regenerator tunnels, perhaps countering the effects of thermal shock, these walls may also have served to retain the make-up used to raise the floor level of the building above the top of the regenerators. They also lie on the same line as the north–eastern of the two internal walls subdividing the building after the laying of a concrete floor (*see Ch 7, p 100; Fig 29*), though they appear to have been of much earlier date.

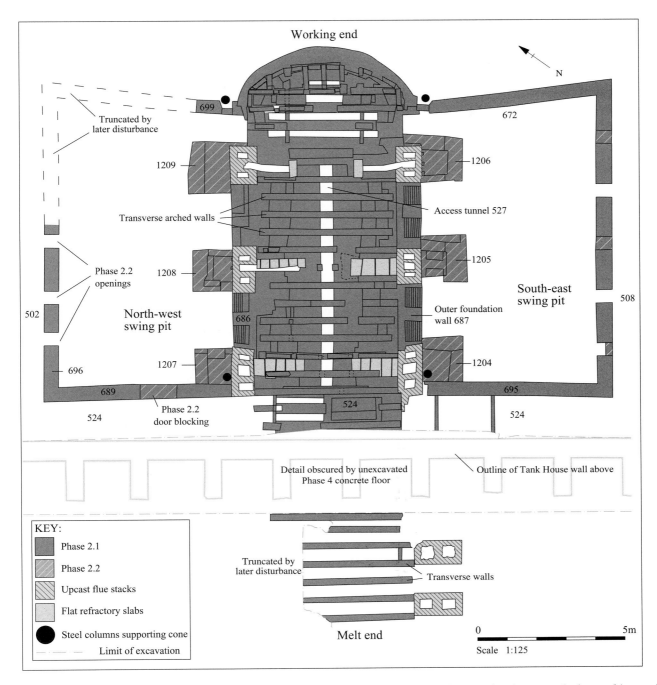

Fig 17 *Basal remains of the Phase 2 furnace. The furnace itself was removed when production ceased; the working end would have been carried by side walls 686 and 687, and by the transverse arched walls which ran between them, spanning the regenerators and central access/ventilation tunnel. Compare with Plate 38. More fragmentary remains of the melt end foundations were found (bottom of figure)*

The basal remains of the furnace

Working end *(Fig 17)*

The remains of the foundations of the furnace were found to be largely intact, despite the removal of the tank itself. In between the foundation walls, the upper surfaces of the crowns of the working end regenerators were visible, built of yellow refractory brick (*see above Working end regenerators and central tunnel, p 49*). Two parallel walls aligned north–east / south–west, 686 and 687, appeared to define the position of the sides

of the furnace (Fig 17, Pls 38 and 39). These foundation walls lay immediately beyond the crowns of the two outer regenerator tunnels, their internal faces being *c* 4.0 m apart. They were built of light yellow refractory brick, in a combination of English and irregular bonds, using a light orange sandy mortar, although the outer surface of the south–eastern wall had been faced with regular red brick. Both walls had been partially disturbed by the foundations for later partitions of the cone house.

Plate 38 *Looking south-west along the foundations of the furnace working end. Transverse arched walls (parallel with scale) supported the furnace base above the regenerators and central access/ventilation tunnel. The side walls were complex structures incorporating vertical upcast flues*

These two outer foundation walls were complex structures, incorporating a number of features. Three sets of vertical flues had been built into each side wall, each set consisting of three adjacent apertures leading up from below (Fig 17). Former glass workers indicated that, in regenerative glass furnaces, these were termed 'stacks', and the apertures into the furnace 'ports' (Parkin 2000, 71, 116; Transcript of interview with Ron Parkin). The positions of the stacks relative to the long axis of the furnace corresponded to those of other flues recorded passing up through the roofs of the regenerators below. Surviving flat refractory slabs were revealed leading down from the inboard faces of the upcast flues to the tops of the regenerator crowns (Fig 17). Evidence of the thermal loads imposed on these features was apparent in their vitrified surface deposits. It thus seems clear that the upcast flues transmitted gases to and from the underlying regenerators.

The upcast flues were roughly rectangular, but varied in exact shape and dimensions (Fig 17). The two pairs towards the centre and north–east of the cone house end of the furnace measured c 1.2 m x 0.8 m. Their three individual apertures were almost rectangular, with dimensions of c 0.37 m x 0.20 m, although the central apertures tended to be slightly larger. The pair of upcast flues towards the south–western wall of the cone house was slightly larger, each measuring c 1.7 m x 0.8 m. They also differed in that most of their apertures were not aligned perpendicular to the axis of the furnace. Former glass workers and Pilkington's principal scientific officer have indicated that the central aperture in each upcast flue, connected to the narrower, inner, regenerator tunnel, would have carried gas, whilst the two outer apertures, fed by the wider, outer, regenerator tunnel, would have carried air. Similar arrangements of flues can be seen in drawings relating to earlier Siemens' patents (British Patent 4763, 1879); they were used both to bring the incoming gaseous fuel mix to the point of combustion, and to allow the passage of exhaust gases to the regenerator bricks in the opposite regenerators. Although the upcast flues have been truncated close to the probable level of the base of the tank furnace, they must originally have risen higher, reaching close to the top of the tank, and delivering the gases for combustion above the surface of the molten glass (Fig 18).

Probable anchorages for vertical 'buckstays' of bull-headed metal (old railway lines) were provided within

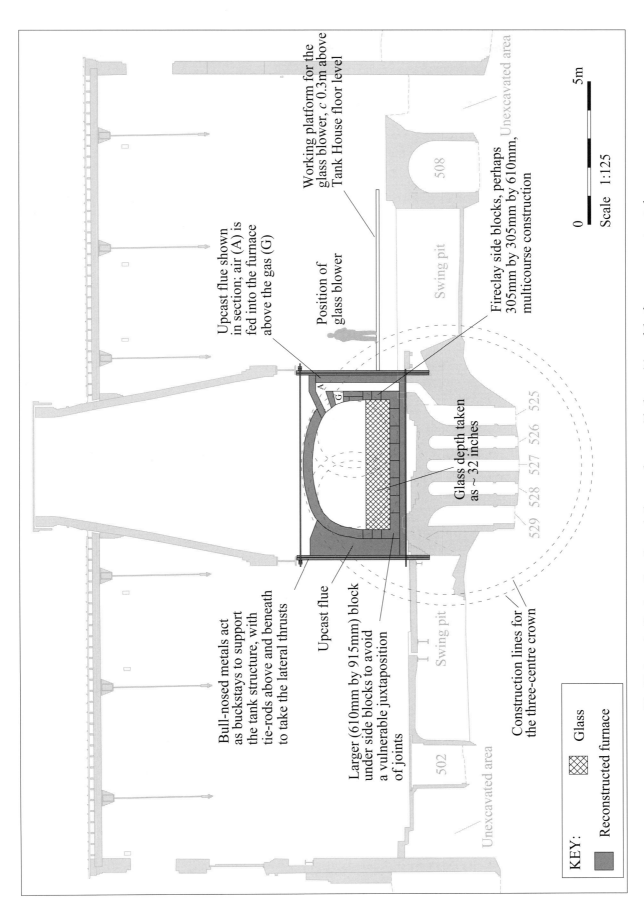

Working platform for the glass blower, *c* 0.3m above Tank House floor level

Upcast flue shown in section; air (A) is fed into the furnace above the gas (G)

Position of glass blower

Fireclay side blocks, perhaps 305mm by 305mm by 610mm, multicourse construction

508

Swing pit

A

G

Glass depth taken as ~ 32 inches

525

526

527

528

529

Bull-nosed metals act as buckstays to support the tank structure, with tie-rods above and beneath to take the lateral thrusts

Upcast flue

Larger (610mm by 915mm) block under side blocks to avoid a vulnerable juxtaposition of joints

Construction lines for the three-centre crown

502

Swing pit

Unexcavated area

Unexcavated area

0   5m

Scale   1:125

KEY: Glass

Reconstructed furnace

Fig 18 Longitudinal section through the cone house, with the position of the furnace reconstructed

the structure of the side foundation walls of the furnace, a platform with stepped recess at either side being built into the wall between each upcast flue (Pl 39). Additional lateral support was provided by large angled buttresses abutting the external faces of the upcast flues, but these represented later additions to the furnace (Fig 17; *see below Changes to furnace buttresses, p 72*); lateral containment seems originally to have been provided by a series of thinner buttresses. Evidence for these could be seen within the later buttresses, and as scars on the floor surfaces surviving in between (1211, 1212, 1213, and 1214, Fig 15).

The two side walls, 686 and 687, supported the ends of a series of transverse arched walls, built of light yellow refractory brick, which spanned the total width of the five tunnels below. In two locations, specially formed bridging tiles were still in position above the arched walls (Fig 17); these would have supported the massive flat slabs, at least 10 ins thick, which formed the furnace base (Fig 19). Nineteen transverse walls had survived in whole or in part, bridging the 4 m gap between the side walls. They were 0.23 m wide, and for the most part, spaced at intervals of 0.40 m. The two walls at the south–western end of this part of the furnace base appeared to have been

supported in part by the roof arches of tunnel 524 below, carried on cast iron beams.

The basal remains of the working end of the furnace had dimensions of 12.7 m x 6.4 m, with buttresses beyond. The upcast flues probably originally passed up outside the tank, the working end of which may have had dimensions of 12.7 m x 4.7 m.

Melt end *(Fig 17)*

The basal remains of the melt end of the furnace had been subject to much more extensive disturbance, but some fragments remained within the footprint of the demolished south–western tank house building, close to the line of the north–east wall. The surviving fragments served to demonstrate that the melt end of the furnace had functioned in a similar way to the working end, although the details of the layout of the brick supports and upcast flues were different.

The lower parts of the two north–eastern upcast flues on the south–eastern side of the furnace had survived (Fig 17). In contrast to the layout at the working end, the upcast flues were aligned perpendicular to the axis of the furnace rather than parallel to it, and were sited straddling the gas and air regenerators, rather

Plate 39 Looking north-west across the south-east swing pit to the working end furnace foundations, after conversion of the cone house for display to the public. Buttress 1206 (Fig 17) is in the centre foreground, and the arched walls that formerly supported the furnace base are visible behind

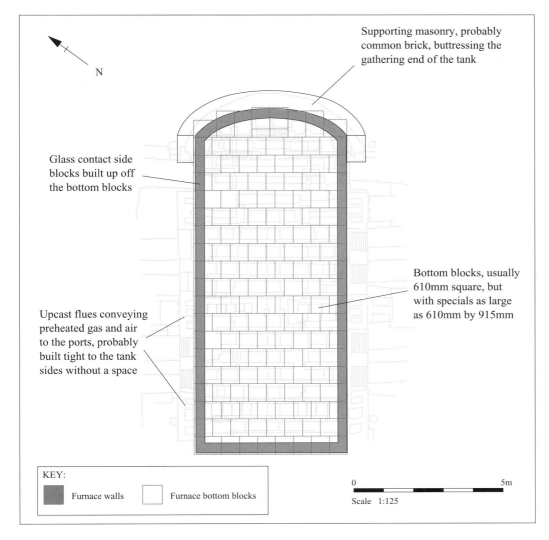

Supporting masonry, probably common brick, buttressing the gathering end of the tank

Glass contact side blocks built up off the bottom blocks

Bottom blocks, usually 610mm square, but with specials as large as 610mm by 915mm

Upcast flues conveying preheated gas and air to the ports, probably built tight to the tank sides without a space

Fig 19 Schematic reconstruction plan of the furnace base at the working end

N

KEY:

▓ Furnace walls ☐ Furnace bottom blocks

0   5m

Scale 1:125

than beyond them. The upcast flues were of similar overall dimensions to the examples at the working end, measuring *c* 1.6 m x 0.8 m. However, they each contained two rather than three apertures, these being larger, measuring *c* 0.46 m x 0.33 m. The location of these apertures suggests that gas and air passed upwards almost vertically from the tunnels below.

To the north–west of the upcast flues, six transverse walls were recorded, 651–657 (Fig 17). These differed from the examples at the working end, in that they spanned only the wide central passage between the melt end regenerators, tunnel 504, partially covering it, but leaving intervening gaps. The walls were 0.20 m wide, and had been built 0.41 m apart. However, these were walls built of regular red brick, and had not supported the furnace base directly; further structures to support the furnace probably lay above, built of refractory brick, but have not survived.

The differences between the furnace base at the working and melt ends is probably largely attributable to the need to attain higher temperatures at the melt

end of the tank furnace. As a result, the regenerators were larger, necessitating different methods of supporting the furnace and introducing gas and air.

The swing pits

The south–east swing pit *(Fig 17)*

Removal of the mid-twentieth century floor surface of the cone house, together with the underlying infill, revealed the presence of a trapezoidal brick-lined chamber below ground level to the south–east of the furnace. Documentary sources, and evidence from retired glass workers, indicate that this represents the remains of an almost intact 'swing pit' (*see below Functional analysis of the tank furnace*, p 74; Fig 17).

The swing pit measured 9.9 m by 5.9 m, and was 2.46 m deep. The south–western wall of the swing pit, 695, butted the southern upcast flue of the furnace, and extended south–east, where it was bonded to the external face of tunnel 508. It was built of orange-red brick constructed in English bond using black ash mortar. The north–eastern wall, 672, was of the same construction. It was bonded to the eastern foundation

Plate 40 View south–east across the south–east swing pit. Three of the five openings in the south-east wall had been partially blocked, from the top down; the first and third openings from the north end of the wall are visible in this photograph

wall of the furnace, and extended in an east–south–easterly direction towards 508, to which it was bonded. It was thus not perpendicular to either the furnace or 508. The south–eastern wall was formed by the external face of 508. A brick floor, 937, covered the bottom of the swing pit, butting against the walls (Fig 15). It had an uneven, irregular, surface, and appeared to have been relaid several times. The north–east end of the floor had been cut away, roughly in line with the northern furnace upcast flue.

A series of five rectangular openings was revealed in the south–east wall, communicating between the swing pit and tunnel 508 (Fig 17; three are shown by Plate 40). The openings were *c* 1.7 m apart, each measuring *c* 1.8 m high by 0.5 m wide. At the head of each opening, an elongated brick 0.77 m long had been laid as a lintel. The northern, central, and southern apertures had subsequently been partly bricked-up (*see below Partial blocking of the openings between the south–east swing pit and tunnel 508, p 72*). Further access to the swing pit would have been provided by a doorway, now blocked, through the south–east wall of the working end switch room.

The north–west swing pit (*Figs 15 and 17*)
The partial remains of a second swing pit were revealed on the north–western side of the tank furnace, the two main surviving walls defining an area measuring *c* 5.9 m x 6.5 m. However, the truncated remains suggest that this pit, in its original form, would largely have mirrored that found on the opposite side, although the openings for access and ventilation differed.

The south–west wall, 689, was constructed of orange-red bricks laid in English bond using black ash mortar. It butted the southern upcast flue on the north–west side of the furnace, and extended north–west as far as tunnel 502, which it appeared to pre-date. The full extent of this wall appears to have been preserved intact. The north–west wall, 696, was bonded to 689, and was of the same construction. The wall thickened towards the base, with the south–eastern wall of tunnel 502 having been added to the existing structure. It had been completely truncated 4.2 m north–east of the western corner of the pit. The remains of the north–east wall were yet more fragmentary, but served to demonstrate that the swing pit had originally mirrored that to the south–east. Wall 699 butted the north–west side foundation wall of the furnace, and extended for *c* 1 m in a north–north–westerly direction, before being truncated.

Most of the floor surface had been removed, but fragments remained in the western corner of the swing pit (936, Fig 15), and between Phase 2.2 buttresses 1208 and 1209 (942, Fig 15). This fragment consisted of red brick irregularly-bonded using black ash mortar. Its surface was at the same height as that of the surviving floor of the south–east swing pit.

The original access to the north–west swing pit was via a wide doorway from tunnel 524 (Fig 15; *see above Access/ventilation tunnels, p 55*), and via a doorway in the north–west wall of the working end switch room. Three additional openings were added after the construction of tunnel 502 to the north–west (*see below North–west longitudinal access/ventilation tunnel, p 71*).

External gas supply flues
Flues 519/521 and 520/522 *(Fig 15; Pls 13 and 41)*
A pair of parallel, contiguous, brick flues, 519 and 520), was revealed running unbroken in a northerly direction from the southern boundary of the site, towards the south–east gable of the cone house. They passed below the eastern corner of the south–east

cone house lean-to, where they were recorded as cutting through the foundations. It seems probable that this relationship reflects the sequence in which the original tank house was built, rather than implying that the gas supply flues date to a later phase; the flues appear to have been essential to the functioning of the furnace within the original tank house, no other gas supply to the working end regenerators being known. Thereafter, the flues turned to run parallel with the exterior face of the north–east wall of the building, here being recorded as 521 and 522. This pair of flues is clearly depicted on a plan of the glassworks flues, reproduced in part in Figure 6; the plan demonstrates that the flues carried producer gas from producer units sited to the south–east of the tank house. Their function appears to have been to supply gas both to the working end of the furnace within No 9 Tank House, and to three furnaces and a number of annealing kilns further to the north–west.

Flue 519 was built of orange-red bricks laid in English bond. It had a semi-circular arched roof constructed of regular bricks, and a brick floor. It was 0.90 m wide and at least 2 m high internally, with the external crown level lying at 28.20 m OD. Flue 520, which was of the same size and construction as 519, lay immediately to the east of 519, the two sharing a common dividing wall.

Plate 41 Looking north along gas supply flues 519 and 520

The exterior surfaces of both flues had been carbonised and blackened, and these charring effects had also been transmitted to the fills covering the flues. By contrast, the interior brickwork, though reddened, carried no such deposits. However, it does not seem to be the case that the interiors of the flues were subject to lower temperatures than the exteriors. Rather, it can be suggested that the internal faces had been seared clean by intense heat and combustion. It appears that the internal surfaces of the gas supply flues used to acquire sooty deposits which were a by-product of the production of coal gas. The accumulation of these deposits was prevented by periodically burning them off, by deliberately igniting the gas within the supply flues, using shafts emerging from the tops of the flues as vents (Transcript of interview with Ron Parkin).

A group of four such shafts was located close to the southern limit of recording, straddling the site boundary (801, 802, 803, 804, Fig 15). The shafts were all near square or rectangular in plan, ranging in size from 1.25 m x 1.15 m to 1.64 m x 1.24 m, and with apertures which ranged in size from 0.61 m x 0.53 m to 0.82 m square. The southern two shafts formed a pair, slightly offset but with a common dividing wall, one opening into each flue. The external surfaces of the shafts were carbonised and blackened, the inner faces being clean. A square shaft c 0.6 m to the north of this pair, 803, opened into flue 520. Its external surface was somewhat blackened, but did not show the same degree of carbonisation exhibited by the three nearby shafts. A further shaft 0.6 m to the north, 804, opened into 519. It was carbonised and blackened on the outside, and heavily eroded and heat-affected on the inside, much of the surface of the bricks having spalled away. The northern wall of the shaft continued to the east across the top of 521, and before disturbance, may have returned to the south to enclose a central area. However, here there was no opening to 521 below, and the function of this part of the feature was not established.

A pair of shafts built as a single structure lay 15.8 m north of shaft 804 (Fig 15). The structure had external dimension of 2.8 m x 1.4 m, and was 0.79 m high. The western shaft, 812, was centrally positioned above 519, and its aperture measured 1.00 m x 0.95 m. Its external surfaces were carbonised and blackened, the brick having suffered severe deterioration. Internally, the brick exhibited a pinkish-yellow colour and severe surface erosion, both characteristics being considered to be the product of intense heat. The eastern shaft, 813, appeared to be of the same form and dimensions, but was sealed by a heavy metal plate.

The remains of a further shaft into 519 lay 5 m to the north (815, Fig 15), but had been extensively damaged.

A possible additional shaft into the same tunnel lay only 0.9 m to the north (816). No upstanding remains survived, but linear arrangements of bricks surrounding a rectangular cut through the tunnel roof may represent the vestigial traces of former shaft walls.

North–east of the cone house, there were three openings in the roof of the south–western flue of the pair, 521, but at least one of these was associated with a mushroom valve, which can be shown to post-date the operation of the continuous tank furnace (807; *see Ch 6, p 88,* Fig 26). Of the remaining openings, one was paired with the only aperture in the roof of the outer flue (opening 808 in 521, opening 810 in 522). Both the paired shafts were circular, but that emerging from 521 had been constructed from wedge-shaped bricks. The two had nevertheless been constructed as a single integral structure, and part of an enclosing wall survived to the south–east of 521 (Pl 42). The interior brickwork of the shafts had a hard surface coating, but no reddening of the bricks was apparent, whilst slight blackening was noted on the external

Plate 42 Shafts 808 and 810, through which gas was drawn from the supply flues to fuel the working end of the furnace. Former glass workers referred to the valve assembly here as a 'jump box'

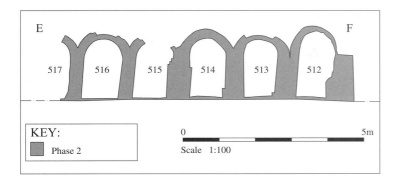

517 516 515 514 513 512

F

KEY:

Phase 2

0   5m

Scale 1:100

Fig 20: Section E–F through gas supply tunnels 512-7 (see Fig 15)

surfaces of shaft 810. These shafts were sited immediately adjacent to the flue passing into the working end switch room from the north–east (*see above The working end switch room, p 51*), and are interpreted as representing the remains of the valves by which the gas to fuel the working end of the furnace was drawn from the gas supply flues. This set of valves, and its enclosing structure, may sometimes have been termed a 'jump box' (Transcript of interview with Ron Parkin). This would have allowed gas to be drawn into the furnace from either supply tunnel, to ensure uninterrupted working during the burn-outs employed to clean the internal surfaces of the supply tunnels.

The third shaft into flue 521 was located to the south–east of the pair of shafts described above (809, Fig 15). It was rectangular in form and brick-built, partly truncated but probably originally measuring *c* 0.87 m x 0.84 m. This shaft was clearly constructed at the same time as the flue below, because the north–west and south–east walls were arched at the level of the flue's internal crown. The internal surface of the shaft was blackened, but had not been reddened by intense heat.

Gas supply flues 512–518 (*Figs 15 and 20*)
To the west of flues 519 and 520, a second multiple group of seven contiguous flues, 512–8, was uncovered. These flues had been truncated at the southern boundary of the site; from here, the surviving structures curved round to the north–west, before appearing to straighten. They were then truncated again at the site boundary. A works' flue plan, probably drawn between 1912 and 1929 (Fig 6), indicates that, beyond the southern site boundary, this group would have continued south to become contiguous with 519 and 520, connecting eventually with gas producer units at least 60 m away to the south–east of the L&NWR railway (Fig 6). To the north–west, the group appeared to lead to the melt ends of the furnaces of four tank houses, including No 9, and at least six annealing kilns. However, the remains of seven flues were excavated and recorded, whereas the flue plan cited above depicts only six in this location. The plan may have been inaccurate, but it seems more probable

either that an additional flue was added after the drawing of the plan, or that one of the flues had gone out of use before the plan was drawn up.

The flues were of the same basic construction as 519 and 520, but showed more evidence of having been repaired. The remains of vertical shafts were recorded communicating with 512, 513, and 514; however, in marked contrast to those on 519 and 520, these were smaller, circular in form, and, although showing signs of being heat-affected, were much less degraded. They resembled more closely the paired shafts 808 and 810 of the possible jump box straddling 521 and 522 to the north–east of the cone house. A square metal plate one inch thick, containing a 0.54 m diameter centrally-located hole and a cast circular plate with eye spigots, was found in isolation close to one of the shafts, and may represent the remains of the shaft control mechanism; it suggests that the shafts may have been used to regulate a flow of gas from the flues below. The shafts at the southern end of 512, 513, and 514 correspond to shafts depicted on the extant plan of the glassworks flues (Fig 6).

Flue 512
This was the outer flue on the eastern side of the group (Fig 15). In common with all the other flues, it was brick-built, with a semi-circular, arched roof. It measured 0.82 m wide by 1.65 m high; the floor was of longitudinally-laid brick. At the southern end, where it was exposed, this floor had a distinct convex profile, with a pronounced central line of bricks forming an apex. Excavation here showed that this floor was laid on a compact deposit of dark bluish black ash, and it is possible that the shape of the floor in this area was a product of the uneven settlement of the footings, rather than being a deliberate feature. The north–east side of the flue had been displaced where it was adjacent to access tunnel 511, suggesting that the gas supply flues might have been built prior to the erection of 511. The whole of flue 512 had been subject to external blackening, whilst the internal brick surfaces showed signs of having been seared by heat, but were clean. This may again suggest periodic burning out to remove unwanted surface deposits.

At the extreme southern end of the flue, just before the point of truncation, a circular brick shaft, 806, opened into the interior. The shaft had an external diameter of 1.20 m, and an internal bore diameter of 0.62 m. It was constructed of wedge-shaped bricks laid radially around the bore of the shaft. The remains of a low rectangular wall to the south–east of the shaft indicate that the shaft was formerly boxed-in in a similar manner to shafts 807 and 808 sited on 521. A circular metal cover plate was found lodged within the shaft bore, further suggesting that shafts 806 and 807 had the same function. The external faces of the shaft were blackened but not degraded, and the internal surfaces appeared to have been reddened by heat. Disturbed brickwork immediately to the north–west of shaft 806 suggested the former presence of a second brick shaft, immediately adjacent, but of square section. This was confirmed by the glassworks' flue plan, which also showed similar, adjacent, square-sectioned shafts above flues 513, 514, and 515 (Fig 6).

Flue 513
This was adjacent to 512, and measured 0.90 m wide by 1.43 m high, with an internal crown level of 28.57 m OD. The exposed south–east and north–west extremities showed that it again had a brick floor with slight upwards bulge or camber to the centre. The vertical walls were built in English bond. The flue had blackened and disintegrating outer surfaces, and reddened inner faces. A shaft, 805, of very similar form and dimensions to that above 512, but in a poorer state of preservation, was present at the southern end. The bricks were blackened but not corroded externally, and reddened internally, the internal colouration being less than that exhibited by shafts opening to 519 and 520.

Flue 514
This flue was adjacent to 513, and measured 0.89 m wide by 1.78 m high, with an internal crown level of 28.72 m OD (Pl 43). The wall surfaces had been heat-affected in the same way as those of 512 and 513. A circular brick shaft at the southern end of the extant length of the flue again closely resembled the adjacent shafts above the flues immediately to the east.

Flue 515
This was adjacent to 514, and measured 0.98 m wide by 1.51 m high, with an internal crown level of 28.50 m OD. The floor was of brick, longitudinally-laid, and with a slightly cambered surface. At the south–east extremity, slight traces of linear brickwork suggested the former presence of a shaft into the flue, but the flue plan showed that this had been rectangular in section, one of four rectangular shafts located immediately to the north of the circular shafts opening from 512, 513, and 514. The surfaces of the brickwork had been affected by heat in the same way as those of 512, 513, and 514.

Plate 43 View south–east along gas supply flue 514

Flue 516
Flue 516 was adjacent to 515, and measured 0.90 m wide by 1.64 m high, with an internal crown level of 28.60 m OD. The western side wall showed a slight lean to the east, and the condition of the brick surfaces differed somewhat from those of the other flues in the group. External blackening was visible, but the internal surfaces showed signs of corrosion and disintegration, and the presence of a light yellowish-brown deposit. Traces of a shaft were observed at the south–east end of the flue; the glassworks' flue plan (Fig 6) suggested that this might be a shaft which straddled flues 516 and 517, opening jointly from both flues.

Flue 517
This was adjacent to 516, and measured 1.15 m wide by 1.55 m high, with an internal crown level of 28.59 m OD. A length of only 7 m remained between the two truncated ends of the flue system, and this was completely excavated. The flue had a level floor of longitudinally-laid bricks, but this had subsequently been covered by a black cinder-like deposit 20 mm thick. In marked contrast to the other flues of the group, the walls were found to be very heavily corroded, especially toward the floor, and encrusted with a light grey, crystalline material, which was flaking away. No red discolouration of the interior

brickwork was observed, but the external surfaces of the flue were blackened.

Flue 518
Flue 518 had been substantially truncated, so that by the time archaeological recording began, no complete profile remained. This was the seventh, and most westerly, of this group of flues; the fact that only six are depicted on the extant plan of the glassworks' flues (Fig 6) may indicate that it had gone out of use before the plan was drawn, for there is no evidence that it was a later addition.

Recording by commercial surveyors in July 1991 indicates that, at that time, a 4 m length of this flue survived intact. It measured 1.9 m wide and 1.55 m high, with an internal crown level of 28.59 m OD. Although wider than the other flues in the group, it was again covered by a semi-circular arched roof. The floor was of bricks laid longitudinally, and was slightly cambered. It showed some red discolouration, but the black cinder-like deposit found in 516 and 517 was absent. The brickwork of the eastern wall that remained at the time of archaeological recording showed heavy corrosion with spalling of the surface, but no reddening. The external surfaces were blackened.

Archaeological evidence — Phase 2.2

Phase 2.2 does not relate to a single episode of alteration of the furnace and its associated structures. Rather, it encompasses all the modifications which could be identified as post-dating the original construction of the tank house, but which are believed to have been carried out whilst the tank furnace was still in production.

North–west longitudinal access / ventilation tunnel (Fig 15)
Tunnel 502 had been truncated at the south–western boundary of the site by the construction of the adjacent hotel. From this truncation, which lay within the footprint of the south–western tank house building, it was traced extending for 6.35 m as far as the north–east foundation wall of the building, aligned roughly south–south–west/north–north–east. Here its direction changed, and it continued for a further 10.8 m, passing under the cone house, on a south–west / north–east orientation. Its north–eastern end had been blocked, but evidence was recovered to suggest that the tunnel had formerly continued for the full width of the cone house, emerging through the north–east wall foundation onto the canal bank: two bull-nose bricks were found low down in the north–east wall, in line with the orientation of 502.

Four similar bricks were found in line with tunnel 508, which is also considered to have passed through the wall.

The tunnel had been built in a foundation trench which truncated the platform, but it also cut through existing masonry, truncating both the tank house foundations, and a wall stratigraphically associated with the regenerators, 639 (see above Walls 629 and 639, p 60). It therefore appears to have been built after both the tank house wall foundations and the underground regenerators, and it can be suggested that it represents a modification to the original layout of the tank house, rather than simply having been constructed late in the original building sequence. As well as truncating foundation walls of the tank house, it was noted that, where openings had been provided from this tunnel to the north–west swing pit, their apertures appeared to have been inserted through the existing wall of the swing pit (see below Provision of additional openings to the north–west swing pit, p 72). The tunnel was not connected to tunnel 524, which provided access between the two sets of regenerator tunnels.

Tunnel 502 was constructed of orange-red brick laid in English bond with black ash mortar. It had a semi-circular arched roof, and was 1.35 m wide and 2.2 m high. Removal of the infill showed that its internal surfaces showed no signs of the effects of heat, suggesting that, like tunnel 508 to the south–east, it had been designed to serve as an access or ventilation tunnel. One entrance to the tunnel may have been through the north–east wall of the cone house, although space here would have been restricted by the presence of gas supply flues 521 and 522; the tunnel rises at a pronounced angle through the cone building, presumably to clear flue 523. However, it is possible that 502 would also have been accessed from the south–west. This remains uncertain because of the truncation of the tunnel. A survey conducted before the archaeological recording of the site began suggested that the south–west end of 502 may have intersected with 501 (see above The melt end switch room, p 60). Such an intersection appears problematic, however, partly because of the different internal crown heights of the two structures, and partly because 501 and 509 appear narrower than the other access / ventilation tunnels, 501 reportedly being two-tiered. Tunnels 501 and 509 may rather be related to the supply of gas to the Phase 3 experimental kiln which probably stood close to this spot (see below Ch 6 Functional analysis of the Phase 3 structures, p 93).

Alteration of the swing pits and furnace
Ramped floor within the south–east swing pit (Fig 15)
A ramped brick floor, 934, located between the northernmost angled buttress of the furnace, and the

north wall of the swing pit, was laid against a bricked-up opening that had led to the working end switch room; its function is not understood.

Partial blocking of the openings between the south–east swing pit and tunnel 508 (Fig 17)

The northern, central, and southern apertures had been partly bricked-up at some stage after their construction. The upper portions of the northern and central openings had been blocked, flush with the face of the swing pit wall, so as to leave apertures of 0.65 m and 0.73 m in height respectively remaining at the base of each opening (Pl 40). The southern opening appeared to have been blocked further back in the depth of the wall. It was unclear whether the original blocking extended for the full height of the aperture.

The fact that at least two of the openings had not been completely blocked, with apertures carefully retained at the base of the former opening, suggests that they continued to have a function at the time of blocking. It seems likely that the blocking represents an adaptation to the form of the tank house, made whilst the furnace was still operating. The blocking may relate to the control of the passage of air into the swing pit and up and over the furnace, and was probably inserted in the light of experience gained in the use of the furnace (see below Functional analysis of the tank furnace, p 74).

Provision of additional openings to the north–west swing pit (Fig 17)

The construction of tunnel 502 allowed the insertion of at least three additional openings to the north–west swing pit, creating a layout more closely resembling the south–eastern pit. The three rectangular openings were of similar size and form to their counterparts on the other side of the furnace, but appeared to be cut through the north–west swing pit wall, 696. This further demonstrates that the north–west swing pit was an original feature of the tank house, but was adapted after the subsequent construction of tunnel 502. The central opening was later blocked, but this occurred when a wall was built to carry an RSJ after the disuse of the swing pit (see below Ch 6 Foundation walls within the former north–west swing pit, p 91).

Changes to furnace buttresses (Fig 17)

Six large angled buttresses were constructed on either side of the regenerators and overlying furnace foundations (1204–1209), each new buttress being positioned adjacent to one of the working end stacks (see above The basal remains of the furnace, p 61). It seems probable that the buttresses were needed to contain some of the lateral expansion that the furnace foundations would undergo during firing; the original, narrower buttresses, identified from scars on the swing pit floors, may have proved inadequate.

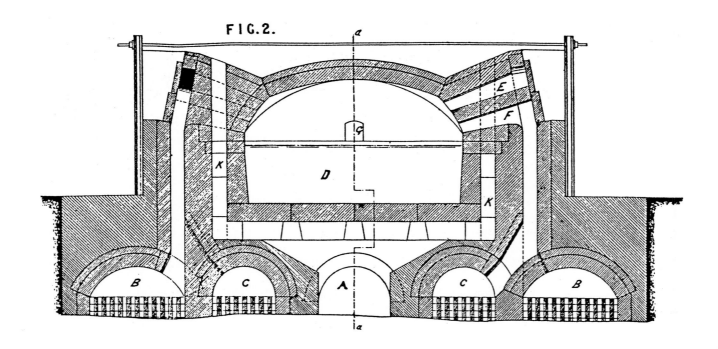

Plate 44 Transverse section across a continuous tank furnace from William Siemens' patent of 1879 (British Patent 4763, 1879, fig 2). A represents the central ventilation/access tunnel below the tank, B the air regenerators, C the gas regenerators, D the tank, E and F the flues carrying up the heated air and gas, and K, flues carrying air to cool the tank

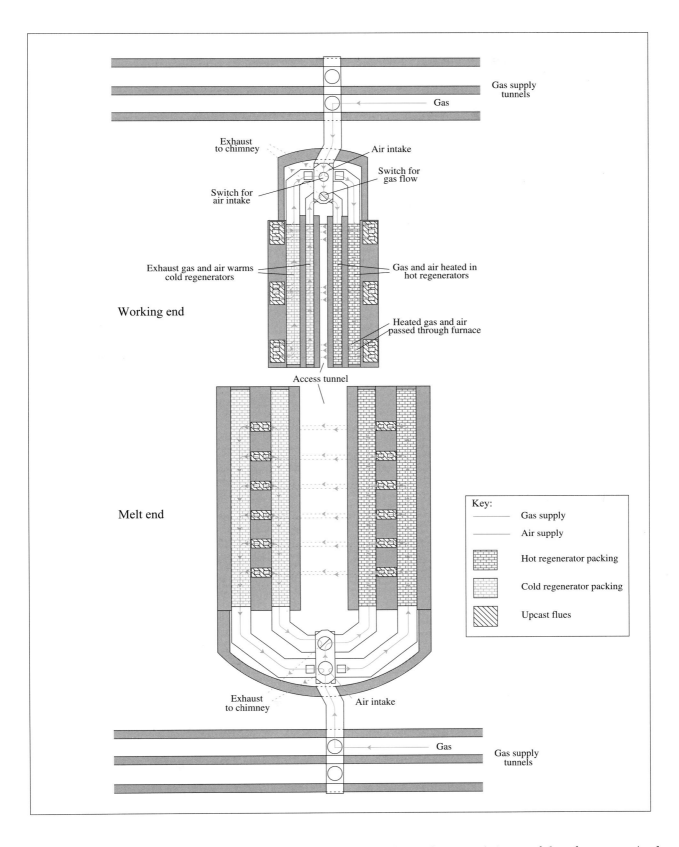

Fig 21 Schematic plan of the regenerators, showing flow of gas and air. The gas and air were fed up from one pair of regenerators, ignited over the molten glass, and the exhaust gases then drawn down to the regenerators on the other side of the furnace

Modification of ancillary structures
Structure adjoining the south–east wall of the south–west tank house building *(Fig 7)*

A small rectangular structure measuring *c* 5 m x 12 m was shown adjoining the south–east wall of this building on the Ordnance Survey 1:2500 map of 1908; its function at this time is not known, although a rather smaller structure in a similar position was labelled 'cullet wash building' on a works' plan of 1933 (PB 665). Wall 567, recorded during excavation, appears to lie in the same position as this structure, but is considered probably to relate to a later rebuild (*Ch 7 Fig 29*).

Structure to the south–east of the tank house *(Fig 7)*

A *c* 7.5 m long section of brick walling, 621, was revealed by excavation to the south–east of the south–western tank house building. It was constructed in English bond of red brick and black ash mortar, and was truncated to the south–west by wall 614 (Fig 29). The position of wall 621 corresponds to the north–west wall of a large structure measuring a maximum of 28 m x 32 m, shown to the south–east of the tank house on the Ordnance Survey 1:25,000 map of 1908 (Ordnance Survey 1908). The original function of this building is not known. However, it is shown on plans accompanying valuation notices of 1933 (PB 665), with the two largest cells apparently labelled 'saltcake stock building' and 'mixing room stock building'.

Functional analysis of the tank furnace

The regenerators

The five parallel tunnels recorded below the cone house, and the similar group found within the footprint of the demolished building to the south–west, are clearly sets of four regenerators, with a central ventilation chamber running down the middle (Fig 15). The layout is very closely paralleled in the transverse section of a tank furnace which accompanies William Siemens' patent of 1879 for Improvements in apparatus for manufacturing and moulding glass articles (Pl 44; British Patent No 4763, 1879, fig 2). Siemens' drawing indicates that the wider tunnels on the outer side of each group of five were air regenerators, flanked internally by narrower gas regenerators. A representation of a pile of refractory bricks is shown within each such structure. At 'The Hotties', the regenerators below the cone house show the same distribution of wider and narrower tunnels, suggesting that, again, the outer regenerators carried air, and the inner ones gas. On the Siemens' drawing, the central tunnel is identified as the 'cave', through, and from which, air currents passed to cool the exterior of the tank base. This was almost certainly the function

of the central tunnels at 'The Hotties', which were not covered by continuous roofs, but rather spanned by a series of transverse arches, with apertures in between. It seems clear that the voids between the arches were intended to allow the passage of cooling air.

The basic concept of a regenerative furnace has been outlined briefly above (*see above Ch 3 The development of the glass furnace 1860–73, p 10*). The published patents for regenerative tank furnaces envisaged two pairs of regenerators being placed below the furnace, aligned along its length, or, alternatively, a pair of regenerators sited at one or both ends (British Patent 3478, 1872; 1551, 1875; 4763, 1879). It is important to note that no more than two pairs of regenerators were used for any one furnace, so that there was effectively only one heating system for all parts of the tank, with the supply of gas and air, and the exhaust gases, being alternately directed to each pair of regenerators.

In contrast, below the two structures of No 9 Tank House, four pairs of regenerators were found, arranged in two separate groups (Fig 21). The two pairs of regenerators below the south–western building of the tank house were both longer and wider than those recorded below the cone house. It might be thought that the regenerators served two separate furnaces, but there is good evidence to indicate that this was not the case, and that they belonged to a single tank:

1)   both groups of regenerators appear to be part of a single integrated network of underground passages and flues (Fig 6); both opened into the transverse tunnel, 524 (Fig 15);

2)   early twentieth century works plans show No 9 and No 10 tanks, and suggest that both spanned two groups of regenerators (PB 222; PB 665);

3)   oral and documentary evidence suggests that, from 1881, Pilkingtons' tanks were divided by a bridge wall. The working and melt ends of the furnace were independently heated, with the temperature of each controlled by separate individuals, who would adjust the air dampers and gas valves (Parkin 2000, 76);

4)   documentary evidence allows the rough estimate that, by 1887, each tank may have been in the order of 30 yards long. This further suggests that both groups of regenerators must have supplied a single tank furnace with two separate sources of pre-heated gas and air.

In the light of this evidence, it seems clear that the smaller pairs of regenerators supplied the cooler working end of the furnace, sited within the cone house building, whilst the larger regenerators supplied the hotter melt end of the furnace, located within the south–western tank house building. It is known that, in order to obtain the oxidising conditions required at the working end of a furnace, the required volumetric ratio of air to gas was 2:1, and indeed, below the cone house, the air regenerators were roughly twice the size of the gas regenerators, whereas below the south–western tank house building, the gas and air regenerators were the same size. This further suggests that the cone house regenerators were specifically dedicated to heating the working end of a tank.

The furnace gas supply, switch rooms, and exhaust

An early twentieth century plan of the works' flues shows that the working and melt end regenerators were independently supplied with gas, probably from separate producer units located about 80 m from the tank house, to the south–east of the L&NWR railway (Fig 6). The working end was supplied from either of two gas flues routed along the edge of the canal to the north–east of the tank house (flues 521 and 522, Fig 15).

These flues continued to the north–west to supply the working ends of tank furnaces 10, 11, and 12, so it seems unlikely that the working end of No 9 can have had a dedicated producer unit; the gas carried by one flue seems to have been available to more than one furnace. In contrast, the melt end regenerators were supplied from a flue which was one of a group of six or seven passing immediately to the south–west of the tank house (*see above External gas supply flues, p 67*; Fig 6). Although the plan of the flues is at a relatively small scale, and is rather schematic, it seems to indicate that the hotter melt end of the furnace may have had a dedicated gas supply, and did not share its supply flue with any other apparatus.

After being drawn from the canal-side flues, gas to fire the working end of the furnace was fed down beneath the floor of the working end switch room, to a point below elevated brick structure 535 (Figs 16 and 22; *see above The working end switch room, p 51*). From here, under-floor flues branched off to each of the gas regenerators, and additional flues led to the

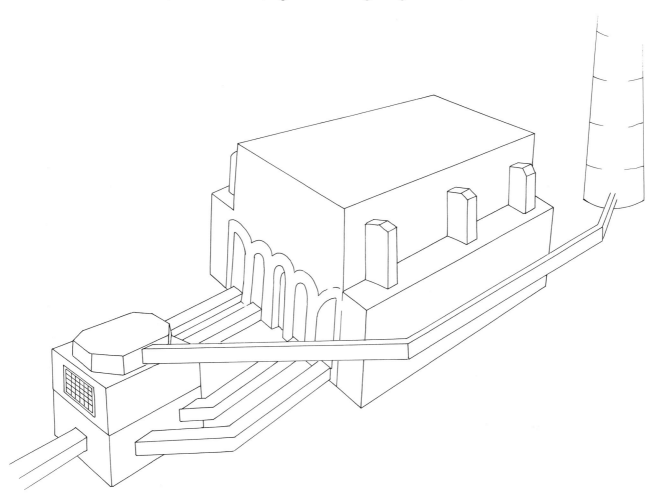

Fig 22 Schematic reconstruction of the working end switch room and regenerators. Air entered the switch mechanism through the grill in the foreground, with gas being fed in via the subfloor flue depicted immediately below (compare with Figure 16). The switches were then used to direct gas and air to alternate pairs of regenerators via sub-floor flues

two air regenerators (Figs 16 and 22). The arrangement of these surviving flues dictates that a switching mechanism must have been sited here, together with an air intake, but the construction in Phase 3 of secondary brick structure 738, sited above the intersections of the side flues with the gas supply flue, had led to the removal of the original apparatus (*see below Ch 6 The working end switch room, p 92*). Such a mechanism must have existed firstly in order to allow the flow of gas to be reversed from one set of regenerators to the other; secondly, to allow the introduction and switching of the air supply to the appropriate regenerators; and thirdly, to allow the exhaust gases to be collected from each pair of regenerators in turn. Air must have been fed into the system from above, and likewise, exhaust emissions must have been channelled upwards to brick structure 535; its position and form strongly suggest that its function was to collect exhaust gases from the regenerator tunnels via the under-floor flues, and funnel the gases into the chimney flue (Figs 16 and 22).

In view of the loss of the original apparatus below 535, it is impossible to determine exactly how the gas and air supplies were directed to the appropriate regenerators; the later introduction of brick blocking into the flues has added to the difficulty. However, it seems clear that gas would not have been allowed to pass from the gas supply flue into the first set of side flues, which led to the air regenerators (Fig 16). It seems probable that the latter were fed with an air supply drawn from above. Rather, it seems certain that the gas was directed in turn into each of the second set of side flues, which led to the two gas regenerators. It has been suggested that simple butterfly reversing valves were used for directing both the gas and air supplies (Parkin 2000, 76), and contemporary diagrams of this type of valve survive (Pls 7 and 45). Further valves or dampers must have existed to regulate the flow of combustion air to the reversing valves, and likewise the flow of exhaust gases out of the regenerators upwards into the chimney flue (*see above The central brick structure and the working end chimney flue, p 54*). A grill which survives in the north–east face of structure 535 suggests that air was simply drawn from the switch room chamber, the recollections of former glass workers indicating that the regulating valve was called the 'natural draught damper' (*see above p 55*).

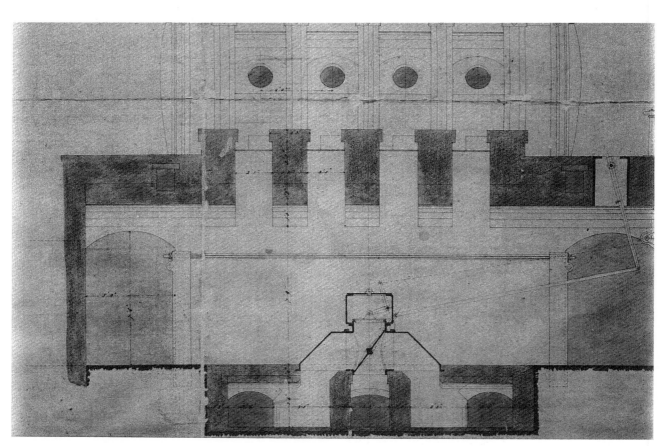

Plate 45 Drawing showing a regenerative furnace butterfly reversing valve, prepared by Siemens Brothers for Pilkingtons in 1873–4. The gas supply enters via the central flue at the bottom of the drawing, and gas is directed in turn to each gas regenerator, via flues to the right and left of the gas supply (photograph kindly provided from the Pilkington Archive by David Martlew)

Both the physical below-ground remains (Fig 15) and plans of the works (Fig 6) indicate that the gas supply flue, dampers, and reversing valves for the melt end of the furnace must have been sited to the south–west of the melt end regenerators. Because of the destruction of archaeological remains in this area, the layout of flues and valves remains uncertain (*see above Entrance tunnel 511 and the melt end switch room, p 59*). However, it would appear that, although the layout may here have been spatially different to that at the working end, the equipment used to direct and control the flow of gas and air was essentially the same (Parkin 2000, 76–7). The melt end switch room, known as the 'cave', was accessed via a passage leading down from the south–east, 511, which may also have served to admit cooling air into ventilation tunnels 504, 508, and 524 (*see below*).

A works' plan demonstrates that No 9 and No 10 furnaces shared one chimney, sited between the two furnaces (Fig 6). However, the working and melt ends had separate chimney flues: the working end of No 9 was connected to the chimney via a flue extending out through the north–west gable end of the cone house from the brick superstructure in the switch room. The plan suggests that exhaust from the melt end was directed to the chimney by a flue running from the melt end switch room along the south–west wall of the melt end tank house building.

Tunnels 508 and 524, and the swing pits

Tunnels 508 and 524 (Fig 15) appear to have had a dual purpose, being used for both access and ventilation. Firstly, they would have allowed maintenance workers to reach the melt and working end regenerators and central ventilation tunnels, and the swing pits; it is known that the refractory bricks within the regenerators had to be replaced periodically (PB 129, 34), and that cullet had to be removed from the swing pits (Parkin 2000, 74). It would probably also have been desirable to have easy access to all areas underlying the furnace so that repairs could be carried out to the base. Tunnel 508 could be entered either from the canal bank, or via tunnel 511, from the gable end of the south–western tank house building. Secondly, 508 and 524 would have provided ventilation air from the canal bank, and this would probably have been drawn into ventilation tunnels 504 and 527 in order to cool the furnace base (Fig 15). The passages would also have ventilated the swing pits; the partial blocking during Phase 2.2 of apertures leading from tunnel 508 to the south–east swing pit demonstrates that the apertures must have been acting as ventilation holes, with the partial brick blocking being introduced as dampers to control the air flow.

The primary function of the swing pits (Figs 15 and 17) was to give space below the level of the cone house floor so that the glass blowers could swing cylinders downwards during blowing (Pl 16). However, they were also entered to recover fallen cullet. Moreover, cool air passing through the pits from tunnels 508 and 524, and up through the swing holes, was probably important in cooling blowing teams working around the furnace. The lack of symmetry in the layout of the two swing pits is difficult to explain. The design of the south–east pit appears to offer the better access and ventilation, and the fact that the north–western pit was subsequently altered to make it resemble this design indicates that its original layout was inferior. One plausible explanation for the initial discrepancy is that an engineering problem was encountered which persuaded the builders not to construct tunnel 502 during the initial building works. A disused mineshaft would be one possible such obstacle (Mick Krupa pers comm).

The furnace

The weight of the working end of the furnace appears to have been carried primarily by the two substantial longitudinal foundation walls which bounded the outer regenerators (Figs 17 and 18). At the melt end, the position of the two surviving 'stacks' (*see above The basal remains of the furnace, p 61*) suggests that the furnace was carried by the particularly substantial walls constructed *between* the gas and air regenerators on either side; for the greater width of the melt end regenerators suggests that the tank could not have been built on foundations flanking the regenerators. The furnace base was supported by elongated fireclay blocks resting on transverse brick walls linking the foundation walls. At the melt end, the arches partially rested on the crown of the inner regenerators.

At the working end, all three pairs of 'stacks' survived at foundation level, each stack here containing three vertical flues rising up from the regenerators (Fig 17). The working end air regenerators were roughly twice the size of the gas regenerators, and it is probable that oxidising conditions would have been needed at this end of the furnace, requiring an air to gas ratio of 2:1 (*see above Functional analysis of the tank furnace, p 74*). It thus seems likely that the flues at either end of each stack carried air, and the central flue gas. It was usual for the flues to discharge the combustion gases close to the top of the furnace's side walls, with the ports for the delivery of air probably sited just above those for the delivery of gas (British Patent No 4763, 1879). This arrangement meant that the crown of the furnace was protected from the flame by a cushion of air, with the air also directing the flame downwards onto the glass below.

Only two individual stacks survived at the melt end (Fig 17). Here, two upcast flues were recorded per stack, probably reflecting the fact that at this end of

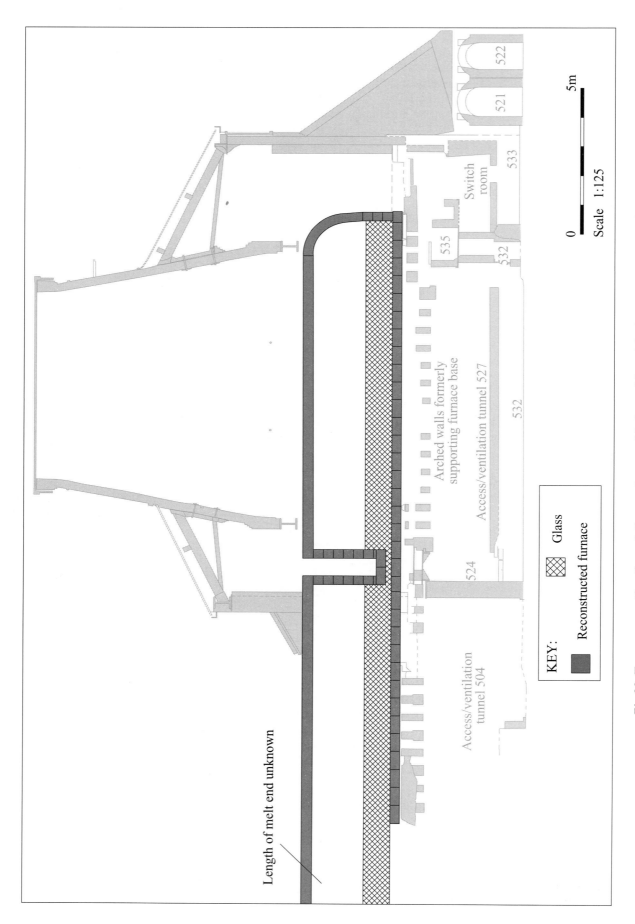

Fig 23 *Transverse section through the cone house, with the position of the furnace reconstructed*

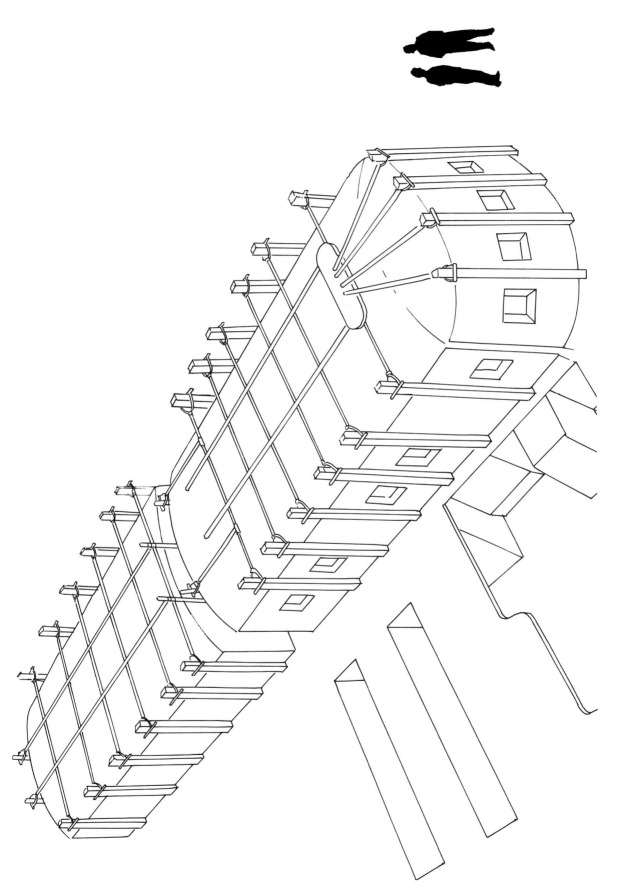

Fig 24 Artist's reconstruction of the furnace, with part of the cone house floor cut away to show the eastern swing pit. Bull-headed metals and tie rods would have provided lateral support to the tank structure

the furnace, the gas and air regenerators were of about the same size, since roughly equal volumes of gas and air were required to create a reducing environment. The total number of stacks at the melt end could not be established from the physical remains because of the destruction of deposits towards the south–west of the tank house, but documentary sources suggest that there were eventually six pairs of stacks here (Parkin 2000, 72). The total surface area of the upcast flues at the two ends of the furnace helps to illustrate the relative power of the melt and working ends; the flue apertures within the three pairs of working end stacks together had a combined total area of 1.33 m^2. If six pairs of stacks are assumed at the melt end, the excavated evidence shows that the total surface area of the flues would have been 3.64 m^2. Clearly, by far the greater volume of gas and air was required by the melt end of the furnace.

The superstructure of the furnace appears to have been demolished in 1929 (Parkin 2000, 78); some inferences about its construction and operation have been drawn from its foundations, but any fuller understanding must be largely dependent on oral and documentary sources. These sources have been used to sketch the likely form of the furnace (Figs 18, 19, 23 and 24; *see above Documentary evidence, p 26*), and one probable characteristic deserves to be highlighted. This is the suggestion that the tank itself was divided into melt and working ends by a fixed bridge, capable of being cooled, comprising two separate walls (Fig 25). This bridge may have reached right up to the furnace crown; in June 1893, the tank repair book noted 'new crown to the bridge' (PB 129, 45), whilst Ron Parkin's reconstruction drawings of the tank's superstructure, based on oral evidence, appear to suggest a bridge as high as the furnace crown, if not higher. If, as he suggests, a walkway crossed the top of the bridge so that water could be sprayed onto runs of molten glass, the bridge must have extended above the furnace crown (Parkin 2000, 78).

Certainly a bridge wall of full height would give a number of benefits. As well as separating partially molten material from refined metal within the tank, it would allow closer regulation of the temperature at the working end by reducing radiant heat from the melt end. Additionally, it would allow the oxidising and reducing conditions in the two ends of the furnace to be more carefully controlled. It is to be expected that oxidising conditions would have been required at the working end of the furnace, and reducing conditions at the melt end, and there are two physical indications that this was the case. Firstly, at the working end only, the air regenerators had roughly twice the volume of the gas regenerators (*see above*), and secondly, deposits found coating the interiors of the

regenerator walls differed between the working and melt ends. Within 507, at the melt end, a coating described as a 'milky white glaze with greenish blue streaks' was recorded; within 525, at the working end, the coating was described as 'dark reddish brown'. No chemical analysis of these deposits was carried out as part of the present project, but the superficial record of the colour of these deposits gives a further suggestion of differing combustion at the two ends of the tank. The presence of a bridge wall, completely dividing the tank from base to crown, would have contributed to the careful control of combustion.

Despite the presence of a fixed bridge, oral and documentary evidence suggests that floating fireclay rings were still positioned by each gathering hole to keep back any scum (Parkin 2000, 77).

Control of the furnace
Oral and documentary sources allow the manner in which the furnace was controlled to be reconstructed. The operation of the furnace has been described in some detail elsewhere (Parkin 2000, 74–8), and thus is only briefly summarised here.

At the melt end, the 'boss teazer' observed the colour of the furnace and the nature of the boil (there were no thermometers), and adjusted the melt end furnace power accordingly. Temperature was controlled primarily by adjusting the apertures of the natural draught damper and the gas valve (*op cit*, 76), both probably sited in the 'cave' or melt end switch room, but the chimney pull damper also needed adjustment to ensure an appropriate amount of pull for the volumes of gas and air being burnt. In addition, tile dampers were fitted to the upcast flues within each stack; full power was usually only required on the first three or four stacks, but control of these dampers was the responsibility of the tank manager. The supply of gas and air was switched from one pair of regenerators to the other every 20–5 minutes.

Control of the working end was very similar, and was the responsibility of the 'boss gatherer'. Temperature was adjusted in the same way on the basis of the stiffness of the gather. It was not normal to alter the power of each individual stack, but the individual stack dampers might still be adjusted to allow fine-tuning of the gas-to-air ratio.

The tank house buildings
The most distinctive feature of the surviving cone house is the cone itself (Figs 13 and 14; Pls 3 and 26). Cones had been constructed over glass furnaces since the late seventeenth- or early eighteenth centuries (*see above Ch 3, p 7*) to provide an up-draught to ventilate and cool the working area around the furnace; this remained the function of the 'Hotties' cone, although

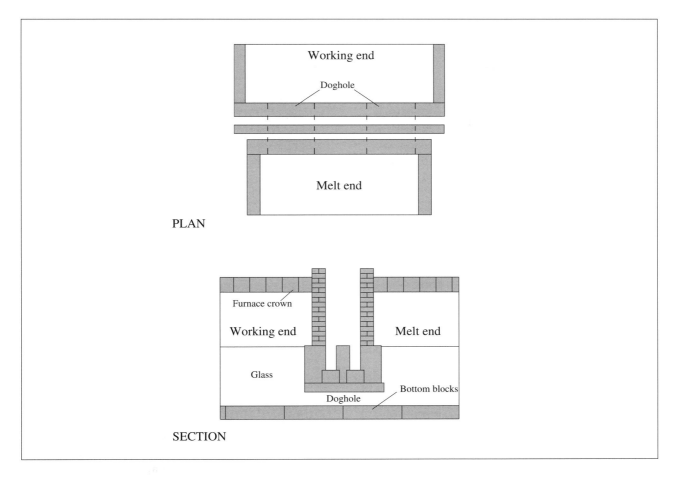

Fig 25 Reconstruction of the bridge wall, separating the furnace working end from the melt end (plan view and longitudinal section; after Parkin 2000, fig 47)

its elliptical shape (at its base the cone measured 7.0 m x 9.9 m, its long axis being aligned with the furnace base below) represents a departure from the earlier form. Ventilation was necessary not only to provide a viable working environment for the glassblowing teams, but also to prevent the cylinders becoming tough and difficult to split. Reference has also been made to 'careful control of the louvres' in order to control the environment around the tank (Parkin 2000, 78); the 'louvres' in question may have been large louvre doors standing between the stanchions of the north wall of the cone house (Transcript of interview with Harry Langtree, 16; *see below, p 81*). The cone itself would have been covered by an overhanging roof to stop water falling down onto the furnace crown below; such a covering is shown on a photograph taken of No 15 Tank House in the 1940s (Barker 1977, plate 57).

If the cone was covered, it is considered that a structure must have also covered and protected the tank where it passed between the melt end building and the cone house. The position of the regenerators suggests that the part of the tank that lay between the two buildings must have been the north–eastern extremity of the melt end, with the bridge being just to the north–east, slightly within the cone house wall. It seems certain that this part of the melt end was not exposed to the elements, but no evidence for the nature of any covering structure was found. An unpublished aerial photograph of the tank house taken in about 1924 shows a low tower linking the two buildings at this point, but this seems to be a post-production addition of the 1920s, perhaps built to cover an experimental drawing tower (Parkin 2000, 81).

Both tank house buildings were probably relatively dark inside to allow the glass workers to see the colour and radiation of the hot glass, and assess its temperature; the brightness of the glass in photographs of contemporary glassmaking appears to confirm that this was the case. In view of these observations, it seems clear that gaps between the cast iron stanchions of the north–east cone house wall were infilled to form a continuous wall, and that the building was not open to the canalside veranda prior to the construction of the later brick north–east wall; on the basis of oral evidence, it can be suggested that the area between the stanchions was formed by louvre doors (Transcript of interview with Harry Langtree, 16), which were probably used to regulate the ventilation of the blowing floor.

Phase 2.2 alterations

Some of the alterations made to the furnace complex were visible in the surviving structures, whilst other changes related to parts of the furnace which have not survived, and are known only from oral or documentary evidence. This is important to appreciate, because the archaeological evidence, if anything, under-represents the extent to which the furnace was rebuilt and improved in the light of experience. This is because the surviving archaeology tells us primarily about the below-ground elements of the complex, the substructure of foundations, regenerators, and ventilation tunnels. These were precisely the parts of the furnace that were least likely to be altered, because, once in place below ground, they were prohibitively expensive to expand.

The most major change made to the surviving substructure was the addition of tunnel 502, and consequent alteration of the north–west swing pit (Fig 15). As noted above, it is puzzling that 502 was not constructed as part of the original build, so as to mirror the design of the south–east side of the complex, especially as it was later thought necessary to remedy its absence by what must have been an expensive alteration. One possibility is that tunnel 508 was an experimental addition to Pilkingtons' usual design, and one which proved so successful that it was desirable to copy it on the other side of the furnace. However, this is only guesswork, and it is perhaps more probable that there was some impediment to the original construction of 502, such as a mineshaft; if the operation of the furnace or glass production was impaired without this ventilation tunnel, it may have proved essential to overcome the difficulty and install it subsequently. Cracking and settlement problems were experienced during remedial works to the lower north–west gable wall of the cone house, suggesting that problems with subsidence, possibly from mining activity, were indeed a factor on this part of the site; a subsequent bore trial within tunnel 502 demonstrated the existence of a voided area at shallow depth. Be that as it may, the new tunnel allowed the north–west swing pit to be ventilated through apertures in the wall opposite the furnace in the same way as the opposing swing pit (*see above The swing pits, p 65*).

Other alterations to the surviving fabric were on a smaller scale. The partial blocking of the apertures communicating between tunnel 508 and the south–east swing pit has already been referred to, and must imply that the flow of ventilation air was being regulated in the light of experience, with each area of blocking acting as a damper (Fig 17). The changes to the buttressing of the side walls of the furnace must similarly have been a response to inadequacies which emerged in the original design; it seems probable that the original, narrow buttresses had failed to give adequate support, hence their replacement with larger, thicker buttresses, one immediately adjacent to each stack (compare Figures 15 and 17), but the alteration might also be related to a possible enlargement of the tank.

These changes evident in the structural remains represent modifications made to improve the operation of the furnace, but do not demonstrate how the tank itself was altered. Documentary and oral evidence, however, has been used to suggest that the size and productive capacity of the tank was being constantly increased (Parkin 2000, 72). It seems that as well as possible changes in the tank length and width, it was redesigned to contain a depth of up to 3 ft 6 in of metal, with the number of 'dogholes' in the bridge wall being increased from one to two. The number of melt end stacks may also have been increased from five to six. Nevertheless, technical change in the glass industry proceeded as rapidly in the early twentieth century as it did in the later nineteenth, and the steady improvement of No 9 furnace was not enough to maintain it for long as a viable productive unit. With tanks eventually reaching a capacity of 1000 tons (Parkin 2000, 70, 76), the 150–200 ton capacity of No 9 was soon outdated, the tank's expansion being limited by the size of its regenerators below ground, and of the tank house building above.

A further matter has yet to be resolved. Whilst being interviewed about the Jubilee Side tank furnaces, an 84 year old former employee suggested that, in the period 1923 to 1926, the Jubilee tanks were operated with floating bridges, and without heat at the working end (Transcript of interview with Harry Langtree). He suggested that No 9 Tank had latterly been operated in the same way, although admitting that he had never been into that tank house: 'The working end we hadn't to heat it…you had canals. Now them was heated with gas but there was no [re]generators at that end[.] No, well it was the same with No 9 and 10 and 11 up to 15'. It seems unlikely that the operation of No 9 tank was radically altered towards the end of its life, or that the other tanks were radically altered after No 9 had ceased production; rather it can be suggested that Mr Langtree may have confused the operation of the of the Jubilee tanks with that of the 'miscellaneous' tank at Ravenhead, to which he moved in 1926.

6

PHASE 3: POST-PRODUCTION TANK HOUSE MODIFICATIONS

Documentary evidence

Jo Bell

Pilkingtons' early and wholehearted commitment to the tank furnace had given them an advantage over competitors and ensured their absolute domination of the domestic sheet glass market. The company showed the same spirit of technological experimentation in the second and third decades of the twentieth century, but this was tempered by a determination that the adoption of new technology should not compromise the quality, and thus marketability, of their glass.

This was a period when the focus of innovation in the glass industry world-wide moved from furnace design, to the problem of how sheet glass could most efficiently be obtained from the molten 'metal'. In the late nineteenth century, as we have seen, the hand-blown cylinder process was universally used, but in 1900, patents for its mechanisation were taken out by Lubber, an American (Barker 1977, 134). The mechanised process was first used by Pilkingtons in 1908 (PB 358/57), though it was not employed in No 9 Tank House. A ring-shaped 'bait' was dipped into the metal and drawn upwards to form a cylinder, which was blown by compressed air (Pl 46). However, the cylinder still had to be subjected to cutting, flattening and polishing operations, each of which incurred a cost and increased the rate of breakage. In view of this, attempts were being made in several countries to mechanise in a more radical way, drawing a flat sheet of glass directly from the tank or from an intermediate pot, thus removing altogether the need to blow a cylinder, and then cut, flatten and polish the glass (*ibid*). A successful method of making drawn flat glass potentially offered enormous improvements in the efficiency of glass manufacture, hence the years of experimentation spent trying to devise a viable drawing machine.

Several flat sheet processes were developed, but only three became commercially successful: the Fourcault,

Libbey–Owens, and PPG (Pittsburg Plate Glass) processes (Cable 1999, 1102). The Fourcault and PPG machines drew glass vertically up into a drawing tower, by means of rollers which gripped the glass above the height at which it had started to solidify; they differed in the method by which the glass was initially guided from the tank, the former method using a clay debiteuse, pressed into the surface of the molten glass, the latter a submerged drawing bar (*ibid*). In Libbey-Owens machines, the glass was drawn from the tank using a submerged drawing bar, but then passed over a roller and was drawn into an

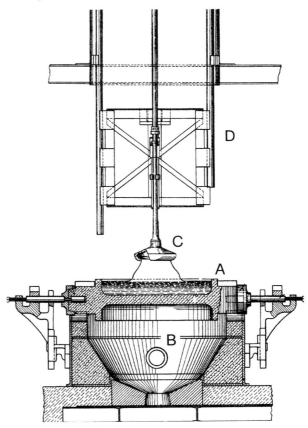

Plate 46 Mechanised manufacture of cylinder glass using the Lubbers process. Glass is cast onto a preheated bowl (A) set above a heated muffle (B). Bait (C) is dipped into the glass, and the blow-pipe unit is raised up the vertical track (D) (reproduced from Cable 1999, fig 14, by kind permission of the author)

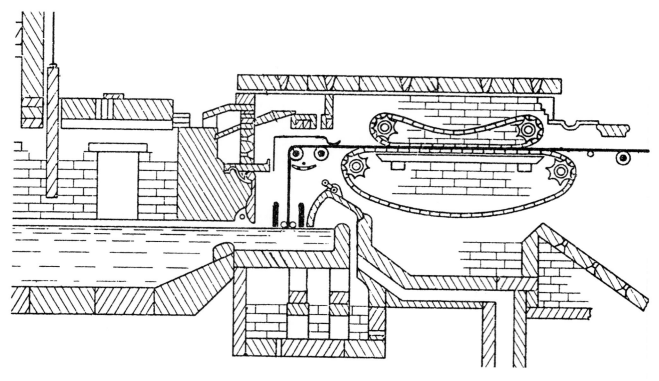

Plate 47 Early version of a Libbey–Owens machine, which drew a sheet of glass directly from the tank, the edges being gripped by knurled rolls. The sheet was drawn upwards between water-cooled boxes, slightly reheated before passing over a bending roll, and fed away horizontally for annealing (reproduced from Cable 1999, fig 16, by kind permission of the author)

horizontal annealing lehr (Pl 47). Fourcault, a Belgian, had begun work on a drawing machine in the 1890s, but the method was not developed to the point of commercial success until the 1920s; similarly, the Libbey-Owens process was under development in America from the 1900s, again reaching commercial success in the 1920s. Experiments started on the PPG process in 1917, with the crucial components not being developed until 1926. All three processes co-existed for several decades, bringing as they did differing advantages and limitations; the processes that used a drawbar had the advantage that corrosion products were locked into the centre of the drawn sheet, and caused minimal optical distortion, but the Fourcault process continues to be used to this day in the production of specialist glasses (Cable 1999, 1103). Other attempts to draw sheet glass direct from a tank were made, but never attained commercial success; these included the Rowat and Danner processes. The former resembled the Fourcault and PPG methods, whilst the latter attempted to flow a sheet of glass vertically downwards through a slot. Unsuccessful experimentation with new glassmaking processes was a costly business; new machines had to provide quality as well as quantity, and it has been observed that 'the road to the glassmakers bankruptcy court is paved with cullet' (PB 358/57).

Until 1929, Pilkingtons' attitude to the new flat drawn processes resembled that of Chances to the earlier development of continuous tank furnaces; the company was doubtful that sufficient glass of high quality could be produced by the available techniques, and were unwilling to invest heavily in unproven technology. Pilkingtons were convinced of the commercial importance of selling good quality glass, and most of their sheet output was still hand-blown in 1926, when it was produced at a loss, wiping out the profit from mechanised drawn cylinder glass production (Barker 1977, 289). However, they were not inactive, combining their own small-scale experimentation with careful monitoring of the processes being developed elsewhere. Very little is known about their experiments; in an industry particularly exposed to technological plagiarism, Pilkingtons was always jealous of its technological secrets. Very little documentation on the matter survives, and it is likely that very little was ever committed to paper, a theory which is partly confirmed by accounts of earlier working methods at the firm (*see above Ch 5, p 25*). However, some facts can be established. The notes made by JB Watts, Pilkingtons' Sheet Works production manager (1925–8), on his visits to glass plants in America and Europe are informative, as is Pilkingtons' 'Valuation' of 1933, which includes an annotated plan showing several

84

structures within No 9 Tank House. This and other evidence has recently been studied by Ron Parkin and we are indebted to him for giving us access to his research in advance of publication (Parkin 2000).

Throughout the second decade of the century, Pilkingtons retained doubts about both the Fourcault and Libbey-Owens methods, the two most developed flat-drawn processes at that time, and in 1919, the company took an option on the Rowat process, which it considered to have greater potential (Barker 1977, 289). In 1920 or 1921, No 9 Tank was taken out of ordinary hand-blown cylinder glass production, and its former melt end was converted into a small four-pot furnace to supply quantities of glass for experiments (Parkin 2000, 80). This furnace is believed to have been sited alongside the two sets of stacks at the south–western end of the former tank, in an area where any surviving remains of the tank house had been destroyed prior to the start of archaeological recording. There are documentary references to 'experimental drawn' No 9 Tank in 1922, and to 'flat drawn experiments' there in 1924, the 1924 Valuation additionally noting 'experimental plant being rebuilt' (Parkin 2000, 78). Although some Fourcault apparatus may have been tried, research in the building appears primarily to have used Rowat patents 182,805 (1921) and 212,545 (1923/4), with glass being drawn up into a vertical tower using a strip of wire mesh as a bait (*op cit*, 80–1); the tower may correspond to the structure known to have stood between the melt and working end buildings (*ibid*). The longest run of glass was reported to be 370 ft, though this probably amounts to the total amount of glass produced in the run, rather than the length of the draw (*ibid*), and the quality of the glass was very poor. The main difficulty was in attaining an even thickness for the drawn sheet glass; it had a tendency to 'waist' or thicken in the middle 'like treacle from a knife blade' (Maloney 1967, 87), and the edges of the sheet were very difficult to control. The company's experiments were abandoned in 1925, though Cecil Pilkington continued his own research into the following year, before being forced to stop in order to conserve energy during the General Strike; by this stage he may have been close to perfecting an adaptation of the Rowat drawing machine, without infringing existing patents (Parkin 2000, 82).

As well as experimenting with Rowat apparatus in No 9 Tank, the company continued to investigate other options. In 1922 the adjacent No 10 Tank was adapted so that some of its glass could feed an experimental Libbey-Owens machine, designed to produce a sheet of glass six feet wide. The trial seems to have been concluded by 1925, when records suggest that the tank was working normally (Barker 1960, 250; Parkin 2000, 82). The period 1925–9 seems to have

been characterised by increasing concern at Pilkingtons over the use of drawing machines by their competitors, and their own failure to find a satisfactory method of mechanising production. JB Watts, who was then the manager in charge of drawn cylinder production at Pilkingtons, visited Fourcault plants in Europe and America at this time. In 1925 he saw a Fourcault plant at Bellevernon, USA, noting several problems including high rates of breakage which stopped the machines and produced glass of irregular quality (PB 358/57). He observed that 'the fundamental problem of making homogeneous glass was not dealt with properly' and that 'nowhere did we see glass that would do for our stock size market' (*ibid*). However, he felt that these problems resulted from sloppy design and management rather than any inherent weakness in the process, concluding that 'the Fourcault process was not being given a fair chance' and required 'far more attention than other processes' (*ibid*).

Given their reservations over flat drawn glass, Pilkingtons invested in the further mechanisation of the cylinder method of production. In 1928, a large new drawn cylinder tank opened at the sheet works (Barker 1960, 207), and in 1928 or 1929, an experimental glass stretching kiln was built in the melt end of No 9 Tank House, designed to flatten cylinders without marking the surface of the blown glass (Parkin 2000, 83). The kiln is listed under Section 3 of the 1933 Valuation (PB 665); the accompanying plan shows one of three installations within the tank house being a rectangular structure straddling the melt end regenerators towards their south–west end, with a narrower arm branching north–east along the line of the north–western pair of regenerators. As the other two installations shown on the plan are identified, it seems safe to deduce that this structure must represent the stretching kiln. Ron Parkin also places the kiln above the melt end regenerators, but towards their north–east end; he provides a description of the working of the kiln, and a plan of its layout (Parkin 2000, 83–5 and fig 52). A split cylinder or 'shawl' was drawn into the kiln, suspended from tongs; it softened and stretched flat under its own weight, and the chamber was then cooled and re-heated slightly so that flattening could be completed on a flattening stone. The stone was then transferred to an annealing chamber for final cooling. Parkin's description indicates that the kiln would need two independent gas jets for the stretching and annealing chambers, but also refers to a third 'warming' chamber (*ibid*). He estimates that the kiln would have had minimum dimensions of *c* 7.0 m x 4.25 m. This investment in cylinder glass may have been intended as a short term measure, rather than indicating that cylinder production was viewed as a long term alternative to the flat drawn processes. In 1928, the licence to operate the Rowat Patent was not renewed, but the company decided to consider lodging an application for a licence for the Libbey-Owens process, as well as authorising further experimentation of its own, as recommended by Cecil Pilkington.

Progress had not been made by 1929, when Pilkingtons was considering operating a single drawn cylinder tank, and purchasing foreign sheet glass in order to satisfy demand. However, later that year, Watts again visited the USA, and was shown an experimental PPG tank at Mount Vernon. 'Locally it is known as the Crazy House', he noted, 'for as [the manager] put it "everything that man could think of was tried there"' (PB 358/57, 39). In November, Pilkingtons decided to pay £ 2000 for an 18 month option on the PPG process; this gave them the right to experiment with a single machine, and it was housed in No 10 Tank House (Barker 1960, 478).

The No 10 Tank was rebuilt to a new design, with the drawing machine placed at the working end (Parkin 2000, 83). The machine itself needed several fireclay components, including a drawbar, and these items of claywork, as well as floaters for the tank, were fired in two burning kilns installed in the adjacent No 9 Tank House. Ron Parkin has suggested that both of these kilns were positioned in the northern corner of the cone house (*op cit*, 79), and notes that as they weighed about 20 tons, new foundations had to be built. He also suggests that gas was no longer available from the supply flues sited alongside the north–eastern wall of the cone house, and may have been supplied by means of a new flue constructed along the middle of the existing regenerators; and further, that the burning kilns needed particularly high firing temperatures, so that a gas-fired preheater was installed. The plan accompanying the 1933 Valuation shows a rectangular structure in the north corner of the cone house, measuring *c* 8.5 m x 6 m (PB 665). It is described as a 'high temperature burning kiln' which was 'in use', and had been built in 1933. It is uncertain whether this structure was a replacement for earlier burning kilns in the same location. A second rectangular structure measuring 7 m x 4.75 m, 1 m to the south–west, was described as a 'ring arch' built in 1930 and also still in use.

The available evidence seems to suggest that No 9 was never again used for glassmaking after the cessation of experiments there in 1926 or 1927. In 1933, it was noted that 'from 1920 to 1927, £ 32,789 was spent on flat drawn experiments…this included additions to plant and buildings which remain today but are not in use' (PB 665). Meanwhile, the experimental PPG machine in No 10 Tank House had been performing relatively well. Cecil Pilkington was convinced that the process was a good one, and in

1931, the manufacture of flat drawn glass as a commercial operation began when the company took up an option to license a four-machine production unit. The machines were installed at No 7 Tank; it was found that they made better glass than could be produced by the Libbey-Owens process, although at greater expense (Barker 1977, 314–5). By 1933, all sheet glass manufacture at Pilkingtons' St Helens works was by the PPG process (Barker 1960, 207), but the fact that a licence was finally obtained to use the Fourcault process in the same year (Cable 1999, 1103) suggests that the company still had reservations about the new technology.

Archaeological evidence

A third broad phase encompasses the subsequent changes that the cone house was subjected to after blown cylinder glass production ceased there. All of the western section of the interior of the tank house beyond the angled furnace buttresses had undergone substantial reworking over several phases. In many cases, owing to the wholesale infilling of the redundant sections of the furnace complex, it was difficult to determine a stratigraphical sequence and recourse to historical records must be made where they survive in order to elucidate the use of the cone house.

Changes to the melt end regenerators
Modification of the melt end regenerators *(Figs 15 and 26; Pl 48)*
After the continuous tank furnace had ceased to function, the north–western pair of melt end regenerators was radically altered. The dividing wall which formerly separated the two regenerators, each with its underlying flue, was knocked through to create a new chamber, 503, centrally located along the length of the former regenerators. The outer walls of the regenerators and underlying flues were largely retained, but the brickwork was replaced towards the tops of these walls. The roofs of the regenerators were also demolished. The bottom part of the springer for a shallow arch was recovered, suggesting that the two semi-circular arches spanning the regenerators were replaced by a single shallow arched roof. To the north–east and south–west, short lengths of the original regenerators remained, intact but abandoned.

At the south–western end of the new chamber, the redundant end of regenerator 531 had been blocked off with a brick wall, constructed in English garden wall bond. A new brick-walled flue, 536D, was constructed at the base of the chamber, parallel with its south–east wall (Fig 26). It measured *c* 4.4 m long x 0.45 m wide x 0.5 m deep internally, and was built in English bond, using refractory bricks. The flue was

Plate 48 Looking north-west at the Phase 3 structures within chamber 503

covered by a number of large refractory tiles, 0.12 m thick, supported in places by metal bars, and laid so that their upper surfaces were flush with the tops of the walls. The internal surfaces of the brickwork were clean. A rectangular vertical shaft, 825, measuring 0.71 m by 0.45 m, had been built mid-way along the flue. It was edged with refractory slabs, and capped by a very heavy metal plate.

Three flues aligned south–east/north–west communicated with 536D, and appeared to be contemporary features (Fig 26; 536A, B, C). The central and north–eastern flues were *c* 2.2 m and 1.5 m long respectively, whilst that to the south–west was at least 2.2 m long, its extremity not being cleared of rubble backfill. All were *c* 0.47 m wide and 0.62 m deep, and were again topped with large refractory tiles. Building techniques and materials varied between flues, though refractory bricks had mainly been used internally. Flues 536A and C were each found to have two apertures through their capping slabs, whilst a single aperture opened through the roof of the central flue. The apertures were mostly rectangular, but the south–eastern opening through 536C was in the form of a narrow slot, and it can be suggested that a flat metal bar found lying on top was part of a mechanism allowing the size of the aperture to be varied. Several of the apertures were edged with refractory bricks or tiles. Although some areas of

blackening were observed, the internal surfaces of the flues and apertures were mostly clean and free from sooty deposits.

Two brick structures, 743 and 745, measuring *c* 1.8 m sq, had been built over flues 536A and C. In both cases, the structures appeared to be contemporary with the flues which passed below them. The south–western structure, 745, appeared to enclose one of the apertures through the roof of the underlying flue, with the brickwork being stepped progressively away from the opening to the north–east and north–west.

The north–eastern structure of the two, 743, enclosed the wider opening through the top of 536C. The stepped brickwork of 745 was absent, the structure having been built with an integral flat brick floor, 947, entirely of refractory brick internally.

After the construction of these two brick boxes, the external area around them had been infilled with a deposit of rubble and sandy clay, 287. A brick wall, 742, was then built on top of the rubble, passing over 536B and joining the south–east faces of the two structures. The area to the north–west of this wall was then floored in brick. In the absence of evidence to the contrary, it can be suggested that this brick wall and floor may also have been constructed during the

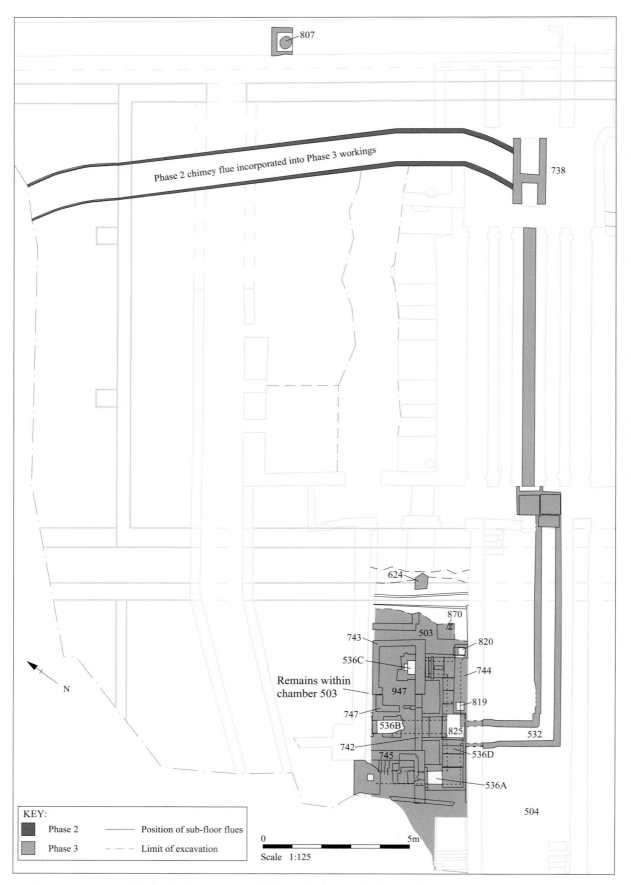

Fig 26 Phase 3 flues and shafts, dating to a period when the furnace had ceased production. The structures built within chamber 503 probably represent the base of a small furnace or kiln, perhaps a 'stretching kiln'

original episode of re-organisation and rebuilding within the area of the former regenerators.

Other features suggest the possibility that the new structures were subsequently altered. A further wall, 747, which butted structure 743, and appeared to extend it to the south–west, may be the product of later modification. Similarly, a third brick structure was built, 744, overlying the south–eastern side of 536D (Fig 26). It measured 1.93 m by 0.47 m, and the aperture associated with this structure had clearly been created by roughly chopping through the tiles of 536D. These characteristics suggested that it was not part of the original design, but was a solution to a problem which manifested itself later. Likewise, another shaft down into flue 536D, 820, may have been a further, later addition to the original configuration.

A further feature, a concrete block supporting a vertical steel stanchion, 870, was recorded in the eastern corner of the chamber, and had been constructed before the north–eastern end of the chamber was backfilled. It may have supported the roof of the chamber, or some installation above, but it is not clear why it was situated close to the chamber's south–east wall. A connection with similar concrete blocks and truncated stanchions located within tunnel 504 seems probable.

Alterations to tunnel 504 between the melt end regenerators *(Fig 26)*

A brick-built flue, 532, was constructed along the bottom of the former central tunnel, 504. It appeared to be connected to the network of flues uncovered immediately to the north–west, having a junction with 536D roughly halfway along the length of that flue, roughly adjacent to the central aperture in its roof. From that point, it was cut through the wall into 504. After a distance of *c* 2 m, the flue turned a right angle, and continued north–east for *c* 7.5 m to the end of the tunnel. Thereafter, it passed below the floor of tunnel 524, and into the central tunnel, 527, between the former working end regenerators, and finally connected with the base of the central brick structure, 738, within the working end switch room. The flue was *c* 0.45 m wide internally. It was built in English garden wall bond, with all internal faces being of refractory brick; these had remained clean.

Higher level flues inserted at the former melt end

A further system of flues existed at a higher level, but several of these had been extensively truncated, hampering their understanding. A brick flue, 603, measuring *c* 0.4 m wide by 0.6 m high internally was recorded cutting through the north–east wall of the south–west tank house building (Fig 12). It immediately turned a right angle, to run between the adjacent walls of the two elements of the tank house.

Here it was recorded bridging the extreme north–east end of the chamber created within the former melt end regenerators, being carried by a brick pier, 624 (Fig 26). The same flue then appears to have turned back to the south–west, running above 504, being carried by the transverse support walls of the former furnace that spanned the top of the tunnel (Pl 37). It was truncated 3 m south–west of the north–east wall of the melt end tank house building. Where this flue was carried above 504, a narrow brick-floored channel, 948, lay immediately parallel to the north–west, carried on top of the re-built upper portion of the wall between 504 and the chamber to the south–west (948 not illustrated; chamber 503 and tunnel 504 are shown on Figure 26). This was subsequently filled with sand and rubble, and a further flue was constructed, 949, running perpendicular to the channel. It butted the south–east wall of the channel, but was truncated immediately to the north–west.

Adaptation of the north–west end of the cone house

The kiln/furnace *(Fig 27)*

A brick and concrete structure contained within the northern corner of the tank house appeared to represent the bottom of an almost square kiln or furnace. The structure had an extensive concrete base foundation, 910, measuring 6.45 m x 5.78 m; it had two rectangular extensions to the south–east, suggesting that the kiln was accessed from this direction. Above, the brick furnace base, 918, survived to a maximum height of three courses of refractory brick bonded with black ash mortar, these being disturbed in places by the footings of later walls. Round iron stay bars were located within the brickwork, and the structure was bound laterally in both axes with metal rods. These presumably contained vertical 'buck stays' of either bull-headed metal (old railway lines) or RSJs, to contain and control thermal expansion. To the north–west of the furnace, a series of seven unmortared brick walls, 778, a single skin thick, enclosed the ends of the tie rods.

The foundations of the structure were found to have been built after the foundation trench of brick box 731 had been backfilled *(see below Brick structures 730 and 731)*.

Brick structures 730 and 731 *(Fig 27)*

A small brick chamber, 730, containing tightly packed vertical steel pipes encased in insulated collars, was constructed 2.1 m beyond the northern corner of the tank furnace. It had external dimensions of 1.08 m x 0.96 m, and had been built in red brick bonded with black ash mortar, the upper surfaces showing signs of subsequent repair. The structure had been constructed within the former position of the north–east wall of the north–west swing pit, the wall having been

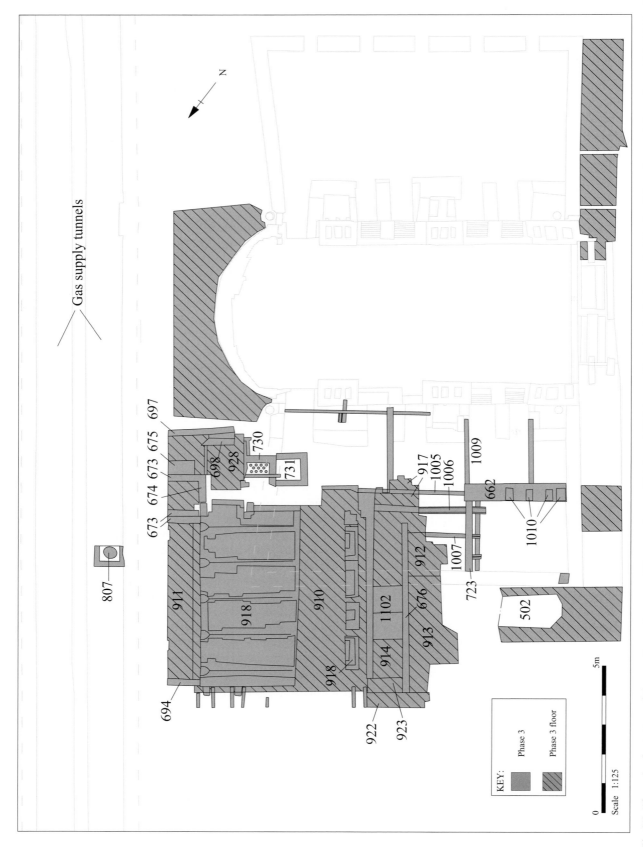

Fig 27 Phase 3 adaptation of the north-west corner of the cone house. Brickwork 918 is considered to be the base of a kiln for firing claywork for adjacent No 10 Tank

demolished with the exception of a short stub remaining at the south–west end. The brick chamber was butted to the south–west by a further brick box, 731, which had a brick floor set upon a concrete base. Box 731 had external dimensions of 1.12 m x 1.05 m x 0.88 m deep; two apertures in the south–west side of chamber 730 opened into box 731, although the upper aperture was sited above the top of 731.

It was noted above that the foundation trench of box 731 was truncated to the north–west by concrete raft 265, associated with the foundations of a kiln/furnace. However, the latter did not appear to have disturbed 730 or 731, so that, whilst it was clear that the kiln/furnace was constructed after these structures, all may have been in use at the same time. Brick chamber 730 post-dated the Phase 2.1 chimney pull flue, 523/534 (Figs 15 and 26), which ran below floor level from the working end switch room out through the north–west gable foundations of the cone house (*see above Ch 5, p 54*), but it seems that there may have been a period when both were in use at the same time; a low level feed or exhaust was discovered connecting brick chamber 730 with the chimney pull flue, suggesting that 730 may have been constructed in this location specifically to give access to flue 523/534. However, it is uncertain whether the Phase 2.1 chimney pull flue still carried exhaust gases in Phase 3; the establishment of a link with flue 532 to the south–west (Fig 26; *see above Alterations to tunnel 504 between the melt end regenerators, p 89*) raises the possibility that this length of flue was now used to feed combustion gases from the former melt end, rather than to provide access to the chimney.

Foundation walls within the former north–west swing pit (*Fig 27*)

The kiln base and its foundations had cut through the northern end of the north–west swing pit, and it is clear that a series of walls built in the southern end of the pit, butting its internal faces, must have been made before or at the same time as the construction of the kiln/furnace. Brick wall 662 was constructed at the swing pit's south–western end, centrally placed and aligned south–west / north–east along the length of the pit. It was built in English bond using red brick and black ash mortar, and stood on a concrete base. The north–eastern end of the wall carried two RSJs, 1005 and 1006, projecting further to the north–east, and to the south–east. A further short length of wall, 723, extended from the north–east end of 662 to the former south–west wall of the swing pit. It was the bearer for two RSJs which in turn carried disturbed brick walls 912 and 919. Additionally, four steel plates were recorded on the upper surface of wall 662, collectively numbered 1010; these may have been footpads for further RSJs, suggesting that a floor or other structure was supported above the former swing

pit, the extent of the reinforcement suggesting that heavy machinery may have been installed in this part of the cone house. It is evident that tunnel 502, the truncated remains of which rise at a shallow angle from the south–western long wall of the tank house, was largely demolished to allow this later activity to occur.

Floors and structures later than or contemporary with the kiln/furnace (*Fig 27*)

Other structures were stratified above the base of the kiln/furnace, and must represent contemporary or later features. A brick-floored walkway, 914, led away from a flight of two steps, 922 and 923, sited just within the central arched opening in the Phase 2 western gable wall. The walkway passed alongside the southern edge of the kiln/furnace, being floored with iron plates, 1102, rather than brick, where it bridged the broken crown of tunnel 502. At its eastern extent the walkway had been truncated; here, an RSJ spanned the former swing pit to the edge of the tank furnace wall. Remnants of a floor surface, 917, had been removed from above this RSJ. The walkway was bounded to the south–west by a section of brick walling, 676, with a further area of disturbed brick flooring, 912, butting 676 to the south–west. The latter floor was in turn butted to the north–west by an area of concrete flooring, 913, carried on metal rails and plates, which bridged access tunnel 502.

The space between the northern side of the kiln and the north–east wall of the cone house was surfaced with a brick floor of dark red brick and black ash mortar, 911, measuring 5.3 m long by 0.9 m wide. The floor was recorded as butting the inner skin of the north–east wall of the cone house, but the latter is considered to have been built during Phase 4, and the cone house wall may in fact have butted the existing floor. Floor 911 was bounded to the north–west by a short length of wall, 694, again built in red brick and bonded irregularly with black ash mortar, and to the south–east, by the north–western wall, 673, of an open brick box structure.

The south–west and south–east sides of this brick box structure were formed by walls 672, 673 and 674, built using red brick, which had become blackened, bonded with black ash mortar. The internal floor space of the box, measuring 1.02 m x 0.94 m, was tiled, but had subsequently been covered by deposits of bitumen; a further rectangular brick wall or buttress, 675, had been built along the exterior of the south–east side of the box. A short distance to the south–east, two almost parallel lengths of wall were recorded, butting one another, 697 and 698. They had been truncated by later activity, obscuring their original function. After the construction of 698, the area immediately to the south–east of the kiln/furnace and to the north–east

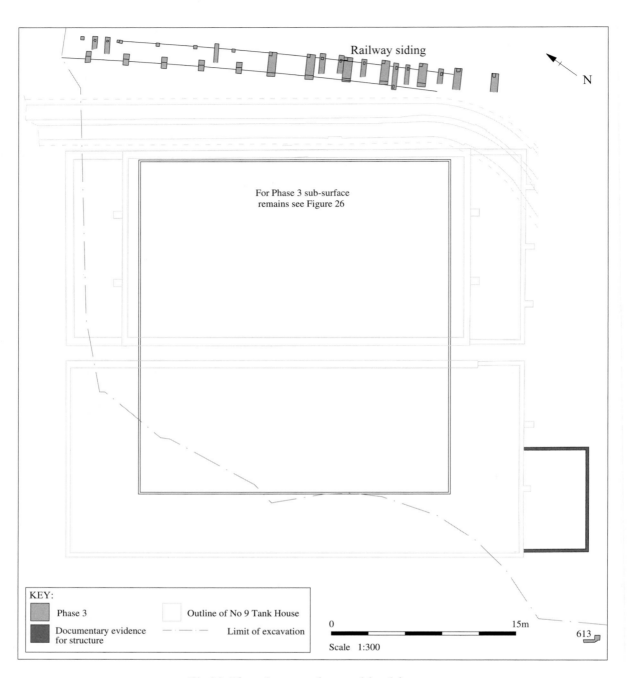

KEY:

Phase 3

Documentary evidence
for structure

Outline of No 9 Tank House

Limit of excavation

0   15m

Scale 1:300

Fig 28 Phase 3: external ground-level features

of the heat exchanger/preheater had been floored with red brick bonded with black ash mortar, 928. The surface had been disturbed to the north–east and south–west, with a thick bitumen deposit subsequently being laid to the north–east, between the brick box structure, and wall 697. A further area of brick floor, 928, lay between the kiln/furnace and the heat exchanger/preheater.

Working end switch room *(Figs 16 and 26)*
The brick chamber in the centre of the room was remodelled during Phase 3. The chamber's H-shaped base, 738, was constructed using irregularly-bonded red brick, obscuring the original form of the structure,

and removing evidence for the switch mechanism which had regulated the flow of gases in Phase 2. Above the new base, the multi-sided brick chamber, 535, was repaired, indicating that it continued to function during Phase 3. Elsewhere in the room, the recess at the northern end of the north–east wall was partially blocked by the construction of an elevated wall in English Garden Wall bond, 665. The blocking of the doorways giving access into the former swing pit may also date to this period.

Modification of the tank house fabric
Little evidence was found for the alteration of the walls or roofs of the two constituent buildings of No 9

Tank House during Phase 3, and, with the exception of a small number of modifications, the structures appear to have been retained largely as constructed in 1886.

Annex south–east of the tank house
A small structure adjoining the south–east end of the building south–west of No 9 Tank House was remodelled between 1908 and 1928 (Ordnance Survey 1908; 1928); the building itself had housed annealing kilns as late as 1914 (unlabelled works plan dated 1914), but had been converted to warehousing by 1927 (Barker 1977). A 1.5 m length of wall revealed by excavation (613, Fig 28) appears to correspond to the position of the north–east wall of the remodelled extension. It was constructed in stretcher bond of red brick and black ash mortar, on a concrete foundation.

Annex south–east of the melt end building
The 'cullet wash building' shown as an annex to the south–east of the melt end of the tank house on plans accompanying the 1933 Valuation (PB 665) appears smaller than the structure depicted on earlier maps (Fig 7; *see above Structure to the south–east of the tank house, p 74*), suggesting that it was rebuilt, although no physical remains corresponding to the smaller structure were recorded.

Evidence for a drawing tower
Some past and present Pilkington employees have attested to the presence, during Phase 3, of a drawing tower, positioned over what had formerly been the melt end of the Phase 2 furnace in No 9 Tank House (*see above p 85*). No direct physical evidence for this has been found, although later aerial photographs from 1939 and 1947 appear to show that the central portion of the roof of the melt end building had either been lowered or removed (PRM/AV/2; PRM/AV/2A), whilst a later post-war photograph shows that this central section had subsequently been re-roofed with a roof covering distinct from the initial slate (Pl 3).

External features
Mushroom valve, giving gas supply to square furnace (Fig 26; Pls 21 and 49)
An intact 'mushroom valve' contained within a small brick chamber was revealed, lying partially covered by later masonry (807). This valve was let into the crown of the inner Phase 2 gas supply flue, 521, and was positioned adjacent to the later Phase 3 kiln/furnace within the tank house. No means of transferring the gas to the kiln was discernible, but gas flues may have been removed or truncated when the north–east wall of the cone house was infilled with brick in the mid twentieth century (*see below Ch 7, p 97*).

Railway line between the cone house and the canal (Fig 28)
Wooden sleepers and iron rail chairs were recorded *in situ* to the north–east of the cone house, indicating the former presence of a railway line. The position of these remains corresponded to that of a rail siding shown on the OS 1:25,000 map of 1928, closely following the canal bank. A works' plan of 1939 (PB 222) indicates that the siding led to buildings labelled 'mixing' and 'melting' to the north–west, and suggests that the siding was constructed to allow the carriage of raw materials.

Functional analysis of the Phase 3 structures

Remains within chamber 503 and tunnel 504
The brick structures recorded in chamber 503, inserted into Phase 2 regenerators 530 and 531, appear to resemble the base level remains of a small furnace or kiln. The long flue aligned north–east/south–west, and three shorter flues branching off to the north–west, are considered most likely to have been built to carry gas, whilst several of the shafts recorded in the chamber may have served to draw gas up from the flues below to a point of combustion within a kiln or furnace sited above.

The documentary study produced no direct evidence to explain exactly how the structures in chamber 503 functioned, but documentary sources do allow the chamber to be tentatively identified as part of a glass stretching kiln (*see above, p 85*). Two pieces of equipment are known to have been installed in the melt end of the tank house after the termination of commercial cylinder glass production in 1920/21: a four-pot furnace with experimental drawing machine, probably used between 1922 and 1926, and the later stretching kiln, built in 1928/9 (Parkin 2000, 79–80). It has been suggested that the former lay close to the south–west wall of the building, beyond the limit of excavation, making any correspondence with chamber 503 unlikely (*op cit*, fig 52), but the Valuation of 1933 implies that part at least of the stretching kiln was located in the position of the north–western melt end regenerators, where chamber 503 was recorded (*see above, p 85*). Little more can be deduced with any degree of certainty. Ron Parkin has reconstructed the approximate plan form of the stretching kiln (Parkin 2000, fig 53), but it is not easy to relate this drawing to the excavated evidence (Fig 26). Similarly the dimensions of the chamber, *c* 7 m x 3.3 m, do not correspond exactly to those of the rather stylised depiction of a structure above regenerators 530 and

Plate 49 The mushroom valve within shaft 807

531 on the 1933 plan, the structure measuring *c* 6.5 m x 1.75 m.

Although a detailed understanding of chamber 503 is not possible on the basis of the evidence presently available, some observations can be made. Gas may have entered the flue system via the south–western flue, 536A, passing north–east to a switch mechanism possibly located below shaft 825 (Fig 26). From this point, it may have been directed to the three vertical shafts, whose purpose was probably to supply gas to burners heating the different chambers of the stretching kiln. We can speculate that the higher level flues recorded within the melt end of the tank house, some passing through its north–east wall foundations, may have been used to fire the kiln at a number of different heights, possibly using very low velocity flames, in order to secure the desired temperature distribution. A further flue, 532, passed through the wall of the chamber adjacent to shaft 825, and into tunnel 504, before leading north–east to rebuilt central brick structure 738 in the Phase 2 working end switch room, which in turn gave access to the chimney pull flue 523 (Fig 26). It is possible that flue 532 carried exhaust gases from chamber 503 to the working end chimney flue, although the exhaust from a small kiln could perhaps have been simply vented to the ambient atmosphere via a short vertical flue, ultimately being

released through the louvres on the ridge of the tank house roof. An alternative explanation for flue 532 is that it carried gas to the burning kiln or kilns in the north–west corner of the cone house (Parkin 2000, 79), but, in view of the Phase 3 mushroom valve adjacent to the burning kiln, apparently supplying gas from flues to the north–east of the cone house, this also remains far from certain.

The excavation evidence suggested that the structures in chamber 503 represented at least one phase of building. This would correspond to the experimental nature of the stretching kiln thought to have stood here.

Structures in the north–west of the cone house

The rectangular brick floor, 918, recorded in the northern corner of the cone house (Fig 27), retained by steel rods and built on a concrete foundation, appears, purely on the basis of the surviving remains, to have been the base of a kiln or furnace, with the tie rods being necessary to counter thermal expansion. Little more can be deduced without referring to oral and documentary evidence. This material, however, allows the structure to be identified as a 'high temperature burning kiln', installed to fire claywork for the PPG tank operating in adjacent No 10 Tank

House. It has been suggested that two burning kilns stood in the cone house and that they were built in, or soon after, 1929, to fire claywork for the first PPG tank (Parkin 2000, 79). Later, plans accompanying the 1933 Valuation give a stylised depiction of a structure in the position of the kiln/furnace; its dimensions on plan are *c* 8.5 m x 6 m, compared with *c* 6.5 m x 5.75 m for the dimensions of the recorded masonry, but the correspondence of location suggests that the two can be related. The valuation text identifies the structure as a single high temperature burning kiln, stating that it had been built in 1933 and was in use in that year. This raises a question as to whether or not a new burning kiln had been built in 1933 on the site of an older kiln erected in 1929/30. A mushroom valve sited over the canalside gas supply flue, 521, was excavated adjacent to the excavated remains of the kiln/furnace; it may have provided gas to fuel the kiln, though it is not clear whether it relates to the 1929/30 kiln, or the 1933 kiln, if they were indeed different structures.

Oral and documentary evidence suggests that the combustion air for the burning kiln(s) was preheated in order to achieve a higher burning temperature, using a preheater possibly fuelled by coal gas rather than producer gas (Parkin 2000, 79). Brick chamber 730, which contained insulated steel pipes, was at first considered to be a possible preheater, but the insulation of the vertical tubes, and lack of space for any gas or liquid outside the tubes, appears to rule out this possibility, and the function of the structure remains unknown. It is also unclear whether the low level connection with the Phase 2 chimney pull flue, 523, carried combustion gas or exhaust during Phase 3 (*see above Brick structures 730 and 731, p 89*).

The foundation walls, RSJs, and steel plates found within and around the former north–west swing pit appear to have supported heavy machinery, but the subsequent removal of all but the foundations of this apparatus means that no assessment of function can be made on the basis of the remains alone. However, the 1933 Valuation and accompanying plan (PB 665) indicate that a 'ring arch' was built in this part of the tank house in 1930, and remained in use three years later. The term 'ring arch' is very similar in meaning to 'claywork burning kiln', and this may be the second of the two burning kilns referred to by Parkin (Parkin 2000, 79). There is insufficient evidence of any kind to allow the function of the remaining floors and brick structures to the south–east of structure 918 to be established; it can only be assumed that further activities relating to the manufacture of claywork for No 10 Tank were carried out here.

7

PHASE 4: MID- AND LATE-TWENTIETH CENTURY ALTERATIONS

Phase 4.1

Initial alteration of the cone house

The side walls of the cone house *(Figs 11 and 12)*
Extensive changes were made to the fabric of the cone house and south–western tank house building during Phase 4. The gaps between the stanchions of the north–east facade of the cone house were infilled with brick laid in English Garden Wall bond, and an additional brick wall was built along the whole length of the wall internally (Pl 23). The south–west long wall was rebuilt and strengthened in a similar manner; externally, the central part of the wall was rebuilt right up to the eaves, filling the Phase 2 opening to the south–western tank house building, and leaving only stubs of original brickwork at either end. In addition, further strengthening of the north–east and south–west walls had been achieved by the provision of external buttressing. Six massive raking buttresses adjoined the north–east wall, these being interspersed by six smaller vertical buttresses, one to the south–east of each raking buttress (Fig 11 and Pl 50). The south–west wall was supported by 11 external buttresses (Fig 12 and Pl 25), which must have rested against the adjoining wall of the south–west tank house building, of which the foundations, 632,

Plate 50 View of the raking buttresses added to the cone house north–east wall during the conversion of the late 1940s

97

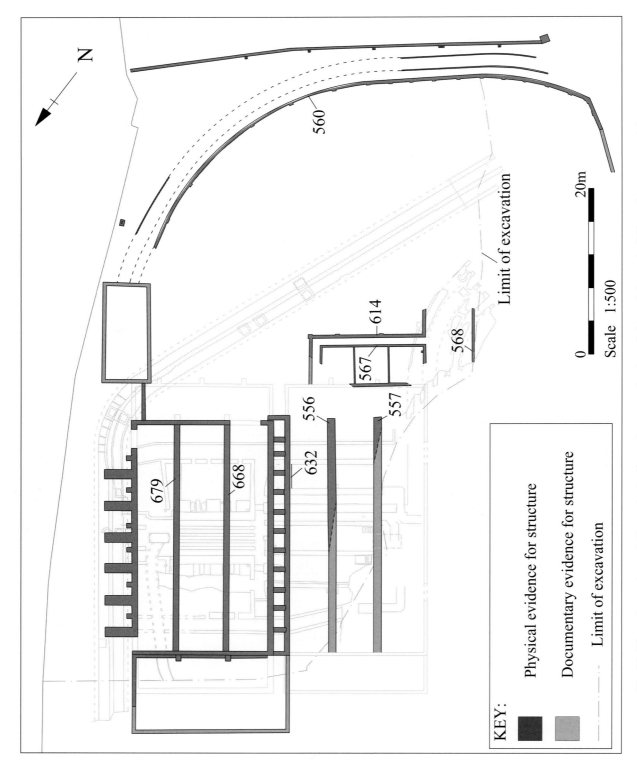

N

560

614
567
568

556
557

632

668

679

Limit of excavation

KEY:

Physical evidence for structure

Documentary evidence for structure

Limit of excavation

0   20m

Scale 1:500

Fig 29 Phase 4 remains, relating principally to the strengthening of the tank house buildings for raw materials storage

remained. The south–west faces of this set of buttresses had been scarred when the south–west tank house building was subsequently demolished (*see below, p 100*).

The south–east gable of the cone house (*Fig 9*)

The gable walls of the cone house were also altered. The circular window at the top of the south–east gable was blocked with wooden shuttering, and red brick blocking was used to fill the seven window apertures below. Lower in the external elevation, an horizontal scar was recorded beneath the windows; it appears to represent the roof-line of the original external lean-to structure adjoining the gable, which was probably removed at this time. A vertical repair to the brickwork at the extreme north–east of the external elevation may indicate the position of the north–east wall of the same structure. At ground level, the upper portions of the large arched doorways into the building were blocked, the doorways being lowered but widened, with RSJs supporting the wall above the apertures. The form of the new central and north–eastern apertures is shown by later brick blocking, inserted when they were in turn closed, whilst the south–western aperture was completely truncated when a larger access was subsequently inserted at the south–west end of the wall.

Replacement of the lean-to adjoining the south–east gable (*Fig 9*)

Further alterations to the external elevation of the south–east gable appear to have been made later in the same phase of construction, or during a subsequent building episode. Five 'I'-section girders were inserted horizontally into the external face of the gable wall, two penetrating the brickwork of the window blocking. The girders were sited 5.1 m above ground level; their stubs remain to the present day. It is suggested that they were erected in order to support the roof of a new lean-to against the south–east gable, with a higher roof-line than the original Phase 2 structure. The removal of two buttresses, evidenced by vertical scars, is considered to have been carried out as part of the construction of the higher lean-to. It was noted that, above the tops of the girders, the external brickwork of the gable abruptly changed colour, being darker above and lighter below. The whitish colour of the lower brickwork seems to suggest that within the lean-to, the gable wall was exposed to a white dust or similar substance.

Cartographic evidence provides some support for this interpretation. The Ordnance Survey 1:1250 map of 1957 shows a structure adjoining the north–east gable of the cone house, on roughly the same footprint as the original Phase 2 annex (Ordnance Survey 1957). However, a further building can be seen communicating with the lean-to, but at right angles to

it and covering a railway siding that had clearly been realigned to the south since Phase 3 (*see below*). By Phase 4, the siding terminated in line with the south–east end of the cone house, with the clear implication that the subsidiary buildings to the south–east of the gable wall were intended to provide cover for the unloading of railway wagons and transfer of materials to the cone house. A later twentieth century plan, viewed at Pilkingtons' Watson Street drawing office in 1997, labelled the area in front of the south–east gable of the cone house 'raw materials stocking area' (Plan of usage, Pilkingtons' Watson Street Drawing Office).

The north–west gable of the cone house (*Fig 10*)

The circular window in the north–west gable wall was blocked with red brick, but the seven windows below were retained, the frames of their sash windows surviving *in situ*. At ground level, the upper portions of the original arched doorways were blocked with red brick, as on the south–east gable, and lower but wider rectangular entrances were inserted, the wall above being supported by RSJs which remained *in situ* above each entrance, and were visible internally.

Internal modification of the cone house (*Fig 29*)

The foundations of two internal dividing walls were uncovered within the cone house, 668 and 679, aligned north–west/south–east. The walls had been built to divide the cone house into three longitudinal bays, and scars visible on the internal elevations of the gable walls demonstrated that the internal divisions had been partially keyed into the gables. In between the divisions, any upstanding remains of Phase 3 structures of machinery had been removed, and a thick concrete floor laid on top of the backfilled glass production areas. Outside the cone house, many of the openings to the former gas flues and access/ ventilation tunnels had been bricked up, and the flues and tunnels which passed beneath the building had been infilled. This had been very systematically undertaken, with cells of random brick infill separated by dividing walls of unmortared brick construction. All this material was removed by hand to allow the original form of the Phase 2 tank house to be established.

Re-roofing

During the repairs to the cone house roof structure an opportunity was made available to examine its components in detail. Evidence for at least one episode of re-roofing was apparent in that the sections of elevated roof seen in early photographic evidence had been removed, leaving the truncated struts still attached to the truss collars. Evidence for this re-roofing is also visible in photographs taken at the start of the Hotties Project, where the covering of the newly lowered area of roof close to the apex is distinguished by its lighter colour (Pl 3).

Other alterations

The south–west tank house building (Fig 29)

The south–west tank house building was demolished in 1984 (Plan of usage, Pilkington's Watson Street drawing office), but the foundations of roughly the eastern half of the structure survived until archaeological recording began in 1991. As described above, the truncated brick buttresses on the south–west external elevation of the cone house were associated with a longitudinal foundation wall surviving from the south–western half of the tank house, 632. This appears to have been built in Phase 4 as a new north–east side wall to the south–western building, covering the remains of the original wall foundation (*see above Ch 5, p 49*). To the south–west, the foundations of two other walls on the same alignment were recorded, 556 and 557; these walls appear to correspond to the internal subdivisions found within the cone house, and suggest that both elements of the tank house were converted for the same purpose in Phase 4. A concrete floor survived between the wall foundations.

Two parallel brick foundation walls, 567 and 614, were recorded during excavation to the south–east of the south–western tank house building (Fig 29). Their position corresponds roughly to that of a building measuring *c* 13 m x 5 m shown on the Ordnance survey 1:1,250 map of 1957. Cartographic evidence suggests that the structure stood in almost the same position as a Phase 2 building (*see above Ch 5, p 74*), although maps of 1928 (Ordnance Survey 1928) and 1933 (PB 665) suggest that larger or smaller structures respectively stood here in Phase 3. A plan suggests that in the period 1962–76, the building was a 'welfare' facility (Plan of usage, Pilkington's Watson Street drawing office).

Structure adjoining the south–east gable of No 9 Warehouse (Fig 29)

A length of wall, 568, aligned south–east/north–west, was recorded during excavation to the south–east of the former No 9 Warehouse. It seems likely that an annex to the warehouse was rebuilt or enlarged during Phase 4 (Ordnance Survey 1957), and that wall 568 represents the north–east wall of the structure. A works' plan suggests that the building variously housed 'Experimental engineering' (1962), 'FD Tech Assist Office' (1967), and 'Sun Cool Offices' (1976–9) (Plan of usage, Pilkington's Watson Street Drawing Office).

External features (Fig 29)

An extensive area to the south–east of the tank house had been surfaced with concrete during Phase 4. This surface was bounded by a curving perimeter wall, 560, the foundations of which survived right up to the east corner of the cone house. The railway siding lay beyond (*see above*), bounded on the far side by fragments of thin linear wall footings.

Date and purpose of the modifications

The major alterations to the tank house buildings have been dated to 1948, on the evidence of a surviving architects' plan, and a 1948 newspaper found in backfill associated with the conversion. An aerial photograph confirms that many of the changes described above had not occurred by December 1947 (PRM/AV/2A), whilst almost all are shown on the Ordnance Survey 1:1,250 maps of 1957 and 1959. Works' plans indicate that both elements of No 9 Tank House functioned as a 'raw materials store' between 1957 and 1976 (Plan of usage, Pilkington's Watson Street drawing office), and other sources refer to the storage of sand and dolomite. There seems little doubt that strengthening and subdivision of the structures in 1948 marked the start of the use of the tank house as a storage facility.

Phase 4.2

Subsequent modification of the cone house

Replacement of the lean-to adjoining the north–west gable (Fig 29)

It is clear that the use of space beyond the north–west gable of the cone house differed from that at the south–east gable. The north–west gable windows were not blocked, girders were not embedded in the existing wall, and the buttresses were not removed (*cf* Figs 9 and 10), hence there is no evidence for a structure comparable with that to the south–east. In the absence of evidence to the contrary, it can be suggested either that the original lean-to was retained at the beginning of Phase 4, or that it was demolished and not immediately replaced.

The south–east and north–east walls of a later building adjacent to the north–west gable survived until the programme of archaeological recording began in 1991. The structure clearly post-dated the beginning of Phase 4, as it was constructed with an unbroken brick wall adjoining the cone house, so that there was no access via the remodelled Phase 4 doors in the cone house's gable, which must have been blocked by this time. The later structure had a pitched roof and was not a lean-to, and with dimensions of 15.5 m x 10.5 m, it was wider than the Phase 2 annex that had stood here; it is shown on the Ordnance Survey 1:1,250 map of 1959, as well as by later photographs (for example, St Helens Library 1974 photograph of the Hotties; rear cover of this volume), and was clearly accessed from a yard area to the north–west created after the demolition of No 10 Tank House (Fig 29). No 10 was still standing in 1947 (Pl 1; PRM/AV/2A), but had been demolished by 1959 (Ordnance Survey 1959).

Further modification of the cone house

In the final phase of use, the internal divisions within the cone house were removed, and the gable entrances blocked, with the exception of the doorway in the south–west end of the south–east gable, which was enlarged. The changes probably proceeded in tandem with the erection of the small structure adjoining the north–east gable. The purpose of these alterations is unclear, although it appears that the cone house was still used for the bulk storage of raw materials; a sign found attached to the wall immediately adjacent to the enlarged single door reads 'Limestone'.

8

WORKING CONDITIONS AND INDUSTRIAL RELATIONS

Work in the tank house

The physical remains of No 9 Tank House, together with oral and documentary accounts, give some impression of the nature of working conditions for the glassmakers of the late nineteenth and early twentieth centuries. At the start of the process, the furnace had to be filled, and lump hooks used to stop the lump of fresh batch floating too far down the furnace; Plate 6 shows a teazer wearing protective equipment to combat the heat. At the working end of the furnace, it is striking that a large number of men would have been required to conduct complex, interlinked, and potentially dangerous tasks in a relatively small space. It is believed that a team of three men worked at each of five gathering holes, distributed along the north–east end of the furnace, which had a width of some 6 m (*see above Ch 5, p 27-8; p 64*). In addition, ten blowers would have worked at blowing holes along the two sides of the furnace working end, approximately 7.8 m long, being supplied with molten glass by men walking round from the gathering holes. The gather of molten glass might weigh 40 pounds, and had to be passed from man to man on the end of a hot pipe; obstacles to be avoided included other pipes being heated up, tubes bringing in compressed air to aid the blowers, and the open holes through the working floor into which the blowers would swing the heavy cylinders of hot glass during blowing. Furthermore, all the tasks had to be carried out in near darkness (the gatherers needed to be able to see and assess the radiation from the hot glass), and in what would have been a choking sulphurous environment if ventilation was not adequate. One member of a gathering team in a furnace comparable to No 9 remembered the wooden face boards, made with strips of blue glass, which the gatherers had to hold in front of their faces for protection when taking glass from the furnace. He also recalled that 'we had to duck down because there was pipes being warmed above you….bits of glass used to fly off and go in your neck and stick to you….sometimes when they stuck you cut your fingers and your neck and they burn…that's how he

used to take his heat' (Transcript of interview with Harry Langtree, 7).

As well as the glassblowing process itself, essential maintenance work had to be carried out, and involved work in confined spaces in great heat. It is clear that as many tasks as possible were carried out as 'hot repairs' whilst the furnace was still operating (*see above Ch 5, p 28*). Ron Parkin recalled the equipment needed for work under a tank at a slightly later period; this then included a felt or asbestos suit, clogs, cone-shaped hat with ear flaps, and a face board (Transcript of interview with Ron Parkin). He also remembered that if the men were too slow operating the valves that reversed the regenerators, gas and air would be mixed too soon, and blow back, producing a 'flush' of flames that would have singed your whiskers. Unattached cast iron plates allowed the flush to escape, to prevent the furnace blowing up.

No records of accidents, deaths, or work-related illnesses from the period of use of No 9 Tank House have been encountered during the course of this project, but it is hard to resist the conclusion that accidents at work must have been commonplace. Nevertheless, despite the toughness of the life, employment in Pilkingtons' glassworks was probably nowhere near as dangerous as work in the ailing late nineteenth century chemical industry of St Helens. In many chemical works, working conditions seem to have deteriorated markedly as the century progressed and foreign competition damaged profitability; there are accounts of workers routinely having their health destroyed by being sent to clean out chemical tanks without protective equipment (Barker and Harris 1959). In contrast, many jobs in the glass industry were highly desirable, and gatherers and blowers remained artisans for as long as hand blowing continued. A man had to serve a five year apprenticeship as a 'time gatherer' before becoming a gatherer; thereafter, if a blower died or left the works, a gatherer might have the chance to become a blower. The gatherers themselves were highly skilled, and had to set the diameter of the gather before passing it to the blower. Harry Langtree remembered that 'it was marvellous because you could get a pair of callipers, say it was twenty inches diameter he wanted, you could bet your life you would not be able to put a sixteenth between it, they were that good' (Transcript of interview with Harry Langtree, 6).

Working hours were long by modern standards. In the 1870s, staff who did not directly make glass, about five out of six of Pilkingtons' employees, worked a $55^{1/2}$ hour week, with three days holiday, on Christmas Day, Good Friday, and the Friday of Newton Race Week in June (Barker 1960, 175). In the days of pot furnaces, the glassmakers themselves had worked 10 hours on followed by 24 hours off; with the coming of continuous tank furnaces such as No 9 Tank, the stand down period whilst the pots were charged was avoided, and the glassmakers appear to have worked six eight-hour shifts a week (*op cit*, 176).

Wages and labour relations

Until the later nineteenth century, glass blowers and gatherers were usually drawn from artisan families specialising in the trade. They were skilled craftsmen who commanded high wages, and moved between glasshouses all over Britain in search of the best wages and conditions (Barker and Harris 1959, 284). Thus, in the early years of its existence, Pilkington Brothers had a relatively small but highly skilled workforce. Even in the early 1870s, the company employed no more than 200 sheet glassmakers, but by 1876 a boom in demand and the introduction of the continuous tank furnace had increased the workforce drastically; there were 1500 employees in all at the Grove Street works. In the years that followed, the relatively large pool of trained labour, and increasing trend towards mechanisation and continuous processes, caused a shift in labour relations, placing the employers at Pilkingtons in a strong negotiating position (Barker 1977, 232f); other companies in the area had been unable to match the firm's successful adoption of new technology, and had shed staff, so that alternative employment was often not available. By the late nineteenth century, the company was a major employer in the town, and by the call-up for the Great War, one manager was able to lament that Pilkingtons had lost 4,000 of its workforce to conscription (Barker 1977, 176).

If glass blowers were seemingly quiet through this period of mechanisation, it was not because of exemplary labour relations. A number of strikes disrupted production in the later nineteenth century, despite the initial absence of a glassmakers' union. The change in working hours, together with three consecutive 10% wage cuts, may have contributed to a strike by some glassmakers in 1878, but this was unsuccessful. The strikers had to return on the employers' terms, and sign six month contracts, probably a much shorter term than had previously been offered (*ibid*), staggered so that only a small number could strike at any one time without breaking their agreements. In 1879, rates of pay were cut again, with the board deciding to impose rates that were 'the lowest that can possibly be gone to'. However, workers who had chosen not to strike in 1878 were granted a bonus of £ 5 a year for life, and there were no further strikes at the sheet glassworks (*ibid*). In 1880, glassmakers were given a 10% rise, after Pilkingtons found that significant numbers of workers were emigrating to take up employment in American glassworks.

American glassmakers, represented by the American Knights of Labour, became so concerned about the influx of skilled workers arriving from Europe, prepared to accept wages below American rates, that they made considerable efforts to organise the glassworkers of St Helens (Barker 1960, 177). A Knights' Local Assembly for British window glass makers was founded in 1884, with a St Helens branch, and Universal Conventions were held in the town in 1886 and 1888. However, Pilkingtons refused to deal with the union, and the secretary of the British Local Assembly reported a complete lack of progress in St Helens by 1887, thanks partly to Pilkingtons' habit of laying-off known union members (*op cit*, 178). At a lower level in the workforce, there is evidence that large numbers of labourers were union members in 1890, but in 1895, one of Pilkingtons' glass blowers asserted that the employees at the sheet works were in no way organised (*op cit*, 179).

This situation finally changed during the war years, when workers were in short supply, and the National Amalgamated Union of Labour was recognised by the company in 1917. In the years that followed, a closer understanding between management and workers was achieved, and despite the rapid technical changes and difficult economic climate in the 1920s, the General Strike of 1926 represented the only serious industrial action in this period (*op cit*, 215). However, this may in part reflect Pilkingtons' growing dominance over employment in St Helens; one commentator said 'It was a time when unemployment was increasing, and it is hard to resist the conclusion that Pilkingtons took advantage of the situation to wring the utmost work out of their employees' (F R Pope, M/PO/237/14/8 at St Helens local studies library). Although union membership was by now tolerated, growing until 'almost the whole workforce had joined' (Forman 1978, 60), the union was said to be 'nothing, not for the glass workers...if you left Pilkingtons' sheet-glassworks, you couldn't get another job — there was none' (*op cit*, 65).

If Pilkingtons' employment practices were often harsh, its tight control of costs allowed it to prosper, securing the jobs of its employees at a time when many other businesses were forced to close with heavy job losses. This was a point which the company was at pains to point out to its workers, telling its men in the 1890s that 'while large works in St Helens have been out and the men getting nothing, you have been at work' (Notes in Board Minutes, quoted in Barker 1960, 181). Certainly business was tight until the turn of the century, and whilst it is known that, from the mid-1890s, sums of £ 100,000–200,000 per year were available for distribution among the Pilkington family, some might argue that it was these profits that allowed heavy family investment in the firm after the First World War (*ibid*).

Pilkingtons' tight control of wages was also counterbalanced, to an extent, by a relatively paternalistic attitude to its employees. A school had been established in *c* 1850 to provide tuition for workers' children and the firm's apprentices, and from 1882, Pilkingtons encouraged and subsidised an employees sickness and burial society. The company also from time to time granted small pensions to long-serving employees, on a discretionary basis (Barker 1960, 112, 180). Welfare provision was increased after the First World War, with a Welfare Department being formed in 1920, providing dental and medical facilities. The impact of mechanisation was softened to some extent by a company compensation scheme established for skilled blowers no longer required when drawn cylinder production was introduced. A staff superannuation fund was set up in 1918, followed by a workmen's pension scheme in 1925. Staff clubs were encouraged, and by 1928 there was an Orchestral section, a Choral section, a Dramatic section, a Photography section, a library, and several clubs for sports including golf, cricket, cycling, football, athletics, angling and 'fur and feather' (*Cullet* 1928). The large workforce effectively become a discrete community within the town, with its own social structures. The staff magazine *Cullet* reported marriages between members of different departments, the deaths of former employees, as well as detailing the activities of the numerous clubs.

9

DISCUSSION

No 9 Tank House, the subject of the 'Hotties' project, dates from a time of rapid technological change in the glass industry, triggered by the development of the regenerative furnace in 1860, and the regenerative continuous tank furnace in 1867 (Cable 2000, 212–6). In combination, these innovations offered dramatic improvements in the efficiency with which glass could be made. However, whilst the application of regenerative technology was easily accomplished in all the major sectors of the glass industry, the continuous tank furnace proved relatively straightforward to apply to the container trade, but difficult to use for the manufacture of sheet window glass. Pilkingtons appear to have been the only major sheet glass producer in Britain to operate continuous tank furnaces between 1879 and 1892, and this undoubtedly contributed to the spectacular expansion of the company; Pilkingtons' output of sheet glass increased four-fold between 1872 and 1900, making the company the largest British window glass producer (Barker 1977, 136). No 9 Tank entered production in 1887, part way through this boom period; the archaeological remains recorded in and below the tank house show, for the first time, how Pilkingtons were able successfully to adapt the Siemens' continuous tank furnace for high quality window glass production, whilst their main competitors remained sceptical of its value.

The use of continuous tank furnaces in the British glass industry

In attempting to introduce continuous tank furnaces, Pilkingtons made use of a design which was aimed at the British glass industry; the company was not seeking out an obscure continental technology. Charles William Siemens had moved to England in 1844, taken a Scottish wife, and acquired British citizenship, and he became one of Britain's leading engineers. He was a close collaborator with his brother Friedrich, and was the family member responsible for obtaining British patents relating to use of continuous tank furnaces in 1872, 1875, and 1879. Friedrich himself had worked in Britain designing and constructing

regenerative pot furnaces, before taking control of the family's Dresden works on the death of Hans in 1867 (Cable 2000, 212, 216). It is clear that the continuous tank furnace design was well known in Britain, indeed the use of tanks for glass melting spread rapidly through the container trade, so that by 1872, there were already 40 tanks for making containers in the UK, although not all were operated continuously (*op cit*, 219). The technology was certainly widely available.

However, if many companies successfully installed continuous tank furnaces for the manufacture of glass vessels, their use for the production of high quality sheet glass for windows was a much more challenging proposition. Bottles could be made with glass that contained tiny bubbles, whereas thorough conditioning of the metal to remove bubbles was a much higher priority in the manufacture of window glass. Since the mid-nineteenth century, the window glass industry had been dominated by three companies: Pilkingtons, Chances of Birmingham, and Hartleys of Sunderland (Barker 1960, 124). Chances, Pilkingtons' main rivals in the sheet trade, were quick to experiment with tank furnaces in the 1870s, but abandoned their attempts to use the technology in 1879, believing that the production of high quality window glass was beyond the capabilities of the available designs (*op cit*, 154). The implication is that the patented continuous tank furnace designs produced glass of inferior quality to that of the existing pot furnaces, and Hartleys, like Chances, do not appear to have adopted the tank furnace for manufacturing sheet. Thus, historical sources suggest that, whilst continuous tank furnace technology was widely understood, Pilkingtons was the only company to succeed in operating furnaces of this type for window glass manufacture. This accords with the known archaeological evidence; 'The Hotties' is the only archaeological site in England where the remains of a nineteenth century tank furnace which produced window glass have been identified (Crossley 1993; Crossley 1996a).

The fact that British companies used continuous tank furnaces for container manufacture, but, with the exception of Pilkingtons, could not apply the technology to sheet glass production, suggests firstly that Pilkingtons' adaptations of the standard patent designs were highly significant, and secondly, that the main effect of the adaptations was to improve the quality of the glass made. It seems highly unlikely that Pilkingtons' adoption of the tank furnace was at the expense of quality; the production of high quality glass was central to the culture of the company, and, in the early twentieth century, it was concern for quality that caused the firm to delay their entry into direct drawn sheet production, instead satisfying their markets with hand-blown cylinder glass produced at a loss (Barker 1977, 292). Given the lack of directly comparable archaeological evidence, the reasons for the success of Pilkingtons' tank furnaces can only be explored by comparing the remains excavated at No 9 Tank House with the documentary evidence for the standard Siemens tank furnace designs which were available to other companies. Thereafter, the remains of No 9 will be briefly compared to those of a surviving bottle glass furnace.

Pilkingtons' development of the continuous tank furnace

The glassmaking technology available in the mid-nineteenth century was little changed from that of the seventeenth and eighteenth centuries. The development by Friedrich Siemens of a gas fired regenerative furnace (British Patent 167, 1861) represented a significant advance, offering cleaner combustion and vastly improved fuel economy, but production was still interrupted by the 24 hour interval required to re-charge and re-heat the pots, preventing efficient use of fuel and labour. However, the Siemens brothers made a further significant breakthrough in 1867, when they succeeded in operating a tank at their Dresden works continuously, and the efficient melting and working of glass in one efficient continuous process now appeared possible. The brothers obtained patents for the use of continuous tank furnaces in 1870, 1872, 1875, and 1879; these designs will now briefly be reviewed, in order that comparison can be made with the furnace remains discovered at No 9 Tank House.

The patents of 1870 and 1872 envisaged use of the same basic regenerative furnace; the second of two provisional specifications registered in 1872 concerned floating fireclay bridges to divide the tank, and working-out mouth pieces to improve the quality of the gather, and stated that these should be used in a regenerative gas furnace 'generally of the form and construction described in…1870' (British Patent 3478, 1872). The 1872 drawings show a short furnace with

a semi-circular working end divided from an almost square melt end by two floating bridges (Pl 8). The combustion gases were provided through six pairs of stacks, the pair nearest the working end being roughly adjacent to the second of the floating bridges. A ventilation cavity was sited below the tank, and additionally, air flues were provided within the furnace sides, being widest where the furnace narrowed to house the floating bridges (British Patent 3478, 1872).

By 1875, the Siemens were proposing rather different furnace designs. Their patent of that year suggested that by placing both regenerators at one end of the furnace, rather than underneath it with burners at both sides, more space could be made available for working-out the glass, and problems of the furnace sides overheating could be reduced (British Patent 1551, 1875). Two variants on this design were suggested, one with a semi-circular working end separated from a near square melt end by a single fixed bridge, the other with eight working-out compartments separated from the melt end by a horseshoe-shaped bridge. Another modification saw the regenerators retained below the furnace as in 1872, but a fixed bridge substituted for floating bridges. Apart from the option to place the regenerators at one end of the furnace, the significant feature of this patent is the use, in all the variants, of a hollow, fixed bridge, in place of floating bridges. A low level aperture or apertures allowed the passage of refined metal, and the whole structure could be ventilated.

Siemens' designs had moved on again by 1879, when another patent was registered (British Patent 4763, 1879). Its key features were the use of a deeper furnace, and the development of boats, fireclay refining vessels to be secured by each working-out hole, which made the use of a bridge unnecessary. Again, two variants were suggested; one was an open, undivided tank, with regenerators sited below, the other a tank divided into four rectangular compartments, with a pair of regenerators at each end. Although, in the latter design, it was specified that the compartments were to be divided by 'bridges', the structures were not intended to allow the passage of refined metal, so in effect, the compartments functioned as four individual open tanks.

The remains uncovered below No 9 Tank House indicate that Pilkingtons' continuous tank furnaces of 1887 differed markedly from any of the designs patented by the Siemens brothers. The differences were so great that, initially, neither the archaeologists nor the former Pilkington employees they consulted could decipher how the structures would have functioned (J Quartermaine pers comm). The structures became comprehensible only when it was realised that the four pairs of regenerators discovered all belonged to a single tank furnace (*see above Ch 5, Functional analysis of the tank furnace, p 74*). The furnace consisted of two separate but interlinked components, one the melt end, one the working end. This in itself was not unique; a number of the Siemens' designs reviewed above allowed for working-out compartments separated by bridges from the melt end. But at 'The Hotties', the two parts of the furnace took the form of separate tanks, housed in separate buildings, whilst crucially, each component had its own set of two pairs of regenerators. This meant that the temperature and atmosphere in the two parts of the furnace could be independently and precisely controlled. The hypothesis that both sets of four regenerators related to a single tank was confirmed by the fact that, below the cone house, the outer, air regenerators were of roughly twice the width of the inner, gas regenerators, whereas below the adjacent south–western building, the gas and air regenerators were of the same dimensions. The former arrangement would have allowed the combustion of a mixture of two parts air to one part producer gas, suitable for creating the oxidising conditions favoured at the working end, whilst the latter would have led to the reducing conditions appropriate to the melt end. This suggested that the working end was sited below the cone building, above the smaller set of four regenerators (*see above Ch 5, p 74*).

Once the rationale behind the No 9 Tank House layout had been understood, it was possible to trace the origins of some elements of the design using documentary sources. It is clear that Windle Pilkington had benefited from direct contact with William Siemens in 1872; Pilkingtons' board minutes refer to a tank furnace which he had seen working in Dresden, and note agreement that Windle and William Pilkington should meet Siemens in London 'to discuss suggestions made to WP as to rings and divisions in furnace' (Barker 1977, 133). This minute was made on the day the provisional specification of the 1872 patent was registered, suggesting that Windle Pilkington was already privy to some of its contents. Pilkingtons' successful development of its own continuous tank furnaces, beginning with experimental tanks lit the following year, was clearly the product of this collaboration; it is known, for example, that Pilkingtons was paying royalties to Siemens in 1877, although at a preferential rate (Barker 1977, 135). Siemens went on to register further patents for the use of continuous tank furnaces in 1875 and 1879 (British Patent 1551, 1875; 4763, 1879), but it can be argued that Pilkingtons' success in developing the tank furnace stemmed from the 1872 collaboration. Thereafter, the company was selective as to which of Siemens' ideas it chose to adopt, using some designs from published patents, but introducing equally significant innovations of its own.

Little is known of the layout of Pilkingtons' 1873 furnaces, so direct comparison with the Siemens' 1872 patents is not possible; the historical evidence outlined above that Pilkingtons' adoption of the tank furnace was based on the Siemens design must be accepted. However, the first furnace has been considered to have failed because the side walls were carried directly by the refractories holding the molten metal (*see above Ch 3, p 14*), yet this seems to be the design suggested by the 1872 patent (British Patent 3478, 1872, fig 4). It is thus possible that the furnace built later in the year, with independent support being provided for the walls and crown (Barker 1977, 134), represented Pilkingtons' own adaptation of the standard design. Letters written in 1876 give a fuller description of Pilkingtons' furnaces three years later (*see above Ch 5, p 26*); the floating bridge and constricted air-cooled waist suggest a resemblance to Siemens' 1872 design, and indicate that none of the ideas from his 1875 patent had yet been adopted. A further source indicates that by 1877, Pilkingtons' furnaces were capable of holding a depth of 2 ft 6 in of metal, anticipating the deeper furnace design patented by Siemens in 1879 by some two years (*see above Ch 5, p 26*). The most major changes in Pilkingtons' furnaces appear to have come in 1881; the use of a fixed bridge appears to represent the application of one aspect of Siemens' design of 1875, but the concept of undivided tanks patented in 1879 was ignored, nor is there any evidence that Pilkingtons ever experimented with regenerators placed at the end or ends of a furnace. However, the year 1881 may also have seen Pilkingtons introduce the crucial innovation of a heated working end, with burners and regenerators completely independent of those at the melt end. No parallels for this design have been found during the present study, suggesting that it may have been a radical innovation first made by Pilkingtons. The application of heat meant that the working end no longer had to be a constricted semi-circle close to the melt end, and allowed the distinctive long, narrow shape of Pilkingtons' furnaces to develop. It solved the problem of lack of space at the working end in a way quite different to Siemens' design of 1879, thus allowing Pilkingtons to make continued use of divided tanks, rather than opting for the open tanks of the 1879 patent.

Compared with the clear archaeological evidence recovered for the layout of No 9 Tank House in 1887, the documentary sources for furnace design are relatively limited. Nevertheless, the references which have been found for the manner in which Pilkingtons' furnaces were designed, and for the working practices of the drawing office, further support the suggestion that Pilkingtons' initial contact with Siemens was highly influential, but that subsequent development was in large measure the product of technical innovation in St Helens. SE Baddeley's recollection of hearing that Windle Pilkington traced out the outline of new furnaces on the ground with his foot has been referred to above, together with his memory that, in *c* 1890, furnaces were built first, and drawn afterwards, if at all (*see above Ch 5, p 26*). It may also be significant that, when in *c* 1890 he tried to find a furnace drawing to use as a stylistic model, the young draughtsman had to resort to one signed by CW Siemens, but dated 1872 (RE 1, 18). Where Pilkingtons' furnace design differs from that of Siemens, the source of the alternative designs remains unknown; however, documentary sources suggest that practical experimentation by Windle Pilkington may have been responsible for much of the innovation, allowing Pilkingtons' tank furnaces to run efficiently, with spectacular results in terms of increased production and financial success (*see below The expansion of production, and further development, p 111*).

The archaeological evidence for contemporary bottle-making furnaces

Although No 9 Tank House appears to be a unique survival of a continuous tank furnace which produced sheet glass, the remains of three later-nineteenth century regenerative furnaces devoted to bottle-making have been identified; these are at the Ouseburn Bottle Works (Tyne and Wear), Hoopers Glass House (Bristol), and the Cannington Shaw Bottle Shop, which lies only 300 m south–east of Pilkingtons' Jubilee Side works in St Helens (Crossley 1996a, 11; Lewis and Philpott 1992). The Ouseburn works has not been excavated, but exploratory excavation at Hoopers Glass House has demonstrated the presence of furnaces adapted from a Siemens' design, which showed evidence of frequent re-building. No details of furnace construction are available in the published note on the excavations (Anon 1989, 61), but it is believed that at least one tank furnace may have been identified (Crossley 1996b).

Much more detailed information is available for the third site, the Cannington Shaw Bottle Shop, a Scheduled Monument (SM 35029, Merseyside no 8) which dates from *c* 1886 (Fig 30; Pl 51 and 52). The surviving elements consist of the brick building which housed the furnace, complete with substantial cone, and five vaulted regenerators below, surrounded by further vaulted rooms, also at basement level. The regenerators and other basement rooms appear to have been cleared out during or before the Second World War, when the structure was used as an air-raid shelter. A limited programme of survey and photogrammetry was carried out in 1989, supplemented by archaeological recording conducted

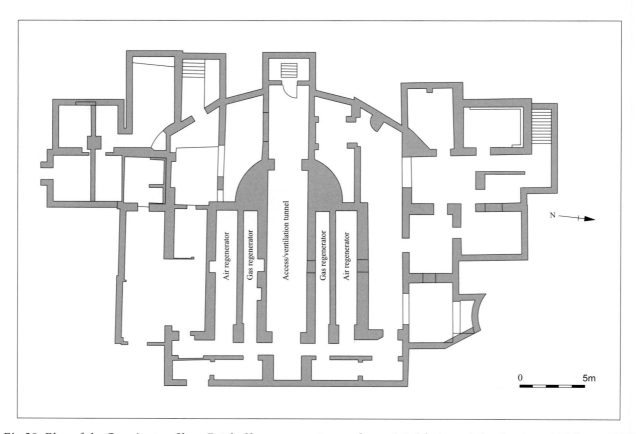

Fig 30 Plan of the Cannington Shaw Bottle Shop regenerators and associated features (after Lewis and Philpott 1992)

Plate 51 The exterior of the Cannington Shaw Bottle Shop, looking south–east

by the Field Archaeology Section at Liverpool Museum and the North West Archaeological Trust (Lewis and Philpott 1992). Brief comparison of the layout of the structure with the contemporary remains recorded on the 'Hotties' site is instructive. The furnace itself would have stood at ground floor level, but had been completely removed. However, the five vaulted tunnels recorded in the basement clearly represent the remains of pairs of regenerators flanking a central ventilation tunnel (Fig 30). The regenerators were *c* 10.5 m long, and together with the central ventilation tunnel, had a combined width of *c* 12.5 m. Foundation walls forming a semi-circular shape suggested that a semi-circular working end had projected *c* 4.5 m beyond the end of the regenerators, with the central ventilation tunnel also continuing below the working end. The combination of short, almost square, melt end and semi-circular working end, corresponds remarkably closely to the furnace depicted in Siemens' patent of 1872 (Pl 8; British Patent 3478, 1872). The dimensions also correspond closely to those of furnaces which Pilkingtons were using in the early 1870s, their tanks then being '15 yards long, with a broad bridge about 5 yards from the gathering end' (1876 letter from James Semple, cited in Keenan 1995, 13). In short, those characteristics of the Cannington Shaw furnace complex which can be reconstructed appear to demonstrate a resemblance to the patented tank furnace designs of the early 1870s, little modified.

The Cannington Shaw remains appear to exhibit conformity with early Siemens' designs, but present a striking contrast to the layout of No 9 Tank House. Indeed, no parallels, in either documentary or archaeological evidence, have been found for the exceptionally long Pilkingtons' furnace, with independent melt and working end regenerators. This, it can be argued, is because, whilst their competitors were harnessing the thermal economy of tank furnaces for the production of bottle glass and rolled plate, products in which glass quality was less important, Pilkingtons was independently but successfully adapting the tank furnace for the efficient production of high quality sheet glass. It is possible that the combination of fixed bridge and independently heated working end, allowing careful control of oxidation, were key features which enabled the metal to be better refined than in contemporary bottle furnaces.

The expansion of production, and further development

Before the introduction of tank furnaces, Pilkingtons' largest recorded weekly output of sheet glass was 350,000 square feet. By 1877, the weekly average was over 500,000 square feet, rising to around 900,000

Plate 52 The base of the Cannington Shaw Bottle Shop cone

square feet in 1887, about 1,250,000 square feet in the early 1890s, and approximately 1,600,000 square feet by the turn of the century (Barker 1977, 136). Although British producers benefited from the difficulties of their major overseas rivals, the Belgians, who were handicapped by high fuel costs in the early 1870s (Barker 1960, 151), Pilkingtons' dramatically increasing sheet glass production seems to have been possible primarily because the adoption of tank furnaces allowed them to satisfy rising domestic demand for cheap, high quality window glass. It can be suggested that the phenomenon should be regarded as an excellent example of technological innovation driving commercial expansion. By contrast, Chances abandoned use of the tank furnace for sheet glass production around 1879, and did not reverse their decision until 1892, thus losing their predominant position in sheet glassmaking to Pilkingtons (Barker 1960, 154). Hartleys, formerly successful window glass producers, fared even less well, and were driven out of business by the strength of competition, the closure of their Sunderland factory in 1894 bringing the end of window glass manufacture in the North East (*op cit*, 157).

Pilkingtons' early and successful introduction of continuous tank furnaces was not repeated in the early twentieth century, when their foreign competitors began to manufacture direct drawn sheet glass in place of cylinder glass. Despite much experimentation, they remained concerned, as Chances had been earlier, that the new technology could not provide a sufficiently high proportion of good quality glass (Barker 1977, 289). The Phase 3 remains recorded at the melt end of No 9 Tank House are a product of the quest to adapt the standard patents for direct-drawn glass machines to meet the company's requirements (*see above Ch 6, p 84–6*). During this period, Pilkingtons managed to retain its market share by a combination of investment in drawn cylinder production, and the manufacturing of blown cylinder glass at a loss (Barker 1977, 292); the firm's earlier successful expansion to all the main types of glass production meant that profits from plate glass manufacture could be used to support the ailing sheet works, until the successful introduction of the PPG process in 1929–31 secured the company's future as a major sheet glass producer. Although the first PPG tank was housed in No 10 Tank House, No 9 still houses the remains of the burning kiln essential to the successful operation of the experimental tank in the adjoining building.

Pilkingtons has continued to develop new techniques and methods, the most significant being the invention of float glass in 1959. By floating molten glass in a sheet across a bath of molten tin, the industry finally achieved its long-desired goal: an entirely fire-polished surface which came into contact with no solid surfaces, and therefore required no subsequent polishing or grinding (Grundy 1990). This was an achievement which revolutionised glassmaking, and can be compared with the impact in the 1870s of the regenerative tank furnace.

Conclusion

In 1991, English Heritage's policy document *Exploring our Past* (English Heritage 1991a, 41) emphasised that the archaeological record is 'notoriously deficient' in industrial period information, and called for 'selective investigation of documented industrial sites to compare the application of new technologies with the historical records of innovation and contemporary technical literature'. The 'Hotties' Project sought to redress the balance, by implementing a programme of multi-disciplinary research of the type advocated by English Heritage. Its subject, a St Helens' glass furnace, was particularly worthy of study, because of the paucity of surveys undertaken on important post-medieval glassmaking remains in the Merseyside area (Crossley 1993), and because so much of St Helens' industrial heritage has recently been destroyed with minimal archaeological recording (Fletcher 1996, 164).

The project combined archaeological, oral, and documentary research. Interviews with former Pilkingtons' employees were particularly important to the process of 'peopling the furnace', and understanding how it would have been operated and maintained, and several personal testimonies were obtained from people who have since passed away; indeed, a former works manager, the late Mr Ron Parkin, was inspired to write his own invaluable monograph describing the making of glass at Pilkingtons' Sheet Glass Works (Parkin 2000). The study of extant documents also contributed essential information, but it was found that detailed records of evolving furnace design were not kept by Pilkingtons, partly because of concerns over industrial espionage. This is important because it means that the detailed form of the furnace, and in particular the specific variations to the standard Siemens' designs, could never have been reconstructed without excavation, demonstrating conclusively the worth of investigating nineteenth century glassworks' structures despite the apparently plentiful records relating to contemporary glass production (Crossley 1996a, 9). The excavations did not merely illustrate what was already known from other sources.

The remains of Pilkingtons' No 9 Tank House are now recognised as 'the most complete known extant [glass] furnace structures' of their era (Cable 2000, 219). The fact that the Cannington Shaw Bottle Shop lies only 300 m to the south–east means that both monuments should be regarded as having enhanced value by virtue of their proximity, offering as they do contrasting pictures of the differing requirements of sheet glass and bottle making. Excavation of No 9 Tank House has enabled knowledge of the standing structure to be supplemented by investigation not only of furnace foundations, but of the regenerators and gas supply flues. Crucially, the clearance and recording of the subsurface remains has led to an appreciation that the tank house was not laid out according to patented designs; rather the success of Pilkingtons and the prosperity of St Helens appear to be products of the ingenious local adaptation of standard furnace technology.

BIBLIOGRAPHY

Primary Sources

Hotties Project Archive (NMGM)

Transcript of interview with Harry Langtree, 2/6/93 LUAU Hotties archive

Transcript of interview with Ron Parkin, 3/6/92 LUAU Hotties archive

Pilkington Archive, held at Information Management & Storage, St Helens

Photo	PRM/AV/2
Photo	PRM/AV/2A
PB 129	Tank repair book
PB 138	Diary of JH Dickinson
PB 222	Pilkington Brothers Sheet Works, 1939; plan showing floor areas of buildings, January 1941
PB 358/57	Notebook of JB Watts, Sheet Works Production Manager (1925–28) including notes on visits to the PPG works in USA
PB 665	1933 Valuation, 7, 8, and 9 Tanks
RE 1	Reminiscences of Earnie Baddeley
RE 2	Reminiscences of James Taylor
	Minutes of Board 17/4/1873

Plans formerly held by the Watson Street Drawing Office, Pilkington Plc

Unlabelled works plan dated 1914
Plan of usage, nd

Plan provided by David Martlew

Plan labelled 'Flues. Crown Glass Works', nd (reproduced in part in Figure 6)

St Helens Library

M/PO/237/14/8 Correspondence of FR Pope
1974 photograph of the Hotties, showing steam over the Sankey Canal

Secondary Sources

Agricola, G, 1556 (rep 1950) *De Re Metallica*, New York

AH Leech son and Dean, 1990 Mining report in relation to the heritage centre at Watson Street, St Helens, unpubl rep

Anon, 1989 Avon: Bristol, Avon Street (ST/597727), note in *Post-Medieval Archaeology*, **23**,61

Ashmore, O, 1969 *Industrial Archaeology of Lancashire*, Newton Abbot

Ashmore, O, 1982 *The Industrial Archaeology of North West England*, Manchester

Ashurst, D, 1970 Excavation at Gawber Glasshouse, near Barnsley, Yorkshire, *Post-Medieval Archaeol*, **4**, 92–140

Aspin, C, 1969 *Lancashire, the First Industrial Society*, Preston

Bailey, B, 1982 *The Industrial Heritage of Britain: a Traveller's Guide*, Somerset

Bailey, FA, 1936 The Minutes of the Trustees of the Turnpike roads from Liverpool to Prescot, St Helens, Warrington and Ashton in Makerfield, 1726–89, *Trans Hist Soc Lancashire Cheshire*, **88**,159–201

Bailey, FA, 1938 Early Coalmining in Prescot, Lancashire, *Trans Hist Soc Lancashire Cheshire*, **99**, 1–20

Barker, TC, 1948 The Sankey Navigation: the first Lancashire Canal, *Trans Hist Soc Lancashire Cheshire*, **100**, 121–55

Barker, TC, 1960 *Pilkington Brothers and the Glass Industry*, London

Barker, TC, 1977 *The Glassmakers*, London

Barker, TC, and Harris, J, 1959 *A Merseyside Town in the Industrial Revolution: St Helens 1750–1900*, London

British Patent 167, 1861 *Improvements in Furnaces,* London

British Patent 1513, 1870 *Furnaces for Manufacturing Glass*, London

British Patent 207, 1871 *Manufacture of Glass*, London

British Patent 3478, 1872 *Glass Furnaces*, London

British Patent 1551, 1875 *Glass Melting Furnaces*, London

British Patent 4763, 1879 *Apparatus for Manufacturing and Moulding Glass Articles*, London

Buckley, F, 1929 Old Lancashire Glasshouses, *J Soc Glass Technol*, **13**, 229–42

Cable, M, 1999 Mechanization of glass manufacture, *J Am Ceram Soc*, **82**[5], 1093–1112

Cable, M, 2000 The development of glass–melting furnaces 1850–1950, *Trans Newcomen Soc*, **71**, 205–27

Cossons, N *Rees's Manufacturing Industry (1819–20) Vol 3: a selection from the Cyclopaedia*, London

Crossley, D, 1967 Glassmaking in Bagot's Park, Staffordshire, in the Sixteenth Century, *Post–Medieval Archaeol*, **1**, 44–83

Crossley, D, 1990 *Post-Medieval Archaeology in Britain*, Leicester

Crossley, D, 1993 Monuments Protection Programme: the glass industry, Step 1 Report, unpubl rep

Crossley, D, 1996a Monuments Protection Programme: the glass industry, Introduction to Step 3 site assessments, unpubl rep

Crossley, D, 1996b Monuments Protection Programme: the glass industry, Step 3 site assessment, Hoopers Glass House, unpubl rep

Crossley, D, and Aberg, FA, 1972 16th-Century Glassmaking in Yorkshire: excavations at furnaces at Hutton and Rosedale, North Riding, 1968–71, *Post-Medieval Archaeol*, **6**, 107–59

Cullet, 1928 *Cullet*, Pilkingtons staff magazine

Dick, WFL, 1973 *A Hundred Years of Alkali in Cheshire*, Birmingham

Douglas, RW, and Frank, S, 1972 *A History of Glassmaking*, London

Dodsworth, R, 1996 *Glass and Glassmaking*, Princes Risborough

English Heritage, 1991a *Exploring our Past; Strategies for the Archaeology of England*, London

English Heritage, 1991b *Management of archaeological projects*, 2nd edn, London

Fletcher, M, 1996 Industrial archaeology, in *The archaeology of Lancashire* (ed R Newman), Lancaster, 157–70

Forman, C, 1978 *Industrial Town: Self Portrait of St Helens in the 1920s*, London

Godfrey, ES, 1975 *The Development of English Glassmaking 1560–1640*, Oxford

Gould, S, and Cranstone, D, 1992 Monuments Protection Programme: the coal industry, Step 1 Report, unpubl rep

Greenwood, J, 1985 *The Industrial Archaeology and Industrial History of Northern England: a Bibliography*, Cranfield

Grundy, T, 1990 *The Global Miracle of Float Glass: a Tribute to St Helens and its Glassworkers*, St Helens

Hampson, CP, 1932 The History of Glass-Making in Lancashire, *Trans Hist Soc Lancashire Cheshire*, **48**, 65–75

Hardie, DWF, 1955 The Muspratts and the British Chemical Industry, *Endeavour*, **14**, 29–33

Harris, JR, 1952 The Early Steam Engine on Merseyside, *Trans Hist Soc Lancashire Cheshire*, **106**, 109–17

Harris, JR, 1968 Origins of the St Helens Glass Industry, *Northern Hist*, **3**, 105–17

Hartley, RJ, 1995 Refractories and the Hotties furnace, paper given at the Jubilee Furnace Seminar, 9/3/95, unpubl doc

Holt, A, 1927 Chemical Industries and Merseyside, in *J Soc Chem Ind*, **46**, 439-444

Hurst Vose, R, 1980 *Glass*, London

Hurst Vose, R, 1994 Excavations at the seventeenth century glasshouse at Haughton Green, Denton, near Manchester, *Post-Medieval Archaeol*, **28**, 1–71

Jackson, JT, 1977 *Housing and Social Structures in Mid-Victorian Wigan and St Helens*, unpubl PhD thesis, Univ Liverpool

Jackson, JT, 1979 Nineteenth-Century Housing in Wigan and St Helens, *Trans Hist Soc Lancashire Cheshire*, **129**, 125–43

Jones, W, 1996 *Dictionary of Industrial Archaeology*, Stroud

Keenan, D, 1995 Conjectures about the Jubilee operation, paper given at the Jubilee Furnace Seminar, 9/3/95, unpubl doc

Kenyon, GH, 1967 *The Glass Industry of the Weald*, Leicester

Lakeland Limited, 2001 *Home Shopping Catalogue*, Windermere

Langton, J, 1979 *Geographical Change and Industrial Revolution: Coalmining in South West Lancashire 1590–1799*, Cambridge

Lewis, GD, 1964 *The South Yorkshire Glass Industry*, Sheffield

Lewis, JM, and Philpott, RA, 1992 Cannington Shaw Bottle Shop, St Helens, Merseyside; archaeological recording of the standing structure, November 1991/March 1992, Field Archaeology Section Liverpool Museum report, unpubl rep

116

LUAU, 1998 Monuments Protection Programme: the Gas Industry, Step 1 Report, unpubl rep

Maloney, FJT, 1967 *Glass in the Modern World: A Study in Materials Development*, London

Newton, RG, and Davison, S, 1989 *Conservation of glass*, London

Ordnance Survey, 1849 5 feet: 1 mile series, St Helens Sheet 7

Ordnance Survey, 1882 1:2500 series, Sheet CVIII.1

Ordnance Survey, 1891 1: 500 series, Sheet CVIII.1.10–4

Ordnance Survey, 1894 1:2500 series, Sheet CVIII.1

Ordnance Survey, 1908 1:2500 series, Sheet CVIII.1

Ordnance Survey, 1928 1:2500 series, Sheet CVIII.1

Ordnance Survey, 1957 1:2500 series, Sheet SJ 5195 SW

Ordnance Survey, 1959 1:2500 series, Sheet SJ 5194 NW

Palmer, M, 1991 *Industrial archaeology: working for the future*, Leicester

Parkin, RA, nd Synopsis: The window glass makers of St Helens, incorporating The Story of No 9 Tank on the Jubilee Site, unpubl doc

Parkin, RA, 2000 *The window glass makers of St Helens*, Soc Glass Technol monog, Sheffield

Pevsner, N, 1969 *The Buildings of England: South Lancashire*, London

Phillips, CB, and Smith, JH, 1994 *Lancashire and Cheshire from AD 1540*, London

Pilkington Brothers, 1926 *Now Thus –Now Thus*, St Helens

Powell, HJ, 1923 *Glass-Making in England*, Cambridge

Rackham, O, 1993 *The History of the Countryside,* London

Redding, C, 1842 *An Illustrated Itinerary of the County of Lancaster*, London

Rosenhain, W, 1908 *Glass Manufacture*, London

Siemens, CW, 1862 On a Regenerative Gas furnace, as Applied to Glasshouses, Puddling, Heating, etc, *Proc Inst Mechan Engineers*, **13**, 21–45

Siemens, F, 1873 A New Method of Heating the Regenerative Gas-Furnace, offprint from unnumbered *J Iron Steel Inst*, London

Tolson, JM, 1983 *The St Helens Railway: its Rivals and Successors*, St Helens

Tomlinson, C (ed), 1860 *Tomlinson's Cyclopaedia of Useful Arts, Mechanical and Chemical, Manufacture, Mining and Engineering*, **5**, London

Ure, A, 1843 *Ure's Dictionary of Arts, Manufactures and Mines*, **2**, London

Vavra, JR, nd *5000 Years of Glass Making: the History of Glass*, Prague

Walton, JK, 1987 *Lancashire: A Social History 1558–1939*, Manchester

Wardell Armstrong, 1991 Report on the results of a site investigation at the site of the proposed Hotties Science and Arts Centre, St Helens, unpubl rep

Welch, CM, 1997 Glass Making in Wolseley, Staffordshire, *Post-Medieval Archaeol*, **31**, 1–60

INDEX

Illustrations are denoted by page numbers in *italics*.

alkali, xii, 5, 9, 14, 30, 31
American Knights of Labour, 104
annealing
    described, xii, 6
    kilns, 67, 69, 93
annexes, tank house, 93
archive, 4

Baddeley, SE, 26, 110
beams, cast iron, 39, 52
Belgium
    sand supply, 31
    sheet glass making, 112
Bellevernon (USA), 85
bicycle machine, 14, *15*, 28
Birmingham, glassmaking *see* Chances
block minders, 28
blowing *see under* glassmaking
blowing holes, 27, 103
boats, 108
bottle glass, 107, 111
bottle-making furnaces, contemporary, *110–11*
brick chamber, *54*, 55, 76, 92
bricks/brickwork
    Phase 2.1
        central tunnel, 57, 58
        cone house, 34–5, 37, 39
        flues, 67, 68, 70, 71
        furnace, 61, 64, 65
        regenerators, 11, 27, 51, 56, 57, 77
        south-western tank house building, 49
        swing pits, 65, 66, 67
        tank, 27, 31
        tunnels, 52, 56, 59, 71
        working end switch room, 52, 53, *54*
    Phase 2.2, ancillary building, 74
    Phase 3
        flues, 86, 87
        kiln/furnace and contemporary structures, 89, 91–2, 93
        swing pits, 91
        working end switch room, 92
    Phase 4, cone house, 97*see also* fireclay bricks/ blocks; silica bricks; tiles
bridges
    fixed, 26, 27, 29, 108, 109
        functional analysis, 74, 80, *81*
    floating, *13*, 26, 108, 109
Bridgewater Chemical Works
    archaeological evidence, *20*, 23, 32–3

    documentary evidence, *18*, 19
Bridgewater Smelting Company, 19
British Cast Plate Glass Company, 9
British Plate Glass Company, 9
buttresses
    cone house
        Phase 2, 37, 39, *42*
        Phase 4, *38*, *97*, 99
    furnace, *61*, *64*, 72, 82

Cannington Shaw Bottle Shop, *2*, *110–12*, 113
'cave', 60, 74, 77, 80
Chalon Court Hotel (Hilton Hotel), 3, 58
chamber 503, 86, *87–8*, 93–4
Chance, JT, 13, 14
Chances (glassmakers), 9–11, 14, 26–7, 107, 112
chemical industry, St Helens, 8, 9, 31, 103; *see also* Bridgewater Chemical Works
Cheshire, salt works, 8
chimney, 27, 77
chimney flues, *53*, 54–5, 77, 91, 94
claywork, manufacture of, 90, 94, 95
coal
    availability, 12, 29–30
    coal-fired furnaces, 7
    conversion of, 12, 14, 30
    see also pit-head; St Helens Colliery; winding house
columns, cast iron, 39, *43*
cone house, *2*
    Phase 2
        brick cone, 39, *43–5*
        functional analysis, 80–1
        original fabric, *34–6*, 37, *38*, 39, *40–1*, *44–5*
        roof, *39–42*, *43*, *46–8*
    Phase 4, *97*, 99–100, 101
cones, glasshouse, use of, 7
contamination, 3, 4, 23
control rods, switch room, *53*, 55
copper industry, 8, 19
cottages, 17
Crank (Lancs), 30
crown glass, xii, 6, 9–10
crucibles/pots, 6, 10, 13, 108
Crystal Palace (London), 10
Cullet, 105
cullet, xii, 5, 77
cullet wash building, *32*, 74, 93
cylinder glass
    blowing, 14, *15*, *17–19*, 103–4
    defined, xii, 6

Pilkingtons' production of, 9–10, *83*, 85–6, 107-8

Danner process, 84
documentary evidence
    Phase 1
        chemical works, 19
        coal mining, *17–18*, 19
    Phase 2
        raw materials and transport, 29–32
        tank furnaces, 25–9
    Phase 3, post-production modifications, 83–6
    working conditions and industrial relations, 103–5
doors/doorways
    chamber 535, 54
    cone house, 37, 39, 81–2, 99, 100, 101
    swing pits, 66, 67, 92
drawing machine, 83–6, 93
drawing towers, 81, 83, 85, 93
drawn glass
    defined, xii
    development of, 83, *84*, 85–6, 108, 112
Dresden (Germany), 13, 107, 108, 109

Eccleston Crown Glassworks, 9
engine house, St Helens Colliery, 17
English Heritage, 3
exhaust emissions, 11, 27, 55, 76–7, 94
exports, 31–2

fieldwork programme, 3–4
fire, 1873, 14
fireclay
    bricks/blocks, 26, 27, 29, 31, 77
    rings, 80
    source of, 9, 31
firestone, 27, 31
First House cone, 25
flattening kilns, 17, 25, 37
float glass, 113
floors
    gas flues, 69, 70, 71
    kiln/furnace, contemporary with, 91, 92, 94
    swing pits, 66, 67, 71–2
    working end switch room, 53
flues, *24*
    chimney, *53*, 54–5, 77, 91, 94
    furnace (upcast)
        archaeological evidence, *58*, 62, *63*, 64, 65
        functional analysis, 77–80, 108
    gas supply
        archaeological evidence
            Phase 2, *20*, *50*, 60, *67*, 68, *69–70*, 71; Phase 3, 93
            functional analysis, 75–7
    regenerators, 51, 57, 59, 75–6

stretching kiln, 86–7, *88*, 89, 93, 94
under-floor, *53*, 54, 55, 60, 75–6
Fourcault process, 83–4, 85, 86
frit, xiii, 5
fuel, 6, 7–8, 10, 12–13, 14, 29–30
furnaces
    development of, 7, 10, 107
        pot furnace, 10
        regenerative continuous tank furnace, *13*, 14, *72*, 107–10
        regenerative furnace, 10, *11–12*, 13
    No 9 Tank House
        basal remains, *43*, 61
            melt end, *61*, 64–5; working end, *61–2*, 64, 65
        buttresses, changes to, 72
        control of, 80
        discussion, 108–10
        functional analysis, 77–80
        position of, *63*, *78*
        reconstruction, *79*
    see also bottle-making furnaces; kiln/furnace

gas
    supply, 25, 27, 75–7, 93, 94, 95
    use of, 10–12, 14, 25, 30
gatherers, 28, 80, 103–4
gathering holes, 27–8, 80, 103
General Strike, 85, 104
glassmaking
    blowing, 14, *15*, *27–9*, 77, 103–4
    historical background, 7–10
    method, 5–6
    see also furnaces
Gloucestershire, glassmaking, 7
Green Lane, colliery, 12, 29
Greenall, Peter, 9, 10
Grove Street, *49*, 104

Hard Lane, quarry, 31
Hartleys (glassmakers), 10, 107, 112
Haughton Green (Manchester), 7
Henzey brothers, 7
Heritage Lottery Fund, 3
Hilton Hotel, 3, 58
Hoopers Glass House (Bristol), 110
Hopton, William, 19
Hotties Science and Arts Centre, 3, 4

inclined-grate producers, 14, 25, 27, *30*, 75

Jubilee Side works, 1, *2*, 3, 14, 25, *48*
jump box, 68, 69

Kenyon, Lady, 8
kiln/furnace, Phase 3
    archaeological evidence, 89, *90*, 91, 113
    documentary evidence, 85, 86

functional analysis, 94–5
see also annealing kilns; furnaces; stretching kiln
Knowsley (Lancs), 30

labour relations, 104–5
ladles, iron, 4
Lancashire, glassmaking, 7, 9
Langtree, Harry, 37, 39, 81, 82, 103–4
Leaf family, 7
lean-to structures, *32*, 34, 35, 99, 100
Leathers, John Knowles, 19
Leblanc process, 9, 14
Libbey-Owens process, 83, *84*, 85, 86
limestone, 5, 30, 31, 101
Liverpool, Drury Buildings, 32
Lloyd, Dr, 13
London, glassmaking, 7
louvres, 47, 81, 94
Lubber process, *83*

machine belting, 22
Manchester and Liverpool Plate Glass Company, 9
Mansell, Sir Robert, 7
May, Thomas, 26
Mersey Chemical Works, 31
Mill Lane, 31
mineshaft *see* pit-head
mixing room, 31
mixing room stock building, 74
Mossbank (Lancs), 30
Mount Vernon (USA), 86
mushroom valve, 68, 93, *94*, 95
Muspratt and Gamble, 9

National Amalgamated Union of Labour, 104
No 7 Tank House, 86
No 9 Tank House
    archaeological evidence
        Phase 1.1, 19, *20–2*, 23
        Phase 1.2, *20*, 23
        Phase 2.1
            access/ventilation tunnels, *44*, *50*, *55*, 56; cone house, *33–6*, 37, *38*, 39, *40–7*; entrance tunnel 511 and melt end switch room, *50*, 59–60; external gas supply flues, *67–70*, 71; furnace, basal remains, *61–5*; melt end regenerators and central tunnel, *50*, 56, *57–8*, 59; raised platform, 32–3; south-western tank house building, *32*, 47–9; swing pits, *61*, 65, *66*, 67; walls 629 & 639, 60; working end regenerators and central tunnel, 49, *50*, 51; working end switch room, *50*, 51, *52–4*, 55
        Phase 2.2

ancillary structures, modification of, 74; north-west longitudinal access/ventilation tunnel, *50*, 71; swing pits and furnace, alterations to, 71–2
        Phase 3
            cone house, north-west end, adaptation of, 89, *90*, 91–2; melt end regenerators, changes to, 86, *87–8*, 89; tank house fabric, modifications to, 92–3
        Phase 4.1
            cone house, *97–8*, 99–101; external features, 100; south-west tank house building, *98*, 100; structure adjoining south-east gable of warehouse, *98*, 100
        Phase 4.2, 100–1
    discussion, 107
        furnace, development of, 108–10
        furnaces, contemporary, 110–11
        production, expansion of, 111–13
        wages and labour relations, 104–5
        working conditions, 103–4
    documentary evidence
        Phase 1, 17–19
        Phase 2
            raw materials and transport, 29–32; tank furnaces, *24*, 25–9
        Phase 3, 83–6
    fieldwork programme, 3–4
    functional analysis
        Phase 2
            furnace, 77–80; gas supply, switch rooms and exhaust, 75–7; regenerators, 74–5; tank house buildings, 80–2; tunnels 508 and 524 and swing pits, 77
        Phase 2.2 alterations, 82
        Phase 3
            chamber 503 and tunnel 504, 93–4; cone house structures, 94–5; listing, 1; location, *xiv, 2*, 14
No 9 Warehouse, 100
No 10 Tank House
    demolition, 101
    experimental work, 85, 86, 94–5, 112
    functional analysis, 74, 75, 77, 82
    location, 25, *32*, *33*
No 11 Tank House, 25, 26, 75, 82
No 12 Tank House, 25, 75, 82
No 13 Tank House, 25, 82
No 14 Tank House, 25, 82
No 15 Tank House, 25, 47, *49*, 81, 82
Nottinghamshire, glassmaking, 7

Oliver, MN & Co, 57

oral research, 113
Ouseburn Bottle Works (Tyne and Wear), 110

'palace', 37
Parkin, Ron
    documentary sources, study of, 26, 85, 113
    on
        bridge, 26, 80
        furnace blocks, 31
        Phase 3 modifications, 85, 86, 93
        protective clothing, 103
        regenerators, 60
        waterboxes, 27
Peasley Glass Works, 2
pensions, 105
Pilkington family
    Cecil, 14, 85, 86
    William, 10, 31, 109
    William Jnr, 9
    Windle
        bicycle machine, 14, 28
        experimental work, 10, 13, 14, 25, 26,
        109, 110
Pilkington plc
    company, development of, 9–10
    drawn glass production, 83, 84–6, 112–13
    furnaces, 25–9, 107–10
        regenerative continuous furnace, 13–14
        regenerative furnace, 10–13
    production, expansion of, 111–13
    raw materials and transport, 29–32
    working conditions, 103–6
    see also St Helens Colliery; St Helens Crown
    Glass Company; St Helens Sheet Glass Works
pipes, steel, 89, 95
pit-head, 17, 18, 19–21, 22–3, 77, 82
Pittsburg Plate Glass process, 83, 84, 86, 94–5, 112
plate glass, xiii, 6, 9
platform, raised, 32–3
ports, 62, 77
pots see crucibles/pots
Prescot (Lancs), 7
protective clothing
    archaeologists, 4
    teazers, 5, 103
pulley wheel, 54

quarries, limestone, 31

railway lines, reused, 54, 62, 89
railways, 17, 30–2, 93, 99, 100
Rainford (Lancs), 30–1
Ravenhead Plate Glass Works, 7, 9, 10, 18, 82
raw materials
    availability, 9
    described, 5
    documentary evidence, 29–32
    preparation of, 14

store, 74, 99, 100, 101
regenerators
    defined, xiii
    development of, 10–11, 12
    No 9 Tank House
        Phase 2
            archaeological evidence, 49, 50–1,
52, 53, 56–9; functional analysis, 73,
            74–5, 80; materials used, 27;
    position of, 108–9
        Phase 3, 86, 87–8
repairs
    No 9 Tank House, 25, 26, 27, 28–9, 103
    regenerative furnaces, 13
ring arch, 86, 95
rods see control rods
roofs
    cone house
        Phase 2, 39–42, 43, 46–8
        Phase 3, 93
        Phase 4, 99–100
    working end switch room, 52
Rotherham, glassmaking, 10, 12
Rowat process, 84, 85, 86

saddle tiles, 51, 57
St Helens
    glassmaking, 7–9
    Pilkington Brothers, development of, 9–10
St Helens Colliery
    archaeological evidence, 19–22, 23
    documentary evidence, 17, 18–19, 30
St Helens Crown Glass Company, 9
St Helens Sheet Glass Works, 1, 2, 11
salt trade, 8
saltcake, 5, 9, 14, 31, 74
sand, 5, 9, 14, 30–1, 100
sandwash plant, 31
Sankey Canal, 1, 2, 8, 9, 31, 32; see also winding hole
school, 105
Semple, James, 26, 111
Semple, T, 27
shafts, 53, 68, 69, 70
sheet glass
    defined, xiii
    production, 14, 25, 31–2, 107–8, 111–12
    see also cylinder glass; drawn glass; float glass
Sherdley Glass Works, 2
shoes, 4
sickness and burial society, 105
Siemens
    Charles William, 107, 110
    Friedrich, 10–11, 12–14, 30, 107, 108
    Hans, 13, 107
    William, 10–11, 13–14, 30, 74, 109
silica, 5
silica bricks, 27
silver sand, 31

slabs, refractory, 62, 64, 87
slates, 46, 47, 93
soda ash, 5, 9
South Lancashire Coalfield, 8
south-western tank house building
    Phase 2, *32*, 47–9, 59, 81
    Phase 4.1, 97, *98*, 99, 100
Southwark, Winchester House, 7
stacks
    archaeological evidence, 51, 62
    documentary evidence, 26, 29
    functional analysis, 77–80, 82, 108
Staffordshire, glassmaking, 7
stanchions
    cast iron, *38*, *39*, *40*, 42, *46*
    steel, 89
stay bars, iron, 89
Stourbridge, fireclay blocks/bricks, 26, 29, 31
stretching kiln, 85, *88*, 89, 93–4
strikes *see* labour relations
subsidence, 82
Sun Cool Offices, 100
Sunderland, glassmaking *see* Hartleys
Sutton (Lancs), glassmaking, 7
Sutton Oak (Lancs), glassmaking, 9
swing pits
    archaeological evidence
        north-west
            Phase 2.1, *50*, 56, *61*, 66–7; Phase
            2.2, 72, 82; Phase 3, *90*, 91, 95
        south-east
            Phase 2.1, *50*, 56, *61*, *64*, 65, *66*;
            Phase 2.2, 72, 82
    function, *28*, 77, 103
switch rooms
    melt end, *50*, 59, 60, 77
    working end
        archaeological evidence
            Phase 2, *50*, 51, *52–4*, 55; Phase 3,
            88, 92
        functional analysis, *75*, 76

tanks
    bottle-making furnaces, 111
    sheet glass furnaces
        development of, 13–14, 108
        documentary evidence, 26–7, 28–9, 31,
        82
        functional analysis, 74, 77, 108
taxation, 9, 10

teazers, *5*, 80, 103
temperature control, 80
textile industry, demand for glass, 9, 10
Thatto Heath (Lancs), glassmaking, 7
tiles, 27, 28, 29, 37, 87; *see also* saddle tiles
time gatherers, 28
trade unions, 104
tramways, 30–1
transport, 7–8, 9, 30–2
tunnels
    access/ventilation
        Phase 2.1, *44*, *50*, *55*, 56, 71, 77
        Phase 2.2, 82
    central
        Phase 2.1, 49, *50*, 51, 56, *57–8*, 74
        Phase 3, 89
    entrance tunnel, *50*, 59–60
    melt end, 60
turnpikes, 8
Tyneside, glassmaking, 7

Union Plate Glass Works, 9

valves, 11, 69, *76*, 77, 80, 103; *see also* mushroom
valve

wages, 104, 105
walkways, 80, 91
warehousing, 25, 31, 93, 100
Warrington (Lancs), glassmaking, 7
waterboxes, 27
Watson, T, 19
Watson Street, 25
Watts, JB, 84, 85, 86
Welfare Department, 105
welfare facility, 100
Widnes (Ches), chemical works, 31
Wilson, J, 19
winding hole, 23
winding house, *20–2*, 23
windows, cone house, 37, 39, 99, 100
wood-fired furnaces, 7
Worcestershire, glassmaking, 7
working conditions, 103–4
World of Glass Project, 3

Yorkshire, glassmaking, 7

Zouch, Sir Edward, 7